PATERNITY AND FATHERHOOD

From the same publishers

ROBINSON CRUSOE: Myths and Metamorphoses (*co-editor with Brian Stimpson*)

Paternity and Fatherhood

Myths and Realities

Editor

Lieve Spaas
Professor of French Cultural Studies
Kingston University

Associate Editor

Trista Selous
Associate Research Fellow
Roehampton Institute London

First published in Great Britain 1998 by
MACMILLAN PRESS LTD
Houndmills, Basingstoke, Hampshire RG21 6XS and London
Companies and representatives throughout the world

A catalogue record for this book is available from the British Library.

ISBN 0–333–64237–6

First published in the United States of America 1998 by
ST. MARTIN'S PRESS, INC.,
Scholarly and Reference Division,
175 Fifth Avenue, New York, N.Y. 10010

ISBN 0–333–64237–6

Library of Congress Cataloging-in-Publication Data
Paternity and fatherhood : myths and realities / editor, Lieve Spaas ;
associate editor, Trista Selous.
p. cm.
Includes bibliographical references and index.
ISBN 0–333–64237–6 (cloth)
1. Paternity in literature. 2. Fatherhood in literature.
I. Spaas, Lieve. II. Selous, Trista, 1957– .
PN56.P32P38 1998
809'.933520431—dc21 97–47027
CIP

10 9 8 7 6 5 4 3 2 1
07 06 05 04 03 02 01 00 99 98

Printed and bound in Great Britain by
Antony Rowe Ltd, Chippenham, Wiltshire

To

the memory of my parents

and

to

Max Marshall

who emboldened me to venture upon the paternity project
when it was merely a shimmering on the outskirts of my mind

Contents

Acknowledgements

A book such as this owes its scope and content to the intersection of different disciplines – in this case the social sciences and the humanities. It arose from an International Colloquium held at the Institut Français de Londres in May 1995. I am grateful to the Research Grants Committee and the Faculty of Arts and Humanities of the Roehampton Institute London, the Institut Français de Londres and the British Academy for their generous support.

My special thanks go to Elaine and English Showalter, who co-organised the Colloquium and whose inspiring support contributed considerably to its success. My thanks also to René Lacombe for his enthusiasm in co-fathering this Colloquium, to Ivonne Holiday for her unfailing support and to Betty Nguyen for her endless good humour in helping with the practical organisation of the Colloquium. My debt to the associate editor, Trista Selous, is immeasurable.

The present collection of essays is the fruit of considerable editorial revision. Trista and I should like to express our thanks to the authors who have carefully followed editorial guidelines and been open to the changes suggested.

Lieve Spaas

Notes on Contributors

Max Andréoli has been a university lecturer for many years and now holds an associate professorship in French Literature at Kossuth Lajos University, Debrecen, Hungary. He contributes regularly to *L'Année balzacienne*, is the author of *Le Système balzacien*, and is completing a book entitled *Lectures et mythes*.

Janet Beer is Principal Lecturer in English and American Literatures at Roehampton Institute London. She is the author of two critical books: *Edith Wharton: Traveller in the Land of Letters* and *Kate Chopin, Edith Wharton and Charlotte Perkins Gilman: Studies in Short Fiction*, both published by Macmillan. She is currently working on a *Literary Life* of Edith Wharton.

Jennifer Birkett holds the Chair of French Studies at the University of Birmingham. Her books include studies on Decadence (*The Sins of the Fathers: Decadence in France 1870–1914*, 1986), women's writing in Europe and America (ed. with Elizabeth Harvey, *Determined Women: Constructions of the Feminine Subject 1900–1990*, 1991), and most recently, the *Macmillan Guide to French Literature: Early Modern to Post-modern* (with James Kearns, 1997).

Philippe Bolusset is Senior Lecturer in French Language and Linguistics at Roehampton Institute London. He is currently completing a comparative study on metaphor in English and French for a Ph.D at the University of Surrey.

Patrick Corcoran taught French at London University and Exeter University before taking up a post at Roehampton Institute London, where he is currently Head of Modern Languages. He has published widely on francophone literature.

Angela Cozea teaches French and Comparative Literature at the University of Western Ontario in London, Canada. She has published on modernity's relationship between literature and philosophy in Baudelaire, Proust, Benjamin, Adorno and Levinas. She is presently working on Renaissance representations of the natural sciences in painting and literature.

Lawrence Danson is Professor of English at Princeton University. His work on Shakespeare and Renaissance drama includes *Tragic Alphabet: Shakespeare's Drama of Language* and *The Harmonies of "The Merchant of Venice"*. He is the author most recently of Wilde's *Intentions: The Artist in His Criticism* (Clarendon Press, 1997).

Mark Ferrigan is Lecturer in French at St Edmund Hall and Lady Margaret Hall, Oxford. He is currently working on a D. Phil thesis entitled 'Writing between the lines: Michel Tournier and the End(s) of Interpretation'.

Béatrice Fink is Professor of French at the University of Maryland and a past Secretary-General of the International Society for Eighteenth-Century Studies who has published extensively on Sade. She specialises in French eighteenth-century culinary discourse/history, and has recently published *Les Liaisons savoureuses: Réflexions et pratiques culinaires au dix-huitième siècle* (1995).

Sander L. Gilman is the Henry Luce Professor of the Liberal Arts in Human Biology at the University of Chicago. He is the author or editor of more than 40 books, the most recent being *Smart Jews* (University of Nebraska Press).

Tivadar Gorilovics is Professor of French Literature at Kossuth Lajos University, Debrecen), where he was also vice-rector of the University from 1983 to 1986. He specialises in the period 1850–1950 (Renan, Zola, Roger Martin du Gard, Jean-Richard Bloch). His publications include: *Recherches sur les origines et les sources de la pensée de Roger Martin du Gard, La Légende de Victor Hugo de Paul Lafargue, Correspondance de J.-R. Bloch et Andre Monglond I & II*. He is general editor of *Studia Romanica*, of Debrecen. He is currently working on an annotated edition of an unpublished correspondence of Jean Richard Bloch, *Lettres du régiment* (1902–1903).

Jean-Jacques Hamm, FRSC, is Professor at Queen's University (Canada) and Head of Department of French Studies. His main interest is Stendhal, on whom he has published several books and numerous articles.

Xavier Martin is historian of law and Professor at the Faculty of Law, Economics and Social Sciences at Angers University. He has published extensively on the ideology of the French Revolution and on the Code Civil of 1804.

Christie McDonald is Professor of Romance Languages and Literatures at Harvard University. She is the author of *The Dialogue of Writing* (1985), *Dispositions* (1986), and the *Proustian Fabric* (1991). She is editor of *The Ear of the Other: Texts and Discussions with Jacques Derrida* (1985) and co-editor of *Transformations in Personhood and Culture After Theory* (1994).

Michaëla Mongelard holds an MA in Romance Languages and Literatures from Birckbeck College. She is completing her Ph. D at Roehampton Institute London on 'Traces of Palimpsest: Sexuality, Evil and Death in the Fiction of Loys Masson'. She has published several articles on Masson.

Carol Mossman has written two books: the most recent, *Politics and Narratives of Birth: Gynocolonization from Rousseau to Zola* was published by Cambridge University Press. She has also to her credit a number of articles and chapters in books. Currently, she is chairing the Department of French and Italian at the University of Maryland (College Park).

Jeff Nunokawa is Associate Professor of English at Princeton University. His publications include *The Afterlife of Property: Domestic Security and the Victorian Novel* and 'The Importance of Being Bored: The Dividends of Ennui in the Picture of Dorian Gray'. He is currently writing a book about the imagination of manageable desire in late nineteenth-century literature and culture.

Trista Selous is an Associate Research Fellow at Rochampton Institute, London. Her publications include a book, *The Other Woman: Feminism and Femininity in the Work of Marguerite Duras*, articles on Duras and on French cinema and several translations.

Yolande de Pontfarcy is Senior Lecturer in French at University College, Dublin. She has published on courtly and Arthurian literature, visions and other world voyages, and Celtic and Indo-European Studies.

Stan Smith holds the established Chair of English at Dundee University. He is the author of a number of books, including *Inviolable Voice: History and 20th Century Poetry* (Gill and Macmillan, 1982) and *The Origins of Modernism: Eliot, Pound, Yeats and the Rhetorics of Renewal* (Harvester, 1994), and of many essays and articles on modern literature. He is General Editor of Longman Critical Readers and Longman Studies in 20th Century Literature.

Lieve Spaas is professor of French Cultural Studies at Kingston University. She has published articles on Rousseau and the eighteenth century and is part of the CNRS Rousseau research team in Paris. Her books include a socio-historical analysis of the letters of Catherine de Saint-Pierre to her brother Bernardin, *Lettres de Catherine de Saint-Pierre à son frère Barnardin* (1996) and *Robinson Crusoe: Myths and Metamorphoses*, co-edited with Brian Stimpson. She is the general editor of the *Polygons: Studies in Cultural Constructs* series for Berghahn Books.

Anna Szabó is Professor of French Literature at Kossuth Lajos University, Debrecen. She specialises in George Sand and has published extensively on this writer. She is the author of *L'accueil critique de Paul Valéry en Hongrie* (1978) and *Le personnage sandien – Constantes et variations* (1991), and is currently working on an annotated edition of George Sand's prefaces to her fictional work.

Neil Taylor is Dean of Arts and Humanities at Roehampton Institute London. He is joint editor, with Ann Thompson, of the *Hamlet* volume forthcoming in the new Arden Shakespeare series. His publications include a number of books and articles on Shakespeare and other Renaissance dramatists.

Lynn Thomas has a BA and MA from the University of Lancaster and a D. Phil from the University of Oxford. She teaches courses in mythology and Hinduism at Roehampton Institute London, and has published a number of articles in these areas. She is currently working on a book exploring the Indian concept of time.

Ann Thompson is Professor of English and Head of Department at Roehampton Institute London. She is one of the General Editors of the Arden Shakespeare series and is co-editing *Hamlet* with Neil Taylor. She has published widely on Shakespeare, most recently concentrating on textual studies and feminist criticism.

Marina Warner is a writer and critic. She is the author of three studies of mythology that have been highly praised: *Alone of All her Sex: The Myth and Cult of the Virgin Mary*, *Joan of Arc: the Image of Female Heroism* and *Monuments and Maidens: The Allegory of the Female Form* (winner of Fawcett Prize, 1986). She has published several novels and biographies, short stories and children's books. She broadcasts regularly on radio and television. The Reith lectures she gave in 1986 are published under the title of *Managing Monsters*. Her forthcoming book is *No Go the Bogeyman: On Scaring, Lulling and Making Mock*.

1

Mythical Constructs and Social Realities

Lieve Spaas

Paternity and fatherhood: is there more than an etymological difference between these two apparently synonymous terms? What do we understand by 'paternity' and 'fatherhood'? These crucial questions lie at the heart of this collection of essays selected from the fields of the humanities and social sciences. In one sense the book is an anthropological document, offering compelling evidence to support the premise that there is a profound difference between the biological reality of paternity and the cultural construct of fatherhood, the procreating *genitor* and the authority-wielding *pater*. At the same time, although psychoanalytical approaches to questions of sex, gender and paternity or the triadic father–mother–son relationship are not specifically addressed here, the theories of Freud and Lacan provide a background for many of the authors' critical explorations. Through a kaleidoscope of literary texts, legal documents, case histories, paintings and letters, a complex picture of fatherhood emerges: filial perceptions of fathers are fraught with ambiguity and conflict, juridical systems constantly redefine paternal claims, privileges and rights, while the founding myths and social realities of many cultures may undermine established notions of fatherhood and paternity altogether. In their exploration of the relations, attitudes, emotions and values generated by the paternity/fatherhood distinction, the essays in this collection broaden our understanding of how the dichotomy has evolved in Western societies and offer insights into its manifestations in some post-colonial cultures.

PATERNITY: BIOLOGY, LAW AND LANGUAGE

The link between ideologies casting the father in the role of *pater familias*, or stressing the importance of the 'family unit', and the evolving political agendas of predominantly paternalistic societies is not surprising. Through metaphorical transference the notions of God (Father of creation), the King (Father of the Nation) or the Catholic priest (Father of one's conscience) have extended the scope of the family structure, offering a 'natural' model for claims to power made by individuals or institutions in political and religious contexts. However, as this book shows, such a model bears little relation to a 'natural' order of things: it is not biological paternity that determines the behaviour, sentiments, authority or qualities of the father. Any investigation of paternity must begin with the fundamental question of biological versus legal paternity.

Max Andréoli explores how, in Western countries, the notion of heredity has been linked to paternity rather than maternity. Generally speaking, he says, 'man has precedence over woman in matters of generation and the transmission of name and inheritance', although 'whether by natural or other means, it is the woman, the female in dioecious animals, who provides the space in which fertilisation and its consequences occur'. Andréoli sees an ideological basis for this division of roles: many scientists and writers have adopted notions which hold little scientific value, such as 'heredity by moral impregnation', a belief that the mother's state of mind at the moment of conception or during pregnancy influences the child. Throughout the nineteenth century in particular, natural versus moral heredity was at the forefront of so-called scientific debate and authors such as Michelet, Balzac, Zola and Goethe exploited the 'new' theories in their works. It is difficult, Andréoli concludes, to decide whether ideology takes its guarantees from science or whether science is guided by ideology. Even with the advances of genetics and the evolution of attitudes, it would be preposterous 'to claim that the questions heredity and paternity pose to men and societies have been definitively solved or left behind'.

The distinction between biological and legal paternity became strikingly apparent in Napoleon's Civil Code, whose use of the paternal function as a political tool is analysed by Xavier Martin. In the later revolutionary period, celibacy was frowned upon by a legislature keen to manipulate the private domain of the family to political ends. Powers which the Revolution had earlier taken from fathers were restored and strengthened. Martin analyses the way in which legal rights of sons were weakened and women deliberately excluded from power in order to make the father an auxiliary of the penal system, thereby easing the burden of law enforcement borne by the state.

Carol Mossman also addresses the question of biological paternity and the implications of recent advances in genetics. What might it mean, she asks, 'that fatherhood can now be somatically located?' Focusing on the persistent partitioning of the real into mind – related to paternity – and matter – related to maternity – she argues that the father is embodied or disembodied to suit political expedience or the needs of authority. Taking the example of pre- and post-revolutionary France, she shows how, under the *ancien régime*, where both class and gender divisions were strictly maintained, the father's body served to uphold class interests, whereas in revolutionary France the rejection and collapse of the class system led to a disembodying of the father. Subsequently the revolution's rejection of the importance of biological paternity was upheld for quite different reasons by the Napoleonic Code, whose famous Article 340 prohibited paternity searches. Concurring with Martin, Mossman sees this legal provision as a reflection of, on the one hand, the need to assert the father's authority in support of that of the state and, on the other, of economic and gender issues. She argues that the repeal of Article 340 in 1912 reflects the ideological ascendency of 'heredity and race' in the early twentieth century. Mossman concludes by expressing the hope that the new possibility of genetically locating the father 'might dismantle some of the age-old dualisms which confine people to extremely unproductive social double-binds'.

Paternal authority is also the subject of Christie McDonald's study of the 'Aurore' case. This concerns a trial held in Quebec in the 1920s, in which a child, Aurore, was 'physically abused to death by her stepmother with the complicity of her biological father'. McDonald investigates the trial and the powerful legend which grew up around the story. Although the father himself actively abused the child, fictionalised representations tend to 'factor the father out' while systematically demonising the stepmother. McDonald seeks to 'factor the father back into' the case history and also to explore the possible links between the way his role has been represented and historical and social changes in Quebec. In so doing she raises important questions about paternal authority and perceptions of paternal absence and throws new light on the cliché of the 'wicked stepmother'. It is necessary, she argues, 'to look beyond nostalgic dreams of paternal power and the Christian nuclear family to find what needs to be reinvented'.

Following these investigations of theories and beliefs concerning heredity and the legal endorsement of paternal power, Yolande de Pontfarcy's essay explores an extensive medieval corpus to trace the growth of the importance of paternity between the tenth and fourteenth centuries. The author shows how the Indo-European transmission of power through women, which had emphasised the relationship of maternal uncle to nephew and made incest between father and daughter a political crime, remained a central issue in medieval literature, especially in stories of succession without a male heir. She also considers the growing importance of the author as 'father' of the text, from the virtual non-existence of the idea of authorship before the end of the thirteenth century to the emergence of the identifiable writer at the end of the fifteenth.

Philippe Bolusset's essay takes us from the analysis of texts to the consideration of contemporary linguistic systems and, in particular, to the question of whether language reflects the social and cultural properties defining the role of the father. Basing his study on the metaphorical use of kinship terms in order to safeguard the distinction between social and linguistic patterns, Bolusset notes that, despite their apparent symmetry, the semantic values and syntactic properties of words such as *père* (father) and *mère* ('mother'), *fils* ('son') and *fille* ('daughter'), show some 'imperceptible dissimilarities'. His analysis of specific examples reveals that, while the two terms might be assumed to be synonymous when used metaphorically, in practice 'the agentive property is fundamental and inherent to the lexical item *père*, in contrast to the word *mère*'. This leads Bolusset to suggest that, like grammatical markers, lexical items may have underlying stable properties, which may themselves be derived from deep-rooted socio-cultural preconceptions.

ABSENT FATHERS

The essays in this volume seem to indicate that fathers, although central and looming large in the subject's psyche, are often experienced as absent. Jennifer Birkett's exploration of the works of several nineteenth century French women writers demonstrates to what extent the absence of the father has marked the lives of their children. Suggesting that the idea of an irreconcilable opposition between father and mother is founded on the Freudian theory of the Oedipus complex and its subsequent rereadings by Lacan, which themselves represent what are in fact age-old Judaeo-Christian theories, Birkett turns to the works of Mme de Staël, George Sand and Rachilde in order to question some of the theoretical positions of psychoanalysis and contemporary feminism. According to Birkett, 'all three recognise the wider social ramifications of rethinking sexual hierarchy: then as now, daughters imagining resistance to the constraints of the father's desire must come to terms with the parallel desire of the brother-clan to overthrow the father'.

As Janet Beer discusses, the stories of Kate Chopin are also marked by the father's absence. When Chopin's husband died prematurely she supported herself and their six children by writing and the absent father became a major theme of her fictional world. Chopin's stories challenged paternal authority, whether it be that of 'God the Father, the patriarch in the system of slavery, or the leisure class father, going about his business'. To defuse their 'potentially explosive nature' she resorted to the popular genre of 'local colour', basing most of her stories in her native Louisiana, with its unique social mix including Creoles and Cajuns. However, Beer shows how Chopin uses the genre to her own ends, portraying the tragedy of the absent father in 'gradations of colour', from the 'slave-father' who is sold away to the morally absent ruling-class father or the 'master-father' who begets children on his slaves. In this way, Beer argues, Chopin denounces the process of usurpation which denies the rightful authority of the slave-father over his child and upholds the abusive authority of master over slave.

By curious coincidence, Mme de Sévigné's daughter left the family home twenty years to the day after her father's death. Angela Cozea's intricate analysis of the subsequent mother–daughter relationship suggests that Mme de Sévigné's 'idolatry' of her absent daughter is marked by this earlier loss of her husband. First, in psychological terms, Cozea argues that M. de Sévigné's death was intolerable not because he was a husband – an unfaithful one, who died in a duel over another woman – but because he became transformed into the father, thereby intensifying identification with the daughter. Secondly, from a philosophical perspective, Cozea takes Levinas' concept of 'deference to death', which Levinas himself saw as reflecting the universal human search for sense in the looming presence of non-sense, and gives it practical application, using it to understand the particular form of Mme de Sévigné's daughter-idolatry as a displacement of her mourning for the husband/father.

The oedipal struggle of sons against oppressive fathers is a recurring theme in many cultures, but what of the son who has no father to struggle with? Jean-Jacques Hamm explores prose works by two poets whose fathers disappeared when they were children, revealing what he calls the 'father effect', the traces left by the father's absence. In both Fernando Pessoa's *Book of Disquiet* and Arthur Rimbaud's *Correspondence* he finds a sense of nothingness, 'perverse, diffuse, destructive and demiurgic', which drives Rimbaud to a relentless search for action and Pessoa to obstinate flight into the sanctuary of dreams. Hamm considers that, in these two cases at least, 'the death of the father, his absence, is the son's breath of life, the possibility for him to exist, even if it is only the terrible existence of an adventurer or drunken poet'.

REINVENTING FATHER

Like Rimbaud and Pessoa, George Sand lost her father when she was still a child; unlike them, as Anna Szabó analyses, she sought to fill the void he left behind. Szabó examines the evolution of Sand's attempt 'to resuscitate the father's *word* in order to give herself at least the illusion of possessing a spiritual father'. The earlier books feature a high occurrence of bastards and foundlings and, when legitimate children do appear, they are antagonistic towards their fathers. In later novels a new image of fatherhood emerges: fathers are present, cruel fathers are replaced by kind ones and absent fathers give way to father substitutes or spiritual fathers. Szabó argues that Sand's novels give precedence to legal and social fatherhood over biological paternity, reflecting the concerns of the period in which she wrote, which was also that of the creation of the Napoleonic Code.

Clearly the father's real presence or absence does not in itself determine the perceptions and emotions of his offspring, although it may be an important element. Patrick Corcoran investigates the relationship between paternity, fatherhood and the context of colonial power in sub-Saharan Africa, concentrating his analysis on Henri Lopes's novel *Le Chercheur d'Afriques*, whose main character is a *métis*, son of a European father and an African mother. Corcoran analyses the way that Lopes's novel raises questions of 'personal, social and cultural identity': the son must find and confront his biological father in order to assert an identity for himself. However, the quest for the father turns to flight when the latter tries to keep his son in Europe and, as the action shifts to and fro between Africa and France, Corcoran shows how the memory of the slave-ships is revived when 'the father becomes the hunter seeking out his progeny'. When the son finally confronts his father, bringing about the latter's death, Corcoran sees this as a reflection of both the African slave-son's revenge and 'the ancient message' that 'in order for the subject to constitute itself as subject the death of the father is required'.

The work of other writers may manifest a desire to reinvent or replace the father altogether. Michaëla Mongelard explores the way that, in the world of Mauritian author Loys Masson, the absent biological father is replaced by father substitutes who themselves prove inadequate and unable to fulfil their duties of surrogacy. The constant search of Masson's characters for a replacement for the failing father is also, Mongelard suggests, that of the author himself: 'Through writing, the writer invents, or rather reinvents himself, he symbolically kills his father and replaces the father's name with a new one, his own.' The text itself thus becomes the site of the oedipal struggle, which must be constantly renewed.

The Marquis de Sade's representation of the father is characterised by hyperbole. 'Sade's star player', Béatrice Fink argues, 'is without doubt the *pater familias*'. But the father who is given privileged treatment by Sade in his novel *Juliette* is none other than the *pater par excellence*, *il Papa*, the Holy Father, the Sovereign Pontiff enthroned on the Holy See. In the lengthy Vatican episode of the novel, Juliette, eponymous heroine and hardened libertine, travels to Rome and sets up an appointment with the Pope. Fink sees the subsequent coupling between the Holy Father and Juliette, representing France, 'the Church's oldest daughter', as one of the most 'intensely transgressive' episodes in all of Sade's fiction. The father's powerful position is both stressed and threatened, and infanticide and parricide are justified in a restating of Sade's paternal paradigm, summed up by Fink as consisting of 'overdetermined, unholy fathers on the one hand, exterminated or exterminating ones on the other'.

According to Sander Gilman, Franz Kafka provides an exemplary case of a son who becomes his father. Kafka's 'Letter to his Father', Gilman argues, is 'an elaborate fiction about Kafka's anxiety about his own body's predestination to become his father's' and 'not the strong, paternal body, but the ill body of a father who manipulates his illness for his own ends, at his son's expense.' The problem for Kafka, as Gilman sees it, is how to 'avert his destiny, which was to become his father and all that his father represented – the ill Dreyfus, the diseased Jew'. Torn in his desire for both a powerful father (whom he fears) and a sickly father (whom he fears to become), 'it is in books that Kafka seeks a "healthy" father and a "healthy" son'; however, beyond the immediate personal conflict, Gilman sees Kafka's case as the story of 'the Jewish patient, whose anxiety is located in the body [inherited from father] but whose real source is the social displacement felt by Jews in the *fin de siècle* European society'.

Jeff Nunokawa finds similar father–son relations at work in a very different context, that of *David Copperfield*, 'the story whose title is also the name of the father'. Here, the father is absent and the son takes 'his proper station as the star of a fatherless household'. Yet while the death of David's father allows him to live with his mother in the 'happiest state imaginable', it does not abolish, Nunokawa argues, 'the other in-house desire grounded in the oedipal plot, namely that of the son for the father himself.' Nunokawa examines how the father, enemy of David's desire, 'turns out to be its object as well'. Exploring the entanglements of heterosexual and homosexual desire, he traces the link between the dead father and the senior schoolfellow to whom David feels attracted. Behind the oedipal plot, for which the father provides the structure, Nunokawa thus reveals the structure of the father who prohibits heterosexual desire, while eliciting its homosexual counterpart.

PATERNITY, SEX, GENDER AND SUCCESSION

Fathers may be associated in the first instance with the act of procreation, but Marina Warner examines cases of fictional and mythical fathers who eat their offspring. The discussion takes her from the fairytale ogre to textual and visual representations of the founding myth of the Greek pantheon, with its 'divine patriarchal prerogative' of cannibalistic infanticide, and ends with the eating of body-parts in paintings and children's lore. Warner suggests that such stories are both a manifestation of eroticism and a response to the problem of the uncertainty of paternal identity. Furthermore, devouring may also be a prelude to birth: being eaten equals incorporation and this, in turn, stands for a surrogate – though unwitting – pregnancy in the male. Considering the relation of stories of ogres and cannibalism to the children who still invent them and pass them on, Warner concludes that such tales contain the implicit message 'that the young suffer the aggression of their elders but can comfort themselves that they will inevitably gain ground on the old'.

Like Warner, Lynn Thomas suggests that stories of parthenogenetic birth to males 'serve, in part, as a vehicle whereby men may begin to overcome some of the fears and insecurities they may have about their role as fathers'. On the other hand she does not agree with critics who have suggested that the primary role of such myths was to denigrate women. Basing her discussion on the story of Athene's birth from Zeus as it relates to the rest of Hesiod's *Theogony*, Thomas shows that the myth's underlying function is to solve the problem of succession posed by Zeus's divine immortality, breaking 'the cycle of filial rebellion' and neutralising the negative aspects of the son as successor and deposer. At the same time, through Athene's relation to the city of Athens, the myth links the genealogy of the gods to the founding of human society. However, Thomas argues, Greek attitudes towards women are reflected in two themes this myth shares with other stories of parthenogenesis: emphasis on avoidance of the womb and insistence on the passing on of culture through a 'second birth' to the father.

The emphasis placed on the father's relationship to the successor in stories of parthenogenesis is completely reversed in the work of Michel Tournier, where, as Mark Ferrigan reveals, it is the successor who holds sway. 'Tournier's major novels' Ferrigan notes, 'all focus on characters whose biological fathers are absent and who are also unable – or unwilling – to become fathers in their own right', while fathers who do appear in the text generally fail one way or another to fulfil their role. The father's absence, Ferrigan argues, is 'the price to be paid for there being a story to tell', yet at the same time Tournier's texts are haunted by absent fathers, both intratextual and intertextual. Discussing the way that Tournier's reworking of other texts betrays 'a distinct unease with relation to his literary precursors', Ferrigan notes that Tournier refuses to acknowledge any indebtedness, to the point of accusing one of his literary fathers, Alain Fournier, of plagiarising Tournier. Ferrigan concludes that 'by encouraging a reading which constantly moves backwards and forwards between stories, without ever establishing . . . a point of origin', Tournier denies 'paternal influence and preempts the threat of filial appropriation'.

Tivadar Gorilovics describes the family in Molière's work as 'a battlefield', where children struggle to free themselves from the control of a father who is always central, while the mother is almost invariably absent. Molière's fathers are interested only in using succession as a weapon for their own material gains: daughters who follow their hearts rather than the paternal interest in choosing a husband are liable to be banished to a convent; sons who fail to abide by their fathers' dictates are menaced with disinheritance. Yet ironically these fathers each have a character defect which threatens to ruin the whole family. In the 'desert of love' analysed by Gorilovics, paternal affection is 'no more than a front behind which the selfishness of the bourgeois may find shelter'. Comedy arises from the potential for catastrophe when filial love is supplanted by parricidal yearnings.

A book on paternity and fatherhood would be incomplete without reference to Shakespeare. Two essays in this collection are thus devoted to him. In the first Lawrence Danson identifies a fundamental difference between Shakespeare's portrayal of father/daughter and father/son relationships, the former characterised by the father's strong urge for reunion with the lost daughter, while the latter is marked by his 'equally strong avoidance of the father–son reunion'. Danson suggests that this difference reflects, on the one hand, 'longing for a union with a woman who must be simultaneously daughter, mother and wife' and on the other, that 'every father is also a son, which is part of every father's and every son's problem' and he goes on to explore the way in which the difficulties of the father–son relationship portrayed in *Henry IV Part I* and *Part II* resurface in *King Lear*, where 'the bad son's wish to supplant the father is also always the good son Edgar's unavoidable destiny'.

The second of the essays on Shakespeare, by Ann Thompson and Neil Taylor, takes a twofold approach to paternity in *Hamlet*. Thompson, noting that Shakespeare 'seems to have been intensely aware that "the first murder" in Judaeo-Christian tradition was not a parricide (more common in stories of the Greek and Roman gods) but a fratricide', suggests that overemphasis on the oedipal aspects of the play have obscured the importance it gives to relations between brothers. Taylor, in his section, concentrates on the problem of the 'fatherhood' of the play's constantly re-edited text, of which he and Thompson are currently preparing a new edition. Looking at the play in both its intratextual and extratextual aspects, Taylor asks who is the father, 'the reader, the author or both? Shakespeare begat Hamnet/Hamlet, but was he the only begetter of Hamlet? Is he alone Father and Mother of that mother and father of a play?'

In the final essay in the collection Stan Smith argues that 'paternity and its problematic nature' is a key theme of T.S. Eliot's *The Waste Land*. Exploring the intertextual elements woven into the *The Waste Land* (Shakespeare, Freud and Hesse), Smith suggests that for Eliot the relation of art to reality is an act of ritual parricide 'in which the body of the material world ... has to be killed in order to be ressurected as "something rich and strange", the work of art'. Smith reveals the guilt and anxiety pervading Eliot's poem as the parricidal son 'seeks to resurrect the murdered father in the body of the text'. Killing the father, Smith argues, whether literally or symbolically, 'is the foundational modern act' by which the revolting sons of Modernism replace patriarchal lineage with a self-constituting brother clan. At the same time, it reflects the general historical context of a century in which 'parricidal revolutions ended by devouring their children'. Smith notes that at the century's end the break with genealogy represented by Modernism still holds, allowing Salim in Salman Rushdie's *Midnight's Children* to state with 'truly postmodern' assurance that 'in the end, everyone can do without fathers'.

The attempt to trace a cartography of fatherhood reveals this concept, as distinct from biological paternity, to be crucial to our understanding of the social structures of Western societies and their political or religious ideologies. However, while at the social level governments have manipulated the notion of paternity to political ends, the father's presence or absence, or even his life or death, do not seem to determine the perceptions or emotions of his offspring. Authors have thus often reinvented fathers. Whether reinvented or surrogate fathers may be seen as an elimination of the biological father would be difficult to argue. Nevertheless, as in classical civilisation, oedipal themes have shaped modern Western culture. Where parricide occurs it happens symbolically through the creation or representation of father figures in literature and art.

If the essays in this collection emphasise the effect of the father on his offspring, they also highlight the fears of fathers concerning their own paternity. These fears were compounded by the lack of proof, since biological paternity could not be formally established. However, a solution to the conflict between paternity and fatherhood seemed available when scientific advances, through the discovery of DNA tests and their use by society, provided the means to ascertain biological paternity. Since the discovery of DNA coincided with profound changes in socio-economic realities the question of the father's significance was raised anew. Biological certainty cannot uphold the *genitor*'s position in complex new family structures, where the father's role may be shared by several parental figures. Old myths return in modern fiction, images of male maternity or female paternity haunt the imagination and new scientific speculations postulate a world where fathers may even become superfluous. The biological reality of paternity and the cultural construct of fatherhood remain distinct: new mythical constructs and new social realities emerge and will continue to do so well beyond the end of this millennium.

I
Biological Paternity in Law and Language

2

Heredity and Paternity

Max Andréoli

For the purposes of this discussion we shall confine the vast subject indicated by the title to a brief examination of the relationships between biology, one of the sciences concerned with heredity and paternity, and the ideological superstructures which these notions necessarily bring into play,[1] as seen through certain literary texts.

Let us begin with a simple observation: in our Western countries, the notion of heredity has long been linked to that of paternity and, although matriarchy is doubtless the most logical way of establishing filiation – with all its consequences for inheritance – it is patriarchy that has been adopted by almost all the so-called advanced civilisations. Paternity and biological heredity have, however, always seemed a profound mystery, the more irritating for being both incomprehensible and banal, prodigious and unexceptional, and this makes them excellent material for the constructions of ideology: 'What a wonderful thing it is', writes Montaigne, 'that the drop of seed from which we are produced should carry in itself the impression not only of the bodily form, but even of the thoughts and inclinations of our fathers! Where can that drop of fluid matter contain that infinite number of forms?'[2] It is no wonder, as Montaigne would say, that he is perplexed, along with all who have investigated this obscure field whose shadows modern genetics is now beginning to illuminate, though not without running into other, no less shadowy enigmas. Until recent decades heredity was a subject covered by an impenetrable veil. Gregor Mendel, founder of modern genetics and the first to go beyond the stage of intuition and analogy, began his investigations in the 1850s, yet, paradoxically, his work remained neglected before its rediscovery – or, as François Jacob would have it, the rediscovery of his methods – forty years later at the beginning of this century. We should add that around 1950, the worlds of both science and politics were shaken by a lively debate around the inheritance of acquired characteristics, due to the publication of the theories of the Soviet agronomist and biologist Lyssenko, who had the support of his country's rulers. This debate offers a perfect illustration of the ideological nature of certain theoretical positions in biology.

These things said, Montaigne's question, for all its humility before the great mystery, nonetheless contains an implicit statement or, rather, presupposition, which is all the more powerful for being unthought and ideological and which I propose to consider more closely: the 'drop of seed from which we are produced' *obviously* refers to the paternal semen and ignores the role of the mother in the process of biological heredity. I am well aware that the word 'fathers' (*pères*) could have the sense of 'parents' and that in his *Apologie de Raimond Sebond* Montaigne offers a critical discussion of the opposing views; yet the context here leaves little room for doubt: the mother is brushed aside. And it is on this brushing aside, implicit in this text, explicit in others, that I intend to concentrate, because it makes manifest the role that ideology allots to paternity in hereditary phenomena. Such a view is accepted so naturally that it goes unnoticed, even by a thinker who, while he tends towards misogyny,[3] is determined, long before Descartes, to doubt everything.

As far as conception was concerned, the opinions of the ancients in fact differed widely, but their beliefs and theories lacked a firm basis or tangible elements and could not counter ideologies that granted the male, the father, the privilege of being the true, if not the only, author of descendence. Patrilinear inheritance, a very old social institution, requires the woman to occupy a necessary but subordinate place in the transmission of inheritance, in whatever form. I need not discuss at length the origins of this institution nor its fluctuating and complex development; suffice it to recall that in *Genesis* (the one in the Bible!) Abraham's wife Sarah has a son by means of her husband's servant Agar, just as Jacob's wives Rachel and Leah give birth through the offices of their servants Bilha and Zilpha. In these three cases the servants, although biological mothers of the children to whom they give birth, are nevertheless what we would today call 'surrogate mothers', whose primary role is to bear the all-important semen of the father. Without taking things to such extremes, we can state that, generally speaking, in our societies, man has precedence over woman in matters of generation and the transmission of name and inheritance. And yet, in all matters of reproduction, whether by natural or other means, it is the woman, the female in dioecious animals, who provides the space in which fertilisation and its consequences occur. How then can we reconcile this obvious function with the pre-eminent role assigned to fatherhood?

The answer lies with ideology, and notably with a religious ideology supported by a scientific ideology from which it is imperfectly separated, which supports the status quo and makes *thinkable* what might otherwise appear as an incompatibility. I have chosen a translated passage from Dante's *Divine Comedy* (*Purgatory* XXV – but there is an equivalent passage in *The Banquet*). The poet returns to the teachings of the all-embracing text of the Middle Ages, Saint Thomas Aquinas's religious, philosophical and scientific work *Summa Theologiae*, in which Aquinas himself adapts the Aristotelian theories outlined by Pythagoras. As they climb towards the summit of the mountain of Purgatory, Dante and his guide Virgil meet the shade of the Latin poet Statius, who describes the stages of the human generation as follows:

> The perfect blood – the blood that's never drunk
> by thirsty veins (like food left on the table
> still unconsumed) but is preserved entire –
>
> acquires, within the heart, formative powers
> to build the members of the human shape
> (as does the blood that serves to nourish them),
>
> then, purified again, flows down into
> the part best left unmentioned; thence it sprays
> in nature's vessel on another blood
>
> and there the two bloods blend. Each is designed
> to play a *passive* or an *active* role
> due to its perfect place of origin.[4]

Statius, Aquinas and Dante (following Aristotle and against the Greek pangermists) thus separate human blood into two types: the more ordinary blood, which irrigates and nourishes the members and which goes to form menstrual blood, from which the material body of the foetus will also be made, and another blood which is purer and more highly developed, the 'perfect' blood whose source is the paternal heart and which, in the guise of sperm, forms the child's soul, as Statius goes on to explain:

> It keeps on swelling, spreading out, my son,
> this force that comes from the begetter's heart
> where nature plans for all the body's parts.[5]

The Italian word *il generante* refers to the male genitor, the father. Supported by the authority of Aristotle and Aquinas, this theory of the two bloods makes it possible to preserve the dominance of paternity by giving paternal semen the active role, while the passive role is accorded to the womb. The two notions of active and passive, which Dante evokes in line 47 as I have emphasised, link this account to the Aristotelian doctrine of form and substance, the male sperm being the active, formal principle and the feminine blood its material substratum.

Thus grounded in tradition they have a bright future in store,[6] acting as points of connection between ideology and science or, perhaps, between a scientific ideology and the other ideologies. They are certainly linked to the great myths; yet generation does take place within the mother independently of her will, although not without intervention on her part. And the spermatozoon's race for life after coitus does show us the competing gametes with the ovum as the end, the (almost immobile) motor and indeed the goal. Still, all this was of course unknown in Dante's time, and for long after.

I can only allude to the debates on this matter, which have divided scientists from the Renaissance almost to the present day. Throughout the seventeenth, eighteenth and even the nineteenth centuries, an interminable quarrel, lacking any concrete element to decide it, split naturalists into two camps along lines which, as in Dante's work, were ideological as much as scientific. New disciplines were being born that were independent of social and religious constraints and drew on the results of observations and sometimes experiments; yet such data were mixed in with considerations which we would not today call 'scientific'. I am referring of course to the quarrel of the 'ovists' and the 'animalculists', with its parallel in the theologico-scientific quarrel between the preformists and the partisans of epigenesis. I shall confine myself to citing a few sentences from the physiologist Richerand, who, in the first part of the nineteenth century, summed up the question in the following terms:

> The only difference that now exists between the hypothetical opinions of the physiologists is this: that according to some the ovum contains the rudiment of the new individual to which, according to them, the sperm communicates the power of life; whereas, according to the others, the ovum is destined only to receive the germ emanating from the male and coming entirely from him.[7]

The basic difference between these opinions and the theory described by Statius seems to me a small one; in both cases it is from the father that comes either the germ itself (for the animaculists) or, for the ovists, the 'power of life' as Richerand puts it, or the *aura seminalis* of the eighteenth century physiologists, which I would link (boldly and without the support of François Jacob[8]) to Dante's *informative power*.

Nevertheless, the mere existence of a fierce debate around the respective importance of the two sexes in the process of generation shows that the scientists' researches were following their own logic, relatively independent of social demands. At the same time, the function of ideology being essentially to reconcile and integrate, we see the formation of a median solution exploiting the old opposition of 'inner life' and 'outer life', in which the social life of relationships – the *active* life – was the preserve of man, while to woman were granted the care of family and home – in other words the *passive* life – without the latter term having the pejorative connotations we give it today, for the inner life is also the life of the soul, while the outer life is that of the body. This schematised duality was condensed in the distinction established by Bichat among others, at the beginning of the nineteenth century, between 'animal life' and 'organic life'. It was thus easy to share out the roles with apparent fairness: the child took its organic life from the mother and its animal life from the father. The interplay of these elements explained the differences in children's characters, while giving each sex a sphere of influence and satisfying social demand, since the male, the father, continued to act and govern and remained the master of heredity. These theories, which I have already greatly simplified, are summed up in a passage from the *Dictionnaire de phrénologie* of 1836 (the entry on *Amativité ou amour physique*) by the Saint-Simonian Théophile Thoré: 'From the point of view of nature the masculine sex represents the active principle, the inciting element, while the female is the passive principle, the fertile element. All observations confirm this metaphysical truth…' And Goethe, in his great novel of 1809, *Elective Affinities*, to which I shall return later, gives his character Charlotte similar words: 'Men attend more to particular things and to the present, and rightly, since they are called upon to act and to influence events. Women, on the other hand, with an equal rightness attend more to the things that hang together in life, since a woman's fate, and the fate of her family depend on such things hanging together and it is up to her to see that they do'.[9] Here we find once more the ideas and indeed the vocabulary noted in Dante's text.

Since I do not have the space to examine how these debates were echoed or merely organised in literary works, I shall confine my discussion to a particular point, one which I believe is often ignored or neglected: I am thinking of what was known as heredity by influence or by impregnation. The expression will be familiar to readers of Zola or Michelet and, of course, to specialists of the history of science, who speak of 'telegony'. So what does it mean?

Again, this was an old belief, reworked in accordance with the tastes of the day in the second half of the nineteenth century by Dr Lucas, author of a celebrated *Traité philosophique et physiologique de l'hérédité naturelle dans les états de santé et de maladie du système nerveux* (Baillère, 1847). This work soon became an authority in literary as well as scientific circles, among those writers who dreamed of giving literature the status of an observational science, or who were looking for scientific guarantees at a time when science had become the new gospel. The naively ideological nature of the very title is plain enough, linking as it does the two adjectives 'philosophique' and 'physiologique'. As is well known, this work was duly condensed by Zola, who referred to it constantly in making heredity the key to his Rougon-Macquart cycle and, in 1868, to his novel *Madeleine Férat*, all of which feature heredity by impregnation. While we should be cautious where the influence of Zola's theories on his practice as a writer is concerned, their effects on what I shall call his 'system' cannot be underestimated; in any case, the family tree of the Rougon-Macquarts, of which some wag said that, had he committed it, he would have hanged himself from the highest tree, is indecipherable without the help of the categories created by Dr Lucas and adopted by the novelist. I am not referring here to the theoretical texts or prefaces which some critics tend to regard as less important than the novels, but to the novels themselves: the tree's 'instructions' are elaborated throughout *Le Docteur Pascal* by the eponymous character.

Now while it is true, as Françoise Gaillard notes in her excellent article *Génétique et mythe de la Genèse* (1985), that the family tree is 'the home of the imaginary realm of the science of heredity', it also had an important function for positive scientific knowledge, as generated by developments in the biology of the period. Certainly Gregor Mendel was establishing the laws of plant hybridation and creating modern genetics at almost the same time, but Mendel was acting independently; he was an outsider whose brilliant experiments were, as I have mentioned, taken up and recognised only much later. Dr Lucas's work, on the other hand, followed the tradition of eighteenth century scientists and the positivist field: his laws were of the kind that was possible before the break marked by Darwin, Mendel and Freud.

Here are some lines from *Le Docteur Pascal* which set out the theories of the hero (the narrator? Zola?), which are also those of Dr Lucas:

> Where heredity was concerned, he had accepted only four possibilities: direct heredity, the representation of the father and mother in the child's physical and moral nature; indirect heredity, the representation of collateral relations, uncles, aunts and cousins; reverted heredity, the representation of ancestors at a distance of one or more generations; lastly heredity by influence, the representation of previous partners, for example the first male who has as it were impregnated the female for all future conception, even when he is no longer the agent of that conception.[10]

New subdivisions follow, based on choice, mixtures, and so on. In the family tree of the Rougon-Macquarts each type of heredity is represented; however I shall consider only heredity by influence, noting at the outset that the mention of 'previous partners' is purely stylistic; Zola could have written: '*the woman's* previous partners', since the woman is the only person involved in this type of heredity. Its most eminent incarnation in Zola's work is the character of Nana, who is the daughter of Gervaise and Coupeau, but physically resembles her mother's first lover Lantier.

This phenomenon of feminine impregnation is no longer granted the slightest element of reality and the so-called facts gathered by Dr Lucas or Dr Pascal rest entirely upon errors, themselves induced by prejudice, in other words by an ideological judgement which disturbed the progress of their scientific work. This prejudice has its secular roots in the belief in the passivity of woman which, as I have shown, led scientists to assume as obvious the influence of the active male principle on the plastic organism of the female, whatever the respective roles attributed to the ovum and the spermatozoon. No one, as far as I know, ever thought that impregnation could operate in the other direction, from the female to the male. Such a bias may well be due in part to physiology: it is 'natural', in a mechanistic vision of the world, to associate impregnation with the mechanism of penetration. Yet this reason is not enough in itself. Ideology remains crucial, and it is clear that here, as in the title of Dr Lucas's book, the relation between science and ideology is one of close symbiosis: science provides society with the theoretical arguments it demands, but in return the other ideologies offer science the structures necessary for understanding, ordering and in some cases constructing the 'considerable heap of observations' as Dr Pascal puts it, that it has at its disposal.

It is hardly surprising then that the ideological context should affect observation. Observation, in the time before Claude Bernard or Pasteur, lacked the rigour we understand it to have today. One need only read almost any scientific work written before – and indeed immediately after – 1880 to see that, as well as properly-conducted experiments, many scientists cheerfully classed as 'observations' a wide variety of comments afforded them without any kind of guarantee by travellers and explorers, or merely by general rumour. They were following an example established down the ages by the ancients, Montaigne and the natural historians of the classical age with their jumbles of 'curiosities'. So that the first task of what we regard today as the true scientific spirit, consisting of objectivity and rigour – an attitude which I also regard as ideological – was to refute the errors of the rest.

The theory of impregnation was very quickly appropriated by many writers, including Michelet, a thinker both anticlerical and religious, who was, like his worst enemies, a fervent supporter of indissoluble marriage and for whom the phenomenon of impregnation offered an opportunity to show that men and women are essentially 'monogamous'. Indeed, if one accepts the idea of impregnation, physiology 'advises' monogamy, since the woman is not the future of man but his creation: according to Michelet, the phenomenon was a 'two-fold prodigy' bringing about both 'the birth of the child [and] the transformation of the mother. The impregnated wife becomes man'.[11] One flesh, but that flesh is masculine. Hence the impossibility of divorce, which would undermine the principle of paternity:

> How dangerous it is for her, when the lover who receives her grows increasingly disgusted at finding you [long before Butor, Michelet created the fiction of a text addressed to the *narrataire*] in this person who has been so completely transformed into you! At coming upon your voice, your words, your gestures! and even more tangible traces!

But above all: 'She belongs so much to you that even if her lover impregnates her, she will most probably give him a child of yours, with your features.' The widow runs the risk of a similar misfortune:

> Once the woman has been impregnated she bears her husband within her. This much has been demonstrated [a verb to savour from the pen of one so indefatigably erudite]. How long does the first impregnation last? Ten years? Twenty years? Her whole life? What is certain is that the children a widow has with her second husband often resemble her first.[12]

This erroneous certainty, which Michelet so imprudently upholds, nevertheless gives him the chance to condemn other errors or false assumptions concerning heredity which might contradict his theories, such as the belief that the adulterous woman's pregnancy was proof that she fully consented to her crime, or the idea that menstrual blood was intrinsically impure, a belief refuted by chemical analyses around 1840. Thus in Michelet's approach a mix of ideological determination and scientific considerations reinforce each other, just as his work combines a discourse which could be considered anti-feminist with a fiercely romantic ultra-feminism.

A curious variant of heredity by influence can be found in heredity by moral impregnation, which is linked to a belief, sometimes accepted by scientists as well as by ordinary people, of the influence on the child of the mother's state of mind at the moment of conception and during pregnancy. This matter, manifested at its most banal in the idea that a pregnant woman has 'cravings', is moreover investigated today with all the apparent seriousness of our modern science. This type of impregnation does not require the physical contact that heredity by physiological impregnation assumes; on the other hand it has never, as far as I know, enjoyed any real scientific support, at least not in the nineteenth century. Be that as it may, writers used it as a plot mechanism, a psychological element and indeed a metaphysical theme. Thus in Goethe's *Elective Affinities*, heredity by influence lies at the heart of the narrative: the 'double adultery' of Edward and Charlotte, one with the Captain, the other with Ottilie, remains entirely emotional; and yet the fruit of this union which is at once both conjugal and criminal, the child whose first name is Othon like that of his biological and spiritual progenitors, resembles the Captain and his imaginary mother Ottilie.

Why did Goethe, who was one of the great thinkers and naturalists of his time, choose to base the plot of his novel on such a premise? Although he presented it as a paraphrase of the words of Christ (Matthew, V, 28) and herein lies one aspect of this complex work, Goethe probably did not regard the episode as having any relation to biology;

in *Elective Affinities* he was applying the discoveries of science, particularly chemistry, to literature, but in a metaphorical or, more precisely, analogical manner, whose aim was to 'embody abstractions' in a 'chemical parabola', as the novel's introductory note puts it. However, readers of his realist narrative, in which concrete details abound, had to be prepared to accept or at least give the benefit of the doubt to the authenticity of this fantastical form of procreation; moreover, the criticisms that were addressed to the author concerned the immorality of the situation rather than its improbability.

The importance of this very specific form of heredity for my discussion however lies in the phenomenon of the child's 'double likeness': 'In his features and in the whole shape of his body the child more and more resembled the Captain, and his eyes were less and less distinguishable from Ottilie's.'[13] It is noteworthy that the child receives his *external* features from his 'father' and his eyes, thus the *internal* aspects, from his 'mother'. These things link Goethe to a tradition whose manifestations in earlier texts I have sought to trace.

The situation is not dissimilar in Balzac's excellent novel *L'Enfant maudit*. Jeanne de Saint-Savin has made an unhappy marriage to the rough and brutal Comte d'Hérouville, a general in the royalist armies during the Wars of Religion, in order to save her cousin, the handsome Georges de Chaverny, whom she loves and who loves her. They have had no carnal relations, apart from 'a few meetings beneath the lime trees, where lack of witnesses made freer speech possible, as well as furtive embraces and surprised kisses, all passion's innocent advances which do not overstep the bounds of modesty'.[14] Jeanne has had to separate from him, she is pregnant by d'Hérouville, but she feels a groundless remorse because, the narrator explains, 'in her innocence she attributed to that last glance, in which her lover sent her his whole life, the power exerted by the angel's Visitation on the mother of Our Lord'.[15] Although the poor countess has every reason to believe that it is not an angel but her rough and nasty husband who is the father of the child she bears and to whom she will give birth prematurely, Etienne, her son, resembles Georges de Chaverny.

Of course, unlike Goethe, Balzac makes nothing explicit, preferring allusions and associations that lead the reader to discover in Etienne, beyond the 'vague resemblance to the cousin beloved beyond the grave' his mother sees, a real identification with de Chaverny. Indeed, while suggesting Jeanne's moral impregnation, the narrator leaves open the possibility of a virgin birth, linking the mother to the Virgin Mary and Etienne to Christ. Yet here too, it is her soul that the mother passes on to her son, while Georges de Chaverny gives him his outward features. Underlying the narrative we can thus discern an opposition of outer and inner which is itself a continuation of the duality of male activity and female passivity. These days, although all references to such beliefs have of necessity been excluded from the field of scientific thought, they remain in a reinterpreted form in literature, as for example in Paul Claudel's well-known use of them for the character of Seven Swords in *Le Soulier de Satin*.

Thus the long quarrel, which seems to have been settled by the advances of genetics and the evolution of attitudes in our European countries, ends up as a literary strategy, like so many of the great ideas that have fed the polemics and thought of the men of the past. Yet what is not clear is the matter with which I opened this discussion, that of the relation between ideologies and the sciences. Jean Borie rightly comments that, in the words of the physiologist Pouchet, as in those of his contemporary Michelet, it is hard to say which 'is more open to the other, the ideology that takes its guarantees from science or the science that offers itself to ideology'.[16] Who could state that any divergence between the two has today been resolved and above all that there is now no convergence? Who would be bold enough to claim that the questions heredity and paternity pose to men and societies have been definitively solved or left behind? Perhaps they are at this moment acquiring new life in other forms, forms that bioethics is currently, and not without difficulty, seeking to codify in a reconciliation – as the composition of its name indicates – of demands that are hard to reconcile because they are not and cannot be of the same order.

Notes

1. It is not possible here to discuss the concept of *ideology*: I give the term a definition wider than that of Althusser.
2. Montaigne, 'On the resemblance of children to their fathers' in *The Essays of Michel de Montaigne*, II, Charles Cotton trans. (London: Dell, 1913) p. 495.
3. Despite the conclusion of Chapter V of Book III ('On a few lines of Virgil').
4. Dante, *The Divine Comedy Vol II: Purgatory*, Mark Musa trans. (Harmondsworth: Penguin, 1981) p. 270.
5. *Ibid.*, p. 271.

6. See the chapter by Philippe Bolusset, which shows how the linguistic unconscious contrasts the agentive value of the word *père* with the instrumental value of the word *mère*.
7. Richerand, *Nouveaux éléments de physiologie* Tome II, (Paris: Béchet 1825) p. 459. Une tretaine d'années avant, Sade avait écrit très directement: '[le foutre] que nous [les femmes] fournissons ne fait qu'élaborer; il ne crée point, il aide à la création sans en être la cause' (*la Philosophie dans le boudoir*, Paris: Grands textes classiques, p. 34).
8. François Jacob, *La Logique du vivant* (Paris: Collection Tel Gallimard, 1970).
9. Goethe, *Elective Affinities*, David Constantine trans., (Oxford: Oxford University Press, 1994) p. 6. See also p. 54: 'Besides, [Ottilie's] whole disposition was towards the house and domestic matters, rather than towards the world and a life in the open air'.
10. Zola, *Le Docteur Pascal*, in *Les Rougon-Macquart* (Paris: Gallimard, Pléiade) Tome V, p. 945.
11. Michelet, *L'Amour* (Paris: Calmann-Lévy, 1859) p. 207.
12. *Ibid.*, pp. 325–6.
13. Goethe, *Elective Affinities*, p. 197.
14. Balzac, *L'Enfant maudit*, in *La Comédie humaine* (Paris: Gallimard (Pléiade), 1979 Tome X, p. 876.
15. *Ibid.*, p. 877.
16. Jean Borie, *Mythologie de l'hérédité au XIXème siècle*, (Paris: Galilée, 1981) pp. 38–9.

(Translated by Trista Selous)

3

The Paternal Role and the Napoleonic Code

Xavier Martin

The role of the father in the 'Civil Code of the French', which was drawn up between 1800 and 1804,[1] was conceived of as *political* in the widest sense of the term, in terms both of the highly specific political context of the years of the *après-Thermidor* and of its underlying theory, the two moreover being confounded in the minds of those who analysed the conjuncture and legislated accordingly.

Modern individualism tends to regard society as a premeditated aggregate of individuals. Ten years of French Revolution was thought to have revealed that human beings were fundamentally bad and asocial, while all the tremors and upheavals had dislocated a society whose fabric was now in need of urgent restoration. In the eyes of the time it was necessary to bind all these individuals together in order to bring about a form of social viability that was already long overdue. In other words the most important space for political action was regarded as lying in the interstices of *individual relations*, whose particular nature, and in the first instance whose solidity, would henceforth underpin the very existence of a society worthy of the name. *Private law*, whose quintessential role is to operate in this inter-individual space, was *ipso facto* given an entirely political mission.[2] In this context the health of the relationships between debtor and creditor was regarded as being of prime concern, but still greater importance was given to the quality of relationships within the family, because these are vital to the social fabric in many different ways. It is not surprising, then, that the legislators should have immediately singled out the role of the father as having vital strategic importance for their purposes.

One could almost begin by saying that, in the eyes of those who drew up the Civil Code,[3] the father of a family has had, by definition, the good taste not to remain unmarried. Hostility to the single state was a marked trait of Enlightenment utilitarianism. The causes of this were of course to do with demographics: producers and consumers were necessary, and so therefore were reproducers.[4] Recalling certain laws of the Ancients (Sparta, Plato, Rome), Morelly sought to make it illegal to remain single,[5] while the encyclopaedist d'Holbach warned that 'A corrupt nation fills up with single people', describing them as 'isolated, selfish, vice-ridden men... who know nothing in this world but the love of pleasure'.[6] For not only did the unmarried fail to play the socially useful game, they were furthermore suspected of using their reproductive faculties in a purely anarchic fashion, thereby damaging society by imposing disturbing elements upon it. Thus Diderot considers that 'in a well-policed state' single people should be seen 'as potential corrupters'.[7] This condemnation of the unmarried state was continually fuelled by the eighteenth century strand of anticlericism.[8]

And yet, in its individualism and marked contempt for everyday values, the current of the Enlightenment also tended, paradoxically, to encourage lay celibacy. D'Alembert objected to the idea that he might be thought of as married and Helvétius, who eventually agreed to marry, was visibly unhappy about it: 'It's true that here I am married. I am surprised at this myself, perhaps even a little ashamed, but in such cases one must put on a brave face and so I am doing'.[9] Chamfort, militantly single, describes how 'to modern philosophy is attributed the fault of having multiplied the numbers of the unmarried'.[10] And it was true that, more generally speaking, the propensity of this philosophy was towards a weakening of family ties.

It was this second trend in fashionable thinking, with its implications for the restriction of paternal power, the breaking of the conjugal tie through the promotion of divorce, or the partial rehabilitation of filiation without marriage that the first stirrings of revolution were most keen to cultivate in their movement towards 'liberation'. And the Revolution soon slipped into anarchy, though of course for quite other reasons than those of family law. However, the postulates of political theory encouraged the thinkers of the period to overestimate the role played by the undermining of the familial base in altering the conjuncture. Thus we find the rhetoric of the Revolution turning against the unmarried state, of the clergy or in general, without mercy. The citizen who enjoyed it was not a citizen but 'the born and sworn enemy of future generations', 'a political monster'.[11] Such people were the dodgers of the social state, whose comfort they enjoyed without relinquishing the pleasures of the state of nature. In Year II a priest announcing his marriage to the Convention accused the unmarried 'of wanting to partake of the benefits... of the social contract without sharing in its fatigues and burdens.'[12] This antagonism grew stronger after the Terror. Just one month after the fall of Robespierre, the jurisconsult Cambacérès, speaking in support of one of the drafts of the Civil Code, asserted that 'Celibacy is *a vice* which the legislator must prosecute', though he emphasised that only 'gentle and unnoticeable means'[13] should be used to counter it, a precaution explained by the fact that he was himself one of the unmarried. He judges accordingly that 'it is more by honouring marriage than by forbidding celibacy that the unmarried state should be combated'.[14]

In fact it is noteworthy that the Constitution of Year III (1795) condemns the single in only an oblique manner, although unambiguously. It provides (Article 83) that, in order to be admitted to the high chamber (the Council of Elders), one must be either *married or widowed*, a condition of a kind which, it is worth noting, had been an idea of Rousseau's.[15] There soon followed fiscal measures against the single, who remained the unloved, and indeed the scapegoats, of civic discourse.[16] In the 1804 Civil Code this trend had led not to any precise measures against the unmarried, but to a general climate of disapproval with regard to this 'lost link, outside the chain of generations and individuals'.[17] Portalis, who acted as the 'theoretician' of the Civil Code, bemoaned the fact that the masculine sex was 'only too disposed towards bachelorhood' and keen to 'flee marriage as one flees servitude and constraint'.[18] In addition to the usual natalist reasons, concern had grown on military grounds. Napoleon inherited the revolutionary practice of conscription and his intensive practice of war meant that human flesh was precious to him in terms of quantity. Reproduction was the order of the day as never before. The emperor wanted his 'peoples' to satsify 'the needs of their organs and the wish of nature'.[19]

But this was doubtless not the only use for fathers, whose role was also, and urgently, one of civic restructuring. The restoration of the social fabric, it was thought, required the rehabilitation of family values. 'No man is a good citizen unless he be a good son, good father, good brother, good friend, good husband.' This well-known article of the Declaration of Rights of Year III already clearly sets the tone, and it is no coincidence that the first concern is that of the relationship of son to father, for the first priority was vigorously to reinstate the authority of fathers, which the Revolution, it was thought, had stamped on far too heavily, with cruelly detrimental effects on public happiness. This is what one of the authors of the Civil Code's first draft seems to have been thinking of when he stated: 'Public interest lies in the good organisation of every family; for from this results the good organisation of the state.'[20]

The Revolution's chief measure against paternal power had been, apart from setting the age of majority at twenty-one, the abolition of the freedom of bequest, so that young citizens tempted by the Revolution would not be deterred by the threat of reprisals against their inheritance.[21] The legislators of the last years of the Revolution were already keen to repeal this decision as part of their plan for social repair, but psychologically speaking, they were in no position to carry out the reversals they would have liked.[22] In the assemblies of the Directoire, some jeered at what they called the 'fathers' faction'[23], which is at least proof that this lobby was growing. Napoleon Bonaparte's arrival in power had the effect of freeing up this propensity to challenge the revolutionary law of succession, with the rearming of fathers as its unambiguous aim.

We may even note that in the month of Germinal Year VIII (March 1800), without waiting for the genesis of the Civil Code, although this was not far off, the First Consul re-established some latitude of bequest within families.[24] The explicit intention, obsessively repeated by the speakers, was urgently to provide fathers with a dissuasive weapon in order to restore the social framework of which their authority was the most important structure. On the day of the final vote the government speaker went so far as to ask, in the strongest terms:

> Who can deny that paternal authority *essentially* depends on the father's right to dispose of his property?... If this faculty is necessary to the maintenance of paternal power, are these not powerful reasons, from both the political and moral standpoints, not to deprive the father of it, nor to tie his hands in its use. Indeed, is there not *a close relationship between the authority of the Government and that of the father*? The Government always seeks to conserve, the father is naturally conservative; the Government seeks order and calm within the state, the father wants these things in his family; the one wants to have *citizens who are subject* to its laws, the other also wants obedient and *docile children*. Work, industry and good behaviour bring prosperity to both state and family and accord with the interest and the wishes of governors and fathers.[25] [He continues] It is impossible to be too hasty in restoring strength and dignity [to paternal authority], now that our concern is simply to conserve. The draft should thus be accepted as a *first step* towards the re-establishment of that authority.[26]

A first step...The words 'a first sign', 'a first effort' and 'first aid' were also used. This legislative decision of spring 1800 was indeed only a foretaste of the Civil Code which, following the same logic, soon increased the power of fathers to exert pressure on their offspring through their inheritance by increasing the quota of property that might be disposed of at will.[27]

It is very important to stress that the effects of this pressure through inheritance were by definition intended to be felt *until the father's death*, thus to guarantee his authority over sons of any age, including and beyond maturity. This observation puts the Civil Code retention of majority at twenty-one in a very different light. Not that this had no effect at all, but it clearly seems to have acted partly as a screen or illusion. Portalis himself said that the age of majority was 'a purely civil invention'.[28] Indeed it would seem that the implicit intention of the Napoleonic Code – and this view is supported by an impressive range of indices – was to establish, in the manner of Roman law although obviously in an oblique way, a form of paternal power which we can only call *lifelong*.[29]

This fact is not always as familiar as it should be to French lawyers, who continue with impunity to praise the so-called encouragement of youth and its power of initiative by the emerging Civil Code. There is a contradiction here, for the last years of the Revolution were a time of distrust of the young. The serious events that had injured society were blamed, as we have said, on the ill-considered enfranchisement of the younger generations.[30] The Civil Code had its place in an undeniably 'gerontocratic' trend. This term is perhaps a little strong, but the reality it is intended to express is not in doubt.[31] It is not unreasonable to suggest that, latently, in the eyes of the law-makers all individuals were sternly presumed to be minors.[32]

Contrary to what might be supposed, this idea in no way represented a break with the thinking of the Enlightenment, whose best supporters had a marked tendency to assume that they alone enjoyed the power of reason and that the masses had no ability to think.[33] The experience of the Revolution encouraged this trend towards contempt for the multitude, giving rise to the pessimistic view of humankind mentioned earlier. The laws of the Terror relating to 'suspects', which described them in such a way that in practice this fearful label could be applied to anyone at all, could be interpreted as being in perfect accord with this pejorative view of human beings which doubts their ability to live in society, in other words, doubts their maturity. The logic was that, while all individuals were suspected of thoughtlessness, this suspicion might reasonably be expected to decrease with the advancing age of the suspects, which thus led the legislators towards favouring a hierarchy of age as a vital factor in social reconstruction.[34]

In this light it might seem surprising that the pressure that the father could exert through inheritance was seen as the main mechanism for strengthening family ties. But the importance it was given is easier to understand if we refer to the dominant ideas of the anthropology of the time, which saw selfishness as the sole motive of all behaviours, necessarily making it also the ultimate basis of the social contract and of all relations between individuals. Illustrations of this presupposition are easy to find in the literature of the Age of Enlightenment.[35] They can also be found during the Revolution. In 1793 Volney wrote that not only was selfishness not incompatible with 'the social state', it was 'the strongest support' of society.[36] Portalis, expounding the theory behind the Civil Code which was then taking shape, states that harmony within the family will result from 'the mutual interest that all the family members have in getting on with each other' and the context clearly implies that the interest in question here is specifically related to inheritance.[37] It is in this sense that we should understand one speaker who very forcefully asserted that 'Property is *the source of all moral feelings*'.[38] One of his colleagues later said that the part of the Code relating to wills was 'the *main basis* of the authority of fathers and mothers over their children',[39] and that it gave the father the '*chief means* of having his authority respected.'[40]

The importance of property in the framework of the French Civil Code is well known, yet it is not always understood that property, in the hands of its owners, was intended to have the precise and socially crucial power of ensuring that the heir apparent remained respectful. Thus the father was regarded only as being, a priori, a property-owner since, according to an appeal tribunal, 'the authority of a dissipated father who has no property to pass on' is very weak.[41] We can see here that the most important connotation of the famous archetype of the Napoleonic Code the *bon père de famille*, which can be roughly translated as the conscientious father, in relation to whom the drafters of the Civil Code had made it their priority to make laws, was patrimony. The *bon père de famille* is a man who manages his patrimony rationally, thus no doubt ensuring or preparing the way for his family's happiness, but primarily maintaining domestic order for the good of society.

In relation to which, it goes without saying that the head of the family is guaranteed not to be female. For although in principle woman was seen as a mechanical egotist in the same way as man, the mechanism did not always work. Diderot thought he had observed this: 'The frail machine of a woman is so subject to breaking down!'[42] In the eyes of the drafters of the Civil Code, the particular disadvantage of woman was that she was liable to emotional disturbances which made her tryingly generous, the 'real enemies which constantly obsess her' being none other than 'her weakness, her goodness, her dangerous sensibility',[43] while Rousseau had already noted that women 'are good in spite of themselves',[44] all of which of course had the effect of threatening a social structure whose framework was thought to be the logic of selfishness and pressure and the judicious use of familial blackmail through inheritance.

Chamfort puts it beautifully: a woman's heart, he says, has 'one fibre more' and her brain 'one compartment less' than those of men.[45] Chamfort's friend Cabanis, whose ideas dominated the anthropology of the years in which the Civil Code was being drawn up and who explained that 'in woman, the cerebral pulp retains the softness of her other parts',[46] simply put the same idea in a more learned manner.[47] Napoleon, who was also on good terms with Cabanis, spoke of 'the weakness of women's brains'.[48] Not surprisingly this is a theme which provides many quotations. Let us merely taste the irony of Tronchet, who directed the drafting of the Code and was in principle little given to irony. To Cambacérès, who pointed out that 'many women have neither knowledge nor character enough to manage a family well', Tronchet pretended to object that there were 'many women capable of the good management of patrimony, who manage it all the better for being sufficiently wary of their own ideas to seek the advice of wise men'.[49] Moreover, unlike men, to whom the passing years brought increased wisdom along with the prestige of their silver hair, who grew 'in authority and majesty' – no small matter in the context of the gerontocratic trend we have noted – woman and her image merely deteriorated with age, 'time has only ravages for her'[50] and time did not even bring her increased maturity.[51] All in all, women were not reliable when it came to the maintenance of the domestic order which the state expected from the father's authority, appropriately augmented by the persuasion of inheritance.

For the paternal role was seen as a *police* role, which the state handed over in order to save its own energies. Montesquieu thought it very wise to arm fathers, making the point that 'Nothing is more soothing to the Magistrates, nothing clears the tribunals more effectively'.[52] In the legislative debates of the Consulate, the recent overcrowding of the tribunals was blamed precisely upon the decline of paternal authority during the Revolution. D'Holbach had praised inflexible fathers who wielded the 'rod of steel' to 'tame unsociable passions'.[53] Following this kind of logic, Maleville, one of the four commissioners involved in the drafting of the French Civil Code, remarkably twice described the function of the father as auxiliary of the state in the Council of State. The first time was in December 1801, when he stressed how important it was

> to give great strength to paternal authority, because it is on this that the preservation of custom and the maintenance of public calm chiefly depends. Paternal power is the providence of families, just as the government is the providence of society: what strength, what tension is necessary in a government obliged to watch over everything by itself, that cannot rely on the authority of fathers to support its laws, to correct behaviour and to foster obedience?[54]

Then again, in February 1803, it was necessary, he said

> to put punishments and rewards into [the] hands [of fathers] to maintain the subordination and calm on which the peace of the state rests.... Fathers are the providence of families, just as government is the providence of the state: it would be impossible for the latter to maintain order if it were not efficiently supported by the former; it would deplete its reserves by constantly using its power and the best of all governments is that which, knowing how to attain its goals through secondary causes, appears to govern least.[55]

Here then we find the political function of the father described at the beginning of this discussion, that of supporting and easing the state. 'In the father's hands', said Portalis, the right to dispose of his property is a 'penal' power; the adjective is used to full effect.[56] The father is thus an auxiliary of penal law, which, it goes without saying, can only concern itself with the punishment of more serious crimes and therefore has an interest in ensuring that the more minor infractions of everyday life, to which the young are only too prone, that disturb society, and which the state would wear itself out pursuing, should be prevented or contained by the pressure that fathers can exert through inheritance. According to one speaker fathers should be given 'the right to punish rebellion, irreverence, laziness, lying...' in other words, 'everything that the law does not punish'.[57]

It is important therefore to understand that, in wishing to restore the authority of fathers, the state that was developing the Napoleonic Code was primarily thinking of itself and its own interests. In consideration of which, and notably, it should not be supposed that this legislative favour towards fathers signified the recognition of an *earlier* form of paternal power, or the concern to respect and protect a function regarded as *natural*. The context was, let us repeat, one of individualism, implying that all social ties were seen as artificial, obviously including those of authority. This philosophical postulate of modern thought emerges clearly in the Declaration of the Rights of Man of 1789, whose third article, referring to nation and its sovereignty, provides that 'no individual may exercise authority which does not emanate expressly from it'.

This general formulation certainly includes the authority of fathers, which the revolutionary state restricted after its own fashion and which the same, post-revolutionary state rehabilitated in the 1804 Code in an entirely artificial and self-interested manner. The artificiality of family relationships was professed, during the very birth of the Napoleonic Code, by First Consul Bonaparte in person, who, speaking of fathers, asked in the strongest terms: 'Is it not understood that, in the social state, it is the law that makes fathers?'[58] *The law that makes fathers...*: let there be no mistake, the father's status and power are entirely constructed by the law, as is the property which is, as we have seen, 'the source of all moral feelings' within the family. Here we are deep in a paroxysm of legal positivism that was the corollary, or the price, of the political artificialism inherent in the doctrines of the social contract and of the imprudent tendency towards relaying the foundations of the legislative acts based upon that doctrine. If the law 'makes fathers' it is just as able to unmake them, depending on the fluctuations dictated by the political interests of the state.

Notes

1. It was named the 'Code Napoléon' in 1807.
2. Cf. Martin, 'Aux sources thermidoriennes du Code civil. Contribution à une histoire politique du droit privé', in *Droits. Revue française de Théorie juridique* 6, 1987, 107–16.
3. By this is meant not only the four members of the commission responsible for drafting the Code (Tronchet, Portalis, Bigot-Préameneu and Maleville), but also all those who spoke during the legislative process of drawing it up (including, of course, Bonaparte himself), at the Council of State and in the Assemblies.
4. It is notable that these two latter words are reputed to have entered the French language with this meaning respectively in 1756 (Mirabeau the Elder) and 1762 (Bonnet). See A. Dauzat, J. Dubois and H. Mitterand, *Nouveau dictionnaire étymologique et historique* (Paris: Larousse, 1971).
5. Morelly, *Code de la nature* (1755) (Paris: Editions Sociales, 1970) p. 144: 'Every citizen, on attaining marriagable age, will be married'.
6. D'Holbach, *Ethocratie, ou le gouvernement fondé sur la morale* (Amsterdam, M.M. Rey, 1776, reprint Paris: EDHIS, 1967) p. 214.
7. Diderot, *Mémoires pour Catherine II* (1773–1774) (Paris: Garnier, 1966) p. 205.
8. The French term 'le célibat' may mean either 'the unmarried state' or 'celibacy', two notions which have become separated in contemporary English. Translator's note.
9. Helvétius, *Correspondance générale* (Toronto and Buffalo: University of Toronto Press and Oxford: The Voltaire Foundation, 1981) p. 274, July 1751 (he was thirty-six); *idem*, p. 275, to his mistress: 'So, since I have to speak plainly, I am the married philosopher. If you knew how much this confession costs me and how ashamed I am you would excuse this foolishness...Go on granting me the same favours.' *Le Philosophe marié* was a play by Destouches (1727).
10. Chamfort, *Maximes, pensées, caractères et anecdotes* (written between 1780 and 1794) (Paris: Garnier Flammarion, 1968) p. 275.
11. From a Rouen elementary school teacher at the Convention, Prairial Year II, *Archives parlementaires*, first series, vol. 93, p. 268/1. Remarks of this type were very common.
12. *Ibid.*, first series, vol. 77, p. 539.
13. Presentation of the second revolutionary draft of a Code civil, 23 Fructidor, Year II, 9 September 1794: P.-A. Fenet, *Recueil complet des Travaux préparatoires du Code civil* 1 (Paris: unnamed publisher, 1827) p. 104 (my emphasis).
14. *Ibid.*
15. Rousseau, *Projet de Constitution pour la Corse* (1760–1769) in *Oeuvres complètes* 3 (Paris: Gallimard, 1964) p. 919: the condition of belonging to the country's highest rank of politicians.
16. This is made particularly obvious in the establishment of a Spouses' Feast Day by the Directorate.
17. The Tribune Carrion-Nisas, 28 Ventôse, Year XI, 19 March 1803: *Archives parlementaires*, second series, vol. 4, p. 398/1.

18. 7 Ventôse Year XI, 7 March 1803: *ibid.*, p. 87/1.
19. To Portalis, 5 March 1807: *Correspondance de Napoléon. Six cents lettres de travail (1806–1810)* (Paris: Gallimard, 1943) p. 136.
20. Bigot-Préameneu, to the Council of State, 21 Pluviôse, Year XI, 10 February 1803: *Archives parlementaires*, second series, vol. 7, p. 445/1.
21. See Martin, 'A tout âge? Sur la durée du pouvoir des pères dans le Code Napoléon', in *Revue d'Histoire des Facultés de Droit et de la Science juridique*, 13 (1992), pp. 227–301, particularly pp. 245–50.
22. *Ibid.*, p. 252 and *circa*.
23. The Tribune Duveyrier complained of having twice been mocked in this way: *Archives parlementaires*, second series, vol. 1, p. 432/2 (March 1800) and vol. 4, p. 439/2 (March 1803).
24. On this episode, whose importance cannot be over-emphasised, see Martin, 'A tout âge', pp. 258–69.
25. Boulay de la Meurthe, President of the Legislation Section of the Council of State, 4 Germinal Year VIII (25 March 1800), *Archives parlementaires*, Second series, vol. 1, p. 509/2 (my emphasis).
26. *Ibid.*, p. 510/1 (my emphasis).
27. Article 913 of the Civil Code (passed in April 1803) extended the quota, which had been set at a quarter in Germinal, to half the property if, at his death, the testator left only one legitimate child, a third if he left two and a quarter if he left three or more.
28. At the Council of State, 30 Frimaire Year XII (22 December 1803): *Archives parlementaires*, second series, vol. 7, p. 742/1.
29. The arguments on this point are fully developed in Martin, 'A tout âge?', *passim*, and particularly pp. 257, 261–2 and 255–6.
30. *Ibid.*, *passim*, and particularly pp. 245–7.
31. *Ibid.*, pp. 236–7, 240–5, 251–2, 269–70, etc.
32. *Ibid.*, for example pp. 232–40.
33. *Cf.* Martin, *Nature humaine et Révolution française. Du Siècle des Lumières au Code Napoléon* (Bouère: DMM, 1994), for example p. 77 and pp. 255–6.
34. There are symptoms of this attitude to be found within the constitution, see Martin, 'A tout âge?', pp. 251 and 269.
35. See *Nature humaine et Révolution française*, e.g. pp. 104–7.
36. Volney, *La Loi naturelle, ou principes physiques de la morale* (1793) (Paris: Garnier-Flammarion, 1980) p. 48.
37. At the Council of State, on liberalities, 28 Pluviôse, Year XI, (17 February 1803): *Archives parlementaires*, second series, vol. 7, p. 446/1.
38. The Tribune Grenier, on property, 6 Pluviôse Year XII (27 January 1804): *ibid.*, 5, p. 247/2, my emphasis. On the significance of these words, see *Nature humaine et Révolution française*, pp. 262–4.
39. Bigot-Préameneu, 2 Floréal Year XI (22 April 1803): *Archives parlementaires*, second series, vol. 4, p. 719/2, my emphasis.
40. *Ibid.*, p. 727/2, my emphasis. Other quotations can be found in Martin, 'A tout âge?', p. 275 and 278.
41. Remarks made at the Riom tribunal of appeal, 14 Fructidor Year IX (1 September 1801): *Archives parlementaires*, second series, vol. 6, p. 774/2.

42. Diderot, *Mémoires pour Catherine II*, p. 86.
43. The Tribune Lahary, 28 Ventôse Year XII (19 March 1804): *Archives parlementaires*, second series, vol. 6, p. 165/2. On this theme *cf.* Martin, 'Madame de Staël, Napoléon et les idéologues', in *Himeji International Forum of Law and Politics* 1, 1993, 39–62, especially p. 54.
44. Rousseau, *Julie ou La Nouvelle Héloïse* (1761) (Paris: Garnier, 1988) p. 255.
45. Chamfort, *Maximes et pensées*, p. 140.
46. Cabanis, *Rapports du Physique et du Moral de l'Homme* (1802, 1803, 1805) reprint of the 1844 edition (Geneva: Slatkine Reprints, 1980) p. 229.
47. *Ibid.*, particularly pp. 235–44.
48. 15 May 1807, notes on the instruction of the daughters of the members of the Légion d'Honneur: *Correspondance de Napoléon*, p. 207.
49. Council of State, 26 Frimaire Year X (17 December 1801): Fenet, *op.cit.*, 10, p. 548. *Cf.* the excellent articles by Yvonne Knibiehler, 'Les médecins et la "nature féminine" au temps du Code civil', in *Annales. Economies, Sociétés, Civilisations* 4, (1976) pp. 824–45 and Michel Delon, 'Combats philosophiques, préjugés masculins et fiction romanesque sous le Consulat' in *Raison Présente* 67, (1983) pp. 67–76.
50. The Tribune Carrion-Nisas, 19 Pluviôse Year XII (9 February 1804): *Archives parlementaires*, second series, vol. 5, p. 435/2. The old man 'is at an advantage when he speaks in a Senate with all the eloquence of his white hair and the weight of his long years. How different is the destiny of woman!' etc.
51. *Cf.* Martin, 'A tout âge?', p. 233.
52. Montesquieu, *Les Lettres persanes* (1721) (Paris: Bordas, 1949) p. 182.
53. D'Holbach, *La Morale universelle, ou les devoirs de l'homme fondés sur sa nature*, Third Part (Amsterdam: M.M. Rey, 1776) p. 43.
54. 26 Frimaire Year X (17 December): Fenet, *op. cit.*, 10, p. 486.
55. 21 Pluviôse Year XI (10 February): *Archives parlementaires*, second series, vol. 7, p. 442/2. '*Appears* to govern the least': I have, in this respect, advanced some ideas concerning the possible nature of liberalism, both liberal individualism and the liberal state, in 'L'Individualisme libéral en France autour de 1800: essai de spectroscopie' in *Revue d'Histoire des Facultés de Droit et de la Science juridique* 4, (1987) 87–144, particularly pp. 132–4.
56. Council of State, 30 Nivôse Year XI (20 January 1803): *Archives parlementaires*, second series, vol. 7, p. 426/2.
57. The Tribune Duveyrier, 26 Ventôse Year VIII (17 March 1800): *Ibid.*, 1, p. 434/2. A few days later his colleague Gary greatly raised the stakes of the debate: if you do not want family order to be maintained through inheritance blackmail, he says in substance, then (while you're at it) 'repeal your criminal laws, break up your scaffolds, open your prisons' (*ibid.*, p. 504/2). Tronchet had already expressed the same idea, although in a very different way, in April 1791: a law which did not allow fathers the weapon of disposing of inheritance would be 'absolutely immoral.... You would prevent only major crimes if you met the aberrations of children with the law's harsh punishments'. *Archives parlementaires*, first series, vol. 24, p. 567/1.

58. Bonaparte, at the Council of State, 4 Nivôse Year XI (25 December 1801): Fenet, *Recueil*... 10, p. 350. Similarly he stated that 'marriage derives not from nature, but from society and manners' (reported in Thibaudeau's *Mémoires*, 14 Vendémiaire Year X (6 October 1801): *ibid.*, 9, p. 261.

(Translated by Trista Selous)

4

DNA and the Stakes in Embodying Paternity[1]

Carol Mossman

Within the last dozen years or so, forensic science has made a breakthrough which may have far-reaching implications. For the first time in the history of human reproduction, it is possible to locate and 'prove' biological fatherhood: that is, to situate, with certainty, the biological father within his body.

I had originally proposed to address the following question. There is a well-established philosophical and narrative tradition in which paternal invisibility is precisely the condition which sets into motion one of Western culture's most cherished stories – that of the son's quest for identity, legitimacy and ultimately authority. Given this cultural investment in the uncertainty of paternity, what might it mean that fatherhood can now be somatically located?

And while this is surely an interesting question, I must confess that I have no ready answers to it. In an attempt to frame this question, the approach I have taken has been first to review some recent feminist and gay thinking on Western culture's ancient but persistent partitioning of the real into mind and matter in terms of the body and its inhabitants. For not everyone lives in the body: some manage to pass through and transcend it. The next stop on my itinerary (by way of an example) will be Freud's 1912–13 psychopolitical variant of the social contract story, *Totem and Taboo,* which explicitly equates the father's immateriality, higher thought and the genesis of patriarchal institutions.[2] As Madelon Sprengnether has pointed out, the father of psychoanalysis delivered himself of this document amid constant pains of childbirth, passing, it would appear, through someone else's body, to arrive at his theory.[3]

Before moving on, however, I would like to enquire as to the stakes involved in founding power through the father. How invisible *are* the structures of authority with which we live, and to what extent do we experience them as 'natural'? In order to 'make strange' the familiar –

our familiar – I will quote from a *New York Times* report on a society in the northeastern reaches of India which is organised according to matrilineal principles. Recently this 800 000 member Khasi group has been yielding to the influence of its neighbouring peoples, and a kind of man's liberation organisation has sprung up under the leadership of Mr A. Swer. 'We are sick of playing the roles of breeding bulls and baby sitters', he explains, while a co-member adds: 'We have no lines of succession. We have no land, no business. Our generation ends with us' (reported in the *New York Times*, 15 February 1994).

If the complaints are disconcerting, they also allow the reader to feel the sheer weight of the father and his law within Western patriarchal culture. Yet the quote does seem to indicate that somewhere in the world, sometime in history, it has been – and indeed remains – possible for biological fatherhood to exist separate and distinct from the abstract and formalised systems which, taken together, ensure that fathers and fathers-to-be (a.k.a. sons) are vested with authority.

I should like to begin by reviewing some of the cultural partitions which ally paternity with the mind, as distinguished from maternity itself defined in terms of materiality. While I agree with the scholarship that has brought to light these alliances, I will be suggesting that, at times when the basis of authority is under contestation and issues of political legitimacy are under negotiation, the body of the father – so often that principle of absenteeism – will materialise.

After a brief review of Freud's construction, in *Totem and Taboo*, of the father figure as ghost, I will explore three literary works – Beaumarchais' *The Marriage of Figaro*, Balzac's *Gobseck* and Gide's *Les Faux Monnayeurs* (*The Counterfeiters*) – which centre on questions of legitimacy and its relation to physical, biological fatherhood. The latter two will be read as responses to the way that French law defined paternity from 1804 to 1912. The argument will conclude with a consideration of the question of the relation between the bodily location of paternity and responsibility within an ideology which seems to privilege paternal abstraction.

Let me begin with Freud's construction of the origins of civilisation, *Totem and Taboo*, which appeared on the very eve of World War I. Freud maps out an already-familiar story in which the brothers, who have no access to the females in the group, band together, murder their sire, and establish kinship systems to regulate the circulation of women. In this narrative, the father looms far larger in death for, by virtue of being no longer bodily accessible, he has become ubiquitous, institutionalised in the law – that network of taboos, constraints and renunciations which makes it possible for a group of people to live together in relative stability. The father is dismembered in the particular in order to be re-membered in the abstract. Freud's text is less a Kiplingesque story of how the father lost his body than an account of why it is important not to have one in the first place. Maternity, Freud later reminds us in *Moses and Monotheism*, is empirically verifiable. Paternity, on the other hand, will always be an uncertainty, a fiction, a speculation and 'thus' represents the 'victory of intellectuality over sensuality – that is, an advance in civilisation'.[4]

With this celebration of cerebration, we recognise the familiar landscape of the mind/matter dualism with its network of racialised and gendered alliances: form/substance, body/soul, nature/culture, public/private. The ancient articulations of this schism reach back to Plato and Aristotle while more recent exponents include noteworthy figures of structuralism and post-structuralism.[5] It is thus hardly surprising that, insofar as it constitutes one of the major modes of cultural expression, Western literature should, time after time, stage and perform the mind/matter split in its relation to the paternal.

It is the vacancy of the paternal position which allows the son to dream an open-ended future, moving through contestation of authority to its embrace. This embrace of authority may take thematic form (comic endings and marriages) or more abstract closural forms, such as the arrival on the scene of a male narrator to close and contain the dream. Paternal absence may be rendered through death or ignorance of origins or, as in the case of Oedipus, both. In its more exuberant mode, the bastard's tale (with its implicit question 'who is my father?') bodes a narrative of unbounded possibility. In a more sombre mode, the father's absence-through-violence opens a tale more existential than social. In Joyce's *Ulysses*, for example, Stephen Dedalus conjures up the image of his drowned father, with tiny fishes dining upon the very loins which sired him. It is hard to imagine a more graphic image of the dematerialising of paternity as a specifically genital function.

In these venerable stories, the vacancy of the paternal position, the abstraction of the father, presents itself as a given, as the unquestionable point of origin. And this is how formalist and structural analysis (starting with Propp in the early part of the century) is bound to construe this originative absence. But to the extent that authority depends on detachment from the material, and then its transcendance, abstraction is also the narrative goal for the son, and the son's quest for identity and legitimacy might be read as the performance or re-enactment of disembodiment.

Would that these mind/matter distinctions were so neat! However, they are not. I am now going to suggest that beyond the familiar epistemological backdrop which installs paternity as transcendental because detached from the bodied particular, certain socio-political contexts do occasionally produce paternity in the flesh. I will be arguing that such 'guest appearances' mark the site of a conflict between competing – albeit still patriarchal – models of authority. I turn for my literary examples to France on the verge of revolution (Beaumarchais), to France during the Restoration (Balzac) and finally, to France just prior to World War I (Gide).

So there are instances in the literature of filial quest in which the father can be bodily materialised and the ideology of corporeal transcendence simultaneously upheld. Such would be the case when the authority of both class and gender must be maintained. *The Marriage of Figaro* provides an example. Because Figaro is a foundling, he can foster the dream that he might, in fact, be anyone at all, even a nobleman, entertaining a cultural fantasy often rehearsed in the eighteenth century. And, of course, this fantasy identity is squelched with the final recognition scene: Figaro's father, Doctor Bartholo, is designated by Marceline: 'There is your father!'

> Figaro: 'Oooh. Ah me!'
> Marceline:'Has nature not told you so a thousand times?'
> Figaro: 'Never.'

If Figaro's class is located through this revelation, thereby aborting the narrative of social ascent, in the end he also gets the girl. Count Almaviva and the aristocratic privileges he represents may be gently chided for their excesses, but things remain in their proper place: class structure is reaffirmed and the problem of ownership of women is resolved. If the son figure's sire is, in fact, designated in the flesh, it is in order to affirm the interests of class. To the extent that this closure supports the prevailing patriarchal values, paternity is abstracted. It is no coincidence that it is the bourgeois father who gets stuck with the body and this corporeality here functions as the stigma of his social inferiority.

At the same time, within the middle-class family context, the father's body may be read as an instantiation of patriarchal *ancien régime* values which require his class subordination, all the while founding his authority within the family. In fact, where there are issues of both class and gender to be negotiated, it is possible for the father to put in a bodily appearance if – and only if – he is superseded by the symbolic.

But what happens in terms of paternal representation when the entire class system collapses, as occurred in France during the Revolution? It is to the Civil Code that I now turn, the Code whose enforcement in 1804 was, in the words of legal historian Bernard Schwartz, 'one of the most notable events in all legal history'.[6] Indeed, the sheer magnitude of the crisis in authority demanded no less a document: with social hierarchy brutally dissolved, property completely redistributed, and Everyman potentially vested with a political voice, the urgent issues to be decided are the very concerns expressed by the Khasi menfolk, namely: who will assume the body in matters reproductive, who can hold property and assets, who can administer these and, most crucially, by what means will authority be reproduced and transmitted down into future generations?

In the absence of king, class and primogeniture, the Civil Code reorganises authority by instituting the nuclear family as the basic social unit with *all* offspring, male and female alike, as legal heirs. More germane to the present topic, however, is the fact that the *paterfamilias* is vested with complete authority within the family. The wife, even if she has property prior to the marriage, can enter into no legal contracts without spousal consent nor can she administer any assets which may be hers. If these legal dispositions make clear who enjoys the support of the law, they come as no particular surprise insofar as the new system remains, after all, patriarchal. What is perhaps more interesting, however, is that the Civil Code vests the father with complete power and privilege *and explicitly considers biological paternity as a fiction*: irrelevant and immaterial.

Article 340 of the Code states that 'paternity searches are prohibited' whereas the following article affirms that 'maternity searches are allowed.' Hence, bodily, biological connection is attributed by the law to the female. The implication here is that paternity is not biological, but rather social in its very essence. Thus for over a century – that is, for as long as Article 340 was to remain in force – paternity is defined solely as a relation to authority, and my claim here is that within a France which is slowly democratising, and given the breakdown of class, the concept must be abstract rather than being tied down to corporeal particulars. There is a sense in which Lacan's latter-day partitioning of the world into the imaginary, on the one hand, with its somatic and maternal associations, and the symbolic, on the other, governed by the law of the father, is the nostalgic resuscitation of a legal reality which had not been in place for more than a century.

The implications arising out of this resolutely abiological and exclusively social definition of paternity are several, and they express themselves as tensions. First, as sheer lived experience, it meant that single, pregnant women, seduced or consenting, could not file paternity suits and were thus left to support their illegimate offspring alone. France experienced an explosion in out-of-wedlock (and thus unsupported) births during the first half of the nineteenth century, a rise attributable in part to urbanisation and new labour conditions, but clearly guaranteed and underwritten by the law as well. By abstracting the body from paternity, the father becomes that ghost – call it Hamlet's or Freud's – which haunts everything and yet remains untouchable. Thus it is that paternal authority, as the Civil Code instituted it in 1804, stands in a problematic relation to personal responsibility.

Out of this definition of paternity as abstraction, a second tension arises which ideologically pits the law, on the one hand, against, on the other, science, which is enjoying increasing prestige as the nineteenth century advances. If one might view the Code's abstract definition of paternity as a response to the Revolution's *tabula rasa* of class difference and as the urgent and a priori stamp of authority in a suddenly created vacuum of power, the slow work of reconstructing difference has been taking place in biology, medicine and anthropology. From the mid nineteenth century, theories of heredity and race firmly anchored in biology begin to evolve. These implicitly challenge the abstractionist legal model of paternity. This particular tension (is paternity social or biological? / 'has nature not told you so a thousand times?' 'Never') will be resolved in the 1912 repeal of Article 340 in favour of heredity and race within the political climate of intense and competitive nationalism leading up to World War I. It can be no coincidence that *Totem and Taboo* dates from precisely this period.[7] For, as during the period around the Revolution in France, authority is once again in crisis.

In order to demonstrate the imbrication of the law and literature with respect to the representation of paternity, I would like to address two literary responses to legal reality, bookends, as it were, responding to Article 340's abstract construction of the father-function, and its repeal in 1912. The first response is Balzac's *Gobseck*, written in 1827, and the second is Gide's 1926 reaction to a heredity-based ideology which he finds alarming.

No one was more aware of the socio-political implications of the Civil Code than Honoré de Balzac. One after another, his novels stage the crisis in authority besetting France from 1800 to 1850. And none is more alert than he to the more obscure consequences – the loopholes – opened up in the transition from one model of authority to another. For if, in proclaiming paternity an operative fiction, this new legal system sought to affirm the nuclear family as the basic social unit under the tutelage of a powerful *paterfamilias* (thereby excluding as illegitimisable any offspring outside the pale of wedlock) it simultaneously defined as legitimate any offspring within the family embrace regardless of blood tie. In a word, if the bastards are locked out, some are locked in as well.

Yet, what if a wife should chance to stray from her vows? Balzac's nightmare throughout the *Comédie humaine* is that there are 'legitimate' bastards in our very midst. In his short story *Gobseck*, he addresses this issue, and redresses the wrong. Beyond being a story about usury, *Gobseck* is a tale about the distortion of true value and the disfiguring of legitimacy. Herein, the saga of *Old Goriot*'s bad daughter, Anastasie, is brought to completion. In that novel, Anastasie had married the aristocratic Comte de Restaud and she has now borne him three children. Alas, she has strayed from her conjugal duties with Maxime de Trailles. Her two youngest offspring are the fruit of this illicit union and yet they are legitimate in the sight of the law. In *Gobseck*'s denouement the count, aided by the canny lawyer Derville, manages to disinherit the two imposters, and leave his intact fortune to his eldest son, repealing the Civil Code in fiction in a nostalgic glance back to the *ancien régime*. In this example, Balzac reassigns paternity to a body in order that the class system be restored.

The opposite bookend, for my purposes here, is Gide's *The Counterfeiters*, written in 1926 but treating the period between 1900 and 1914.[8] Like *Gobseck*, this is also a tale about legitimacy subsumed under the metaphorical aegis of an inflationary, distorted economy. The novel opens on a son figure in the very process of realising that he is not his father's son, after all. Bernard Profitendieu is rifling through his mother's drawers when he thinks he hears his father's magisterial footsteps. His putative father, that is. Because what Bernard has just discovered in his indiscreet probe is an old love letter to his mother from his 'real' father: 'What does this initial mean? A V, which could just as well be an N... Should I ask my mother?...' wonders he. But he decides in favour of Figaro's liberating uncertainty: 'Let's give her credit for good taste. I'm free to imagine that he's a prince' (p. 59). Then, Bernard adds, 'All searches place one under obligation' [*Toute recherche oblige*] (p. 60), an apparent allusion to the new legal understanding of paternity as biological.

When Bernard does return to the paternal hearth at novel's end, his journey has concluded with his acceptance that his father is the man who loves him and has raised him. The body of the father is thus immaterial. Just as Balzac's short story is a reaction to a new legal reality, an attempt to repeal the Code's definition of paternity in favour of blood line and primogeniture, Gide is responding to the law's reversion to the 'truth of the blood,' and rewriting it in favour of paternity as abstract principle, in favour of Figaro's 'Never'.

To conclude this discussion, my point here has been that despite the persistent epistemological schism which gives the mother the body, thereby allowing the father to transcend it, occasionally the paternal body is produced. When this occurs we should look very closely, for these apparitions are the symptomatic sites where two ideological systems – both patriarchal – surface and clash. In Balzac's case, it is aristocracy versus impending democracy.

Moving to the other bookend, the male body which is being produced in the pre-World War I climate which emphasises heredity and race (and against which Gide is reacting) might be read as a virile body asserting itself against Gay Paree's decadentist 'feminised' representations of masculinity. In other words, paternity cannot afford to remain disembodied when its class, gendered or heterosexual base is being challenged.

It is within the framework of the foregoing discussion that I would like to pose the question of what it might mean that technology can now 'pin down' the body of the father. For it is not simply that the father's bodily absence authorises the son's quest, but that it keeps the mother firmly anchored as the-all-too material object of this quest. And as for the daughter, well, her choices in literature have often been to remain confined within a convent or literally locked out of her mind, and more broadly, locked out of the Mind.[9] Perhaps one of the consequences of the forensic locatability of paternity will be to launch the dismantling of some of the age-old dualisms which confine us – all of us – and lead to extremely unproductive social double-binds. Such, in any case, is my hope.

Notes

1. I wish to thank the General Research Board of the University of Maryland for a semester grant which enabled me to write this article.
2. For a discussion of social contract theory which includes its relation to Freud's account, see Carole Pateman, *The Sexual Contract* (Stanford: Stanford University Press, 1988).
3. Madelon Sprengnether, *The Spectral Mother: Freud, Feminism, and Psychoanalysis* (Ithaca: Cornell University Press, 1990).
4. Sigmund Freud, *The Complete Standard Edition of the Psychological Works of Sigmund Freud*, 23, James Strachey (ed.) (London: The Hogarth Press and the Institute for Psychoanalysis, 1953–74), p. 114.
5. There is a wealth of feminist criticism on the gendering of mind and matter. See, for instance, Wendy Brown, *Manhood and Politics* (New Jersey: Rowman and Littlefield, 1988), Dorinda Outram, *The Body and the French Revolution* (New Haven: Yale University Press, 1989) and, especially, Judith Butler, *Bodies that Matter* (New York: Routledge, 1993).
6. Bernard Schwartz (ed.), *The Code Napoleon and the Common-Law World* (Westport, Connecticut: Greenwood, 1975). p. vii
7. Freud's French connection in this regard has gone largely ignored. For his direct and avowed debt to Emile Zola's *Fécondité* see Carol Mossman, *Politics and Narratives of Birth* (Cambridge: Cambridge University Press, 1993) pp. 226–7.
8. André Gide, *Les Faux-monnayeurs* (London: Methuen, 1986).
9. Some novels which readily come to mind are Mme de Lafayette's *La Princesse de Cleves* or Mme de Staël's *Corinne*, George Sand's *Lélia*, Charlotte Brontë's *Jane Eyre* and its Caribbean 'daughter' *The Wide Sargasso Sea* by Jean Rhys.

5

Factoring the Father [1]

Christie McDonald

The problem of fathers and fatherhood, subsumed under the heading 'family values' in North America, has been much debated at both social and political levels.[2] Whereas in the 1960s and 1970s the women's movement brought about a re-evaluation of the importance of the mother and the revolution in reproductive technologies of the 1980s questioned her definition and changing role in the family and society, in the 1990s the unsettling of family relations has necessitated a review of the father's role: how has this changed or not changed during the twentieth century?[3] For although men are increasingly demanding their rights in custody cases,[4] the situation predominantly blamed for many of the ills in North American society during the 1990s is the absence of fathers who have abandoned their children, both materially and spiritually.[5]

David Blankenhorn's book *Fatherless America. Confronting Our Most Urgent Social Problem* (New York: Basic Books, Harper Collins, 1995), discusses the crisis in society brought about by fathers who default, not only in their financial payments to their children but also in their ability to provide them with a model and structure of authority. In an effort to rehabilitate fatherhood, nostalgia has set in for the good old days of nuclear families in which the father had an important role as the one out in the world earning an income and protecting both wife and children at home. The underlying premise of Blankenhorn's book is that fatherhood neutralises natural male aggression by socialising the man through his relationship to his children and their future.

In the light of this debate I will analyse a court case from the 1920s in Quebec in which a child was physically abused to death by her stepmother with the complicity of her biological father. In relation to this case, changing conditions have revealed over time that a fascination with the mother figure had occulted serious flaws within the perception of fatherhood. The case became a legend in French Quebec, symbolising first martrydom, then abandonment and victimisation, as the reasons for its extraordinary success changed with the decades. I will review the follow-up to the case which, by focusing the blame on and depicting the evil violence of the stepmother, whitewashed certain ethical problems raised by the father's traditional role at a time when that role was under threat. The term 'factoring' combines the French sense of *facteur* as one who is a 'partisan, adherent, approver' (*OED*) with the mathematical sense of 'an element which enters into the composition of anything' (*OED*). My aim is to factor the father back into a history from which he has been largely factored out: it is his absence not only from the story, but also from the history of its reception that is at issue.

According to newspaper reports at the time the case unfolded as follows: one week after the death of Aurore Gagnon's mother in January of 1918, Télésphore Gagnon married a woman who had been living in his house and nursing his sick wife, Anne-Marie Houde. The newly remarried spouses were responsible for the children of the previous marriage, among them Aurore (aged nine). In February of 1920 a concerned neighbour reported the extremely debilitated physical state of the child, but by the time a serious inquiry began, Aurore had died. The coroner found fifty-four wounds on her emaciated body. The stepmother was accused of first degree murder and there ensued a sensational trial, extensively followed in the daily newspapers. Testimony revealed that Mme Houde had beaten the child, burned her scalp and hands, deprived her of nourishment and made her eat 'slices of soap'. Witnesses also revealed that Houde had denounced the ten-year-old to her father as lazy, impure and licentious. The jury found the stepmother guilty of first degree murder and the judge condemned her to death by hanging. However, because she was pregnant there was a stay of execution. Houde gave birth to deformed twins, was exempted from the death penalty and died two years later in the psychiatric section of a prison.

In a second, less spectacular trial, the father was found guilty of involuntary manslaughter and sentenced to prison. In its headline of 26 April, 1920, *Le Soleil* quoted Télésphore's comments about beating his daughter: 'I wasn't about to let myself be pushed around by [Aurore].' Given the relative size and position of this frail child to her father, such excuse-making would appear to be the statement of a man who feels he has lost paternal power. There had been two physical beatings and a witness reported that the father had used a 'plaited whip, the kind used for horses... He held her with one hand over the head, she was naked and he beat her.' Télésphore admitted that 'when he beat Aurore, blood ran down her legs.'

The argument of the defence relied on the father's reputation as a farmer and member in good standing of his community: the same witness, when asked if the father was a violent man, replied, 'I've never worked with him, but he never seemed to me to be a violent man . . . He was a good guy, sober, to my knowledge' and the article in *Le Soleil*, while underscoring the violence of the acts, nevertheless points out that the father was within his rights to beat his own child. The defence also sought further to incriminate the wife: 'Anne-Marie Houde, the wife of the accused, created a system in the family because she wanted to demonstrate to her husband that Aurore was a thief, a dirty and impure child, and so on. The father has been the victim of a plot hatched by his wife.' The Crown prosecutor then asked some crucial questions: was it possible not to perceive the state of the child, who had fifty-four lacerations on her body? 'How is it that [the father] did not see what everyone else saw? . . . There is the fact that he could not see the child was in such a state, bloody, bent over, emaciated, near death; only those who do not want to see could not have seen.' The court wanted to know how a man could ignore what was happening in his very own home (where he was supposed to be master).[6]

It took the jury only twenty minutes to render a verdict of involuntary manslaughter; it had taken ten for the decision on the stepmother. According to *Le Soleil*, 'The end of th[is] trial . . . marks the epilogue of one of the most revolting dramas in our judicial annals, a drama in which the mother played the most odious role.' Télésphore was imprisoned, but was released when he was diagnosed with terminal cancer; he then underwent a successful operation, later remarried and lived quietly until his death in 1961.

The judicial decisions marked the end of the trial and the beginning of a process of interpretation. The story of this young girl's torture and death evoked horror and outrage, not only in the judge and jury and the Quebec public of the 1920s, but over several generations to follow.[7] Schoolchildren in Quebec may not know the origin of the story, but they still recognise the name of Aurore the Child Martyr, symbol of the young victims of family violence.

For thirty years a play re-enacting the story of Aurore and the trial ran to full houses all over Canada and in New England.[8] First performed in January 1921 by a troupe called Petitjean-Rollin-Nohcor, its success was immediate. When, after a few years, the manuscript was lost, the actors were able to reconstruct the scenes by heart and several companies ran versions simultaneously. In 1927 a second part was added, *The Trial of the Stepmother*, and the play was billed as a melodrama in five acts. It continued to run successfully until the production in 1951 of a successful film, *La Petite Aurore: L'enfant martyre*, based on a novel by one of the play's actors, Emile Asselin (stage name Marc Forrez).[9] Four other novels were written: Robert de Beaujolais, *La petite martyre, victime de la marâtre* (date unknown, perhaps written between 1927 and 1930); Benoît Tessier (pseudonym for the prolific novelist Yves Thériault), *Le drame d'Aurore*, 1952; Pascal Hubert, *Le roman d'Aurore, la petite persécutée*, 1966; and André Mathieu, *Aurore, une histoire vécue*, as recently as 1990. All these productions were marked by melodrama and a moral victory of the law over evil; none was considered high art.

In all the different versions of the Aurore story, as in *Cinderella* and other fairytales, the portrayal of the stepmother and even of Aurore herself is relatively consistent: the stepmother is malevolent and unrelenting, Aurore innocent and submissive. The main story-line and the repetition of certain scenes also remain constant from one version to another. The main variations are to be found in the representation of the father. In one text he is a farmer, in another a worker in the city. Always absent from the home and blind to the torture of his daughter, he is exonerated to varying degrees within the different texts; in Tessier's novel, for example, the father bears no responsibility and testifies against his wife at the trial. Thus where one finds a consistent demonisation of the stepmother and martyrisation of the child, various stories of the father emerge which tend to accord him no strength or power and to let him off psychologically, socially and even legally.

In all the productions of Aurore, the stepmother's depravity is a sign of evil. The sense was, especially in the early reception and criticism of the play, that the mother figure was central: the good and true mother, the sweet and loving mother, dies leaving her daughter behind; the stepmother, on the other hand, can never love the child, who is a threat to her happiness and home, since in her youthful beauty she resembles her biological mother. In other words, the stepmother cannot be anything other than a denatured mother because of the lack of a biological relationship.

All the same, the father's inaction, viewed as moral weakness, often incited outrage in men in the audiences who would yell threats at the actors during the performance and even challenge them to fights after the play was over.[10] To the extent that the limits between fact and fiction were blurred, the play accomplished what Alonzo Leblanc suggests it was meant to do, instructing widowers who remarry and showing how the punishment fits the crime.[11]

In the novels of both Tessier and Asselin the father abandons his prerogatives to the mother; she is the one supposed to know best what is appropriate for the children. In Asselin's version, the father (whose name is Théodore) explicitly abdicates his right to corporal punishment of the child. The wife hits her own biological son when she sees fit and she cagily expresses the desire for her husband to do the same with his daughter. The following is from a scene in which the wife's duplicity wins her domestic power:

> – She's your daughter; you must raise her properly. She is very delicate, but she must be straightened out every now and then, like the other children.
> – What do you want me to do?... I'm never at home.
> – Well, if it were my daughter....
> Théodore stopped still, his eyes raised to meet his wife's. Leaning over the cradle, she put the pacifier in Marcel's [their baby's] mouth. The man was struck by the appearance of maternal tenderness in this gesture. Now she is the mother of Aurore. He asked straight away:
> – Why don't you act as if she were your daughter?
> Marie-Louise hesitated for a moment. Her answer might seem a bit daring. But she went ahead anyway.
> – I would thrash my own daughter if it were necessary.
> ...
> He responded:
> – Punishment of children is the mother's business. You are the mother here. It is up to you to punish them, Aurore just like the others.
> – If you give me permission.
> – It is your business.[12]

In this scene, the father delegates his paternal authority to the stepmother who takes over the role of both mother and father and the consequences suggest that in so doing *she* perverts the power of both. Manipulation has ostensibly won out over good feelings (in the father). Implicit is that in abdicating the traditional position as master of his house, the father has not negotiated any new role for himself. His sole function will be as accomplice.

Although the displacement of power from the father to the mother is not as clearly marked in Thériault's novel, the father's constant absence from home for long periods of time corresponds *de facto* to the voluntary abdication of power in Asselin's text. Indeed, this followed closely the teaching of the Church that marriage itself is for the purpose of procreation; one of the main justifications for men to remarry was to provide children with a new mother. Nothing is said of the stepmother's son who in turn receives a new father. The division of duties leaves the stepmother in the home, but the hierarchy of power relations appears to have been reversed: the woman is strong and capable of violence; the man, although himself brutal, is no match.

Asselin ably exploits the sadistic and cruel aspects of the story. He shows the pleasure that the stepmother takes in inflicting pain and, more troubling still, the pleasure that her foetus seems to exhibit, inciting her to physically abuse Aurore. It all begins with the scene of the curling iron when the stepmother accidentally burns Aurore's scalp. An unknown and perverse pleasure comes over her which becomes the motivation for her sadistic acts. Such connections between mother and foetus and between sadistic desire and pregnancy were not uncommon in late nineteenth and early twentieth-century views of women and gave rise in the courts to the notion of 'mental abnormality' to account for the violent behaviour of pregnant women; the court's leniency with young mothers who committed infanticide grew out of a phenomenon one critic calls 'myth making by legislation'.[13] In the story of Aurore, such psycho-social explanations turn demonic.

Beyond the mental imbalance created by the jealous impulses of a pregnant woman unable to stand her budding stepchild, the stepmother comes then to demonstrate how the evil side of women works itself out in society and threatens men. It is in order to possess her husband that the wife sacrifices his child, and clichés about the attributes of gender abound: the jealousy of women and their ruses, the need to possess a man and his strength, the absence and insensitivity of men. So that although the father appears secondary next to the stepmother and child, he always remains a pivotal figure of the drama. Paternity has not been destroyed; it has been rendered ineffectual: the father has given too much power to the woman who has misused it. It is that for which he is punished, not his own acts of brutality. When the father is finally able to exert some authority, the stepmother acquiesces without contest; however, he only does so when it is too late to save Aurore.

As for the critical reception, the story took on a life of its own, as though after a while the original trial became superfluous. Yet the popular success of the story depended on the premise that it was located between fact and fiction, neither one nor the other, but a tangle of the two. Just as men in the audience were moved to yell out threats to the father during performances, so people offered to adopt the actress Thérèse MacKinnon, who played the part of Aurore for years, and harassed the woman who played the stepmother, Lucie Mitchell, so that she would leave the theatre through the back door.[14] Later, an unsuccessful attempt on the part of the family to suppress the release of the film resulted in a defence of both play and film as *fiction*, not fact; the producers ultimately agreed to put a disclaimer at the beginning of the film stating the fictive status of the story.

The history of Aurore the Child Martyr can be divided roughly into three periods. With each period, and these are rough historical outlines, the interest in the case shifts, reinterpreting the importance of the story. During the first period, from the 1920s to the early 1950s, the play and criticism of it raised questions about the morality of choice and remarriage through the horror of violence to the child; during the second, from the 1950s to the 1980s, a political allegory of the child emerged; in the period since the 1980s, echoes of the first two have continued, but critics have begun to look at the history of the case as a cultural event.

During the first period, the morality of choice and remarriage appeared to be one of the underlying issues and, as a morality play, performances ostensibly addressed those capable of judging the horror of it all, in particular men and fathers, the present and future heads of households. Performances of the play were organised in everything from regular theatres to small rooms and the basements of churches. The clergy not only hosted but advertised performances by the touring troupe in their Sunday sermons. This was important because they billed the play as instructive: the death of the child, a vision of Paradise, and especially forgiveness for the guilty parents in Aurore's final vision. However, the producers of the play targeted their public by publicising not only the moral aspects of the production but also spectacular scenes that became household knowledge:

> See the red hot poker, the buttered soap, the good priest, Aurore's last prayer.
> Not an animation – but a real drama.[15]

In 1927:

> The Trial of the Stepmother. Melodrama in four acts.

> The buttered soap, the glass of detergent, the whip, the red hot poker, the good priest's visit, Catherine and Abraham, the fall down the stairs, the confession, the death of the child, the couple's punishment, the priest's testimony, the doctor, the testimony of Aurore's little brother, prison, the defence speech, the judge's instructions, the vision of Aurore in heaven asking forgiveness for her parents from the judges, the condemnation of the stepmother.[16]

The brutality unleashed in the repeated scenes of abuse brought people for a kind of sadistic entertainment, enjoyment of a violence absolved by the representation of the trial and its outcome.

Melodrama here gave the power in matters of family relations to the law,[17] which re-established the ascendency of the forces of good over evil and took over from both the Church and the real father who failed to protect the child; if it could not bring Aurore back, the law nevertheless restored order. Moral order here is not religious; it is juridical and social. The play's success itself suggests an anxiety about social change and the inability of the Church to dictate moral behaviour at either an individual or a collective level.

Resistance to the sensationalism of the play came from certain members of the bourgeoisie, as well as dramatists and writers who expressly demanded that performances of it be banned.[18] Critics like Jean-Cléo Godin and Laurent Mailhot explain that in the early part of the century, 'the theater had to confine itself to traditional subjects and avoid the slightest suspicion of immorality. Religious and historical subjects were numerous, safeguarding morality – not quality.'[19] The moral disdain on the part of critics in the early period served moreover to reinforce the paternal authority of social institutions.[20]

The second period, from the 1950s to the 1980s, focused on the child martyr and the production of the film in 1951 coincided with the end of the theatrical performances. In the film what dominates is vengeance; even the testimony of Houde's biological son against her is considered revenge by the father. Moreover, as Réal Ouellet writes, the entire social body cries vengeance, exemplified in the moment when the emotional judge passes the death sentence because 'the condemnation of the stepmother guarantees the consciences of everyone else'.[21]

At the same time, critics began to develop the legend's potential for political interpretation. Questions of the triumph of good over evil shifted away from representations of the family to a representation of Quebec as the child abandoned by her mother (France, which ceded

Quebec to the British in 1763), and mistreated by her stepmother (England) as her father watches on in complicity with a powerless Church and state.[22]

Since the 1980s, roughly the third period of reception, the cultural aspects of this story point to ways in which a public reflects on the unknown, both personal and political, through modern tales of anxiety.[23] Le Blanc's publication of a large dossier of historical material about the play, as well as the play itself, has made an important contribution to understanding its remarkable success as a cultural event.

By the time that intellectual critics began to take something of an interest in Aurore, the popular audience was losing theirs, so that social and political criticism took over where the religious and cultural event left off. A revival of the play in 1984, for example, could not command the kind of audience it had had from the 1920s to the 1950s and was unsuccessful in transforming stark melodrama into a complex analysis that could take account of the psychology of the stepmother.

When one includes all of the versions of the play, the novels and the film, along with the criticism, the scandalous case-turned-myth demonstrates a form of social jurisprudence,[24] one promising a kind of judgement beyond the decision of the court itself, which could not address the larger questions at issue. These differ, as we see, for each period, though certain questions persist, especially perhaps those that remain unanalysed.

Why did this particular case hold such fascination for almost thirty years? I would like to suggest that several factors from the 1920s are only coming into focus now, and these involve a vision of paternity – and its lack. Only in recent times has the silence surrounding suffering within the family begun to be probed. What conception of fatherhood can be gleaned throughout the different versions of Aurore, as the blindspot or unthought area of a legend which raises questions not only about martyrdom and the evil of false maternity, but also the exoneration of abusive and abdicating paternity?

Three aspects of the changing socio-political conditions of the time are important to the timing of public reaction to this scandal. They involve the lack of a strong male model within Quebec, new political strength for women outside Quebec and the spectre of a society threatened by radical change through divorce laws and suffrage. First, there was no prevalence of a heroic model for men and absent fathers as soldiers in Quebec after the First World War, which was viewed by the French Canadians as a British war. Second, the status of women in the public arena was changing as discussions of universal suffrage got under way between 1916 and 1918. From 1916 the western provinces began to give the vote to women and the federal government later granted them the vote in 1921. Women in Quebec could thus vote in federal elections, but they could not vote in provincial elections until 1944. Finally, at the very moment when the trials were taking place in 1920, the Quebec press published heated discussions around the passage of a law legalising divorce in Canada, but again not in Quebec. *La Presse* castigated the Quebec senators on 19 April 1920, for their abstention from voting on the law, interpreted as a compromise of Quebec's moral superiority. Not only had the principle of divorce been voted into Canadian law, but its effects, the article contended, were sure to be destructive: 'It has been proven, by experience from other countries, that laws on divorce drastically change modern society and bring with them all kinds of abuses.'[25]

Although separating marriage as a sacrament from marriage as a social contract only became possible in Quebec during the twilight years of the Church's domination in the 1960s, discussions about divorce were already clearly a threat to the clergy in the 1920s. No surprise then that the Church welcomed the melodrama of Aurore, which seemed to show quite conclusively, albeit perversely, that remarriage could lead to perdition. Melodrama here, as in its beginnings during the French Revolution, addressed the problem of legitimising choice, in the absence of the deciding authorities of faith or reason, purporting to restore morality to the social order through the family by returning the father, the Church and God to their rightful place. Marriage was used as a 'paradigm of the ethical' through which radical questions of choice could be channelled.[26]

The lack of any conception of a father's role was symptomatic of the impending split between the religious and social order in 1920s Quebec. Réal Ouellet suggests that, as the father and the law pulled apart, women – whose emergent status as legal partner and citizen loomed on the political horizon – became able to impose the violence they had internalised from paternal law: the Church had long fostered fascination as well as disgust in relation to the physical and sexual humiliation of women.[27] In this light the Aurore story could be read as showing how the father's ancient right of life and death (*potestas patrias*) under Roman law had been illegally passed on, not to the mother (whose purity, like the child's, remained protected through death), but to the stepmother.

However, even if the father no longer had the right of life and death, he retained his long-held right to physically redress his child through beating. Far from being neutralised through family relations as Blankenhorn suggests, his violence was excused. The fictionalised depictions of a father absent to his surroundings and a martyr's forgiveness do not solve the social and even philosophical problems of the destructiveness of that father's role. Réal Ouellet is virtually the only recent critic to have pointed out how continued representation of Aurore indicates a sadism within society about which it is necessary to speak out. When, he asks, will society ('we') have the lucidity and courage to oppose depictions of women to whom violence is done, for whatever reason: religion, publicity or art?[28]

Perhaps the lines between the inside and the outside, the private and the public, have become so crossed and confused, and power relations so shuffled in the process, that the continued interest in this story of brutality and its reinterpretations speak of the explosive power inherent in change. It is surely as necessary now as it was then to look beyond nostalgic dreams of paternal power and the Christian nuclear family to find what needs to be reinvented.

Notes

1. This piece was written from research originally supported by the Social Sciences and Humanities Research Council of Canada. I would like to thank Yannick Portebois who was the assistant for that project during the year 1991–2 at the University of Montreal. I thank also Jenny Lefcourt for her contributions and Maurie Samuels for his comments during a seminar at Harvard University in the spring of 1995.
2. *Newsweek* proclaimed 1995 the year of the father in an article that states that 'fathers have become almost mythic figures – manning the barricade safeguarding America against further decay'. The article contends that 'it is necessary to instill in the next generation of fathers the belief that fatherhood is a sacred trust'. Ellis Cose, 'The Year of the Father', *Newsweek* (31 October 1994).
3. An editorial in *The Independent* summed up the situation for men somewhat drastically: 'Educationally less proficient, economically less valuable and biologically less important, there is a looming and genuine crisis of masculinity.' 'New Lines in the Sex Wars', *The Independent*, 29 May 1995.
4. In the United Kingdom, groups like the UK Men's Movement and Dads for Divorce have sprung up; in the United States, organisations like Promise Keepers bring men together to solidify their roles as fathers and relations. Men interviewed during a meeting that drew

media attention felt that 'the example set by fathers and grandfathers has become outdated'. *New York Times*, 8 June 1995. On October 5 1997, there was a huge gathering of Promise keepers in Washington: 'hundreds of thousands of christian men hugged, sang and sank to their knees..., repenting for their own sins and what they see as a secular and socially troubled America' (*New York Times*, October 5, 1997).

5. A campaign launched to track down 'Deadbeat Dads' in order to force them to pay child support has received widespread media coverage. A headline in the *Burlington Free Press* reads: 'Court orders deadbeat dad to pay $583,685', *Burlington Free Press*, 8 February 1995.
6. *Le Soleil*, 26 April 1920. All translations from French are my own.
7. The judge broke down at the moment he pronounced the sentence of death by hanging. He was reported to have retired from the bench shortly after the end of the trial. *Le Soleil*, 22 April 1920. For coverage of the trial, see *Le Soleil* from February to May 1920.
8. See the dossier prepared by Alonzo Leblanc, *Aurore l'enfant martyre* (Montreal: VLB Éditeur, 1982).
9. The production was filmed in 1951 by Jean-Yves Bigras and produced by France-Film.
10. Roch Carrier, Director of the Canada Council and a well-known poet, recounted how he attended such a performance, during a conversation following a presentation at the Canada Seminar, Harvard University, Spring, 1995.
11. Leblanc, *op. cit.*, p. 97.
12. Emile Asselin, *La Petite Aurore: L'enfant martyre* (Montréal : Alliance Cinématographique Canadienne' 1952), p. 46.
13. 'The Crime of Infanticide: Throwing out the Baby with the Bathwater', *Canadian Journal of Family Law*, 6, (1987) 48. Unlike Houde, the young women, mostly without means, were seen as victims and not in themselves a threat to society. Despite the English Infanticide Act of 1922, women were often not prosecuted. Infanticide was common in nineteenth-century Canada as a way of dealing with unwanted children. For Catholic Quebec, the stakes were quite different.
14. See Leblanc, *op. cit.*, pp. 67–77.
15. *Le Courrier Fédéral*, 5, 8, 9 December 1921, 5. Cited in Leblanc, p. 57.
16. *L'Événement*, 21 May 1927, 30, and *Le Soleil*, 21 May, 1927, 14. In Leblanc, *op. cit.*, p. 61.
17. See Peter Brooks, *Balzac, Henry James, Melodrama, and the Mode of Excess* (New Haven: Yale University Press, 1976).
18. See Leblanc, *op. cit.*, pp. 98–9.
19. *Le Théâtre québécois* (Montreal: Hurtubise HMH, 1973) p. 20.
20. Léopold Houlé, in his *Histoire du théâtre au Canada* (Montreal: Fidès, 1945), gives only one line to Aurore: 'The theatre of art is understood and appreciated just as much as that dreadful melodrama *Aurore, enfant martyr*' (p. 167).
21. Réal Ouellet, 'L'Aurore l'enfant martyre de Léon Petitjean et Henri Rollin', *Lettres québecoises*, 29, 60.
22. See Heinz Weinmann, *Cinéma de l'imaginaire québécois. De La petite Aurore à Jésus de Montréal* (Montreal: L'Hexagone, 1990).

23. See my 'Modern Tales of Anxiety', *Diogenes*, 43/1, 169, Spring 1995.
24. I thank Yannick Portebois for finding this term.
25. *La Presse*, 19 April 1920.
26. Alisdair MacIntyre, *After Virtue* (Notre Dame: University of Notre Dame Press, 1984).
27. See Ouellet, *op. cit.*, p. 60. Many schools carried inspirational information about Maria Goretti, who preferred death to life after being raped and was canonized, and pregnant teenagers were put to death by religious 'stepmothers' in the 1920s, according to Ouellet.
28. Ouellet, *op. cit.*, p. 60.

6

The Heredity of Power and Paternity of the Text in some Medieval Works

Yolande de Pontfarcy

Between the beginning of the tenth and the middle of the eleventh centuries, as Georges Duby has shown, political and socio-economic structures underwent a transformation. The weakening of royal power, the multiplication of sources of authority, the breaking-up of tightly-knit groups, the crumbling of fortunes and the progressive settling of members of the aristocracy on their patrimonial lands emphasized the role of paternity and the importance of the son as heir and perpetuator of the lineage.[1] Duby sees proof of this in the growing use throughout the eleventh and twelfth centuries of the patronymic, which emphasizes paternal ancestry as the mark of territorial ownership, whereas hitherto a man had usually borne a single name appertaining to a family group on either the paternal or the maternal side.[2] The greater importance accorded to the image of the father and the concomitant exaltation of the son led, in the latter's absence, to a reflection on the relationship between father and daughter and that other privileged relationship between the maternal uncle and his nephew. The literature of the period will be the terrain of this examination of paternity and the inheritance of power.

Paradoxically, until the end of the thirteenth century the idea of authorship was practically non-existent (anonymity was the norm and in the best of cases one finds only a name) and the idea of the authenticity of the text was unknown before the end of the fifteenth century (there were many versions of each work and each copyist left his own imprint).[3] Nevertheless, one can find considerations of the relationship between the writer and his work and his conception of the act of writing.

Due to the laws of exogamy in ancient Indo-European society, power was transmitted through the woman. Thus Pelops won the hand of Hippodamia and the kingdom of Pisa in Ellis by his victory in a race over his future father-in-law (Diodorus Siculus IV, 73) and the reason that the Thebans gave Oedipus his own mother as a wife in reward for having got rid of the Sphinx was because Jocasta was the incarnation of the sovereignty of Thebes. This ancient conception persisted in the Middle Ages, even when there was a male heir: Charlemagne, for example, avoided marrying off his numerous daughters because he feared the multiplication of pretenders to his throne. To suppress the menace which a son-in-law would represent, without at the same time wishing to lose the advantages of new alliances, the right of daughters to inherit from their father was diminished.[4] In a system in which power is transmitted through the woman, incest between father and daughter becomes a political crime because it signifies an abusive appropriation of this power. The taboo of incest comes to the fore in medieval literature when there is a question of succession in the absence of a son.

In the *Lai des Deuz Amanz* by Marie de France, who lived in the second half of the twelfth century, the king of Pîtres in Normandy is encouraged by his entourage to marry off his daughter, since the exclusive affection of the old king for the young princess has led to talk and people are worried because of the absence of a male heir.[5] To avoid a marriage, the king imposes on the suitors the almost impossible task of carrying the princess in their arms to the top of a hill without rest. After a few suitors have failed, a young knight passes the test with the connivance of the princess, who sends him to get a magic potion; but having refused to drink the potion in order to succeed solely by the strength of his love, he dies of exhaustion on reaching the top of the hill. The princess in turn drops dead from shock and the potion falls on the ground, making the region fertile. The hill was named 'The Two Lovers' in memory of this misadventure and the Bretons composed a lay which was retold by Marie.

I showed some time ago that the source of this lay was a royal inauguration ritual, complete with human sacrifice, signifying the creation and birth of the sovereign.[6] But another meaning has been grafted on to the original sense of the memorised ritual because this story of fatal love – with the bitter triumph of the father punished through his affection (he faints from sorrow upon hearing of the princess's death) – condemns both the king's abusive love of his daughter and his love of power, a condemnation perpetuated in the name of the hill and the Breton lay retold by Marie.

Even though Marie speaks in the first person in the story, bearing witness to the real existence of the places mentioned (lines 8, 19, 230) or adding a commentary here and there (lines 18–20, 54), she does not present herself as the author, but as one who continues a collective voice which had memorised the tragedy of the legitimate love of two young people. The story is introduced by a prologue which gives the origin of the lay:

> *Jadis avint en Normendie*
> *une aventure mut oïe*
> *de deus enfanz ki s'entreamerent;*
> *par amur ambedui finerent.*
> *Un lai en firent li Bretun :*
> *De Deus Amanz reçuit le nun.*
>
> (lines 1–6: éd. Jean Rychner)

[A long time ago, in Normandy, there was an event which was much talked about. It concerned two young people who loved each other and died of love. The Bretons made up a lay about it which was called 'The Two Lovers'.]

This theme is repeated in the epilogue:

> *Pur l'aventure des enfaunz*
> *Ad nun li munz 'des Deus Amanz'.*
> *Issi avint cum dit vus ai;*
> *Li Bretun en firent un lai.*
>
> (lines 251–4)

[Because of the story of the two young people, the hill was called 'The Two Lovers'. In that place what I have just told you happened and the Bretons made up a lay about it.]

The return in the conclusion to the theme of the prologue makes Marie's lay a mirror of the Breton story, repeating the original act and implicitly the condemnation of incest. Marie's voice is therefore like an echo within the tradition, an echo of the collective voice which named the hill and the lay.

The story of *Apollonius of Tyr*, which was rewritten many times between the third and the eighteenth centuries (I shall follow here the

Vienna version which dates from the fourteenth century),[7] tells of the difficulties which Apollonius has to overcome in order to regain his heritage and the various relationships between fathers and daughters and between kings and sovereignty. It also illustrates the analogy proposed by Lévi-Strauss between marriage and communication and between the movement of women and messages.[8] The first part is a dark story of incest. The regent Antiochus, who governs the young Apollonius's four kingdoms, not only makes his subjects hate him because of his heavy taxes but also, on the death of his wife, takes his consenting daughter as his mistress because of her resemblance to her mother. To rebuff his daughter's prospective husbands while at the same time giving the impression of acceding to the desires of his subjects, Antiochus gives the suitors the task of solving a riddle which would result in the public revelation of his incestuous relationship. As the suitors are unable to find the solution, their severed heads (a significant mutilation) are exhibited on the palace tower. But a similar fate awaits whoever might publicly reveal this crime, as Apollonius almost learns to his cost when, having discovered the meaning of the enigma, he is accused of lying and has to flee to escape Antiochus's wrath.

By breaking the sexual taboo, concealing the truth and endangering the prosperity of his people, Antiochus presents a totally negative image of the moral, spiritual and physical paternity that a just king should exercise. His daughter becomes a double of her mother, in other words a shadow of death. She is voiceless (she allows herself to be adorned and brought without a word into her father's bedroom), a symbol of the silence of death that the king imposes all round him. God does not wait long to punish this incestuous couple by having them struck by lightning. Apollonius on the contrary shows the qualities proper to a just sovereign in his feats as a warrior (he vanquishes the red knight), his respect for the law (he was ready to marry Antiochus's daughter according to the wishes of his counsellors and the terms imposed by the king), his mastery of the word (he solved the riddle) and his generosity (he distributed corn to the Tarsians and saved them from famine).

The second part is the story of the king of Cyrene and his daughter in whose country Apollonius is shipwrecked. This couple provide the reverse image to that of Antiochus and his daughter. Antiochus's greed is contrasted with the generosity of this king, shown not only in his promise to the princess to marry whomever she likes but also in his magnificent life-style, the quality of his hospitality, the freedom of speech he permits and its revelation of truth. The young princess falls in love with Apollonius who, while remaining incognito, through his sporting, intellectual and musical talents brings himself to the notice of the king who employs him as his daughter's tutor. The young princess at first speaks discreetly to her father, then sends him a letter whose meaning modesty renders unclear, in which she reveals that she loves Apollonius rather than other suitors. The king understands neither the oral nor the written message. Apollonius is asked to explain the letter and the blushing young man reveals what seems to be a riddle. The king is delighted with his daughter's choice.

How can one account for the princess's embarrassment at expressing her desire since her father is disposed to grant her request? And why does he not understand what she is trying to say? Michel Zink[9] and Jean Scheidegger[10] see in this 'hermetic' communication the expression of an unconscious sexual desire. It seems to me more likely that what is being suggested here is that it is not proper for a girl to choose her husband without her father having had his say, as to do so would destroy his authority and his paternal duty to marry her off. The passivity of the king seems to be a sort of auto-castration (he does not know whom she loves nor does he understand either her oral or written message) and without the help of Apollonius he would have been vanquished in the war waged against him by the rejected suitors. Once more, by his many talents, by his knowledge of the secret meaning of words and by his mastery of the art of war, Apollonius has shown the qualities of a sovereign.

The final trial that Apollonius must face is the temptation to incest. Having learned of the death of Antiochus, Apollonius sets sail with his wife to repossess his heritage. A storm rises and the young woman, flung this way and that by the sea, gives birth before her time to a girl called Tarsienne. The young mother is thought to be dead and her coffin is buried at sea. Apollonius leaves his daughter to a couple whom he believes he can trust, declares that he will neither shave nor cut his hair until he has married her off (a way of protecting himself against such incestuous desire as he might inspire by means of his repulsive image)[11] and goes on his way. Tarsienne becomes a young woman and is kidnapped by Saracen sailors, who sell her as a virgin for a good price to a pimp from the kingdom of Anastagoras. Despite all the dreadful situations in which she finds herself – first of all with King Anastagoras, then with his knights and finally in a house of prostitution – she succeeds in keeping her virginity by telling the story of her life, for which her listeners, moved by pity, pay her so much that the pimp thinks it would be more profitable to exploit her talents as a musician and story-teller than to exploit her body. The pleasure of Tarsienne's story-telling becomes a substitute for carnal pleasure and, as Scheidegger states, an erotic economy has been replaced by an economy of discourse.[12] Because of her art of speech, the substitute for a carnal act, Tarsienne finds her father.

Apollonius, believing his daughter dead and disgusted with life, sets sail and refuses to leave the hold of the boat. He eventually arrives in the country of King Anastagoras. The latter, who now loves Tarsienne as his daughter because of her virginity, guesses that Apollonius is the girl's father and sends her to him so that she may bring him some comfort by her talents. He in fact acts in the same way as the king of Cyrene did when he sent Tarsienne's mother to entertain the young Apollonius at the time of his shipwreck. Tarsienne's songs serve only to revive the pain of Apollonius, who pays her and sends her away. But sent back again by Anastagoras, she sets Apollonius riddles and threatens to give him back his money if he refuses to answer. Apollonius, not wishing to take anything from her, solves all the riddles. Then, while trying to push the young girl away when she makes a gesture of tenderness, he causes her to fall. Wounded in one knee and in pain, she tells the story of her unfortunate life.[13] Apollonius, full of joy, recognises her, celebrates their meeting and immediately gives her to King Anastagoras who has asked for her hand in marriage. Having now married off his daughter, Apollonius deserves to enjoy his kingship and his father's legacy. Furthermore, God has sent him a vision which helps him to find his wife, who was not in fact dead and who, as a supreme reward, will give him four sons to succeed him at the head of his four kingdoms. Apollonius has his adventures and those of his family written down. These are set out in two books, one of which he places in the temple of Diana in Ephesus, keeping the other in his library.

The daughter, image of the word, is the mediatrix of sovereignty only if father and king use her in a system of communication and exchange. In this context Antiochus, the incestuous king, is evil; the king of Cyrene, who refuses to intervene in his daughter's choice of husband, is weak; and the procurer, who is the perverted image of a father, is a criminal and is sent to the stake by general accord. As speech cannot be communicated without the support of sounds or signs, so a woman cannot live without male support: Tarsienne's absent father is symbolically replaced by the procurer and by King Anastagoras (who initially would happily have raped her but who, having accepted her virginity, begins to love and protect her as a father); it is Anastagoras who helps her find her father and, this done, asks for her hand in marriage, as he could not have married her beforehand without the paternal consent of Apollonius. Thus the marriage of daughters is the business of fathers, in the same way that the Logos is the power of the father or husband and can be exercised by a woman only in order to guard her virginity or her chastity, in other words to remain the daughter of her father or the faithful wife of an absent husband.

As the given author of this story is none other than Apollonius, the voice of the anonymous compiler reading the story restores to us the unique voice of the author, the father and the king. This sort of circularity, which unites past and present in one voice, is expressed in another manner in the story. When Tarsienne puts the riddle to her father, she associates herself with the original word at the source of life, whose meaning is full of mystery. And Apollonius, who solves the riddle, finds himself associated with the fertilising Logos, that which reveals meaning. The one engenders the other, but the latter is the father of the former. The circular relationship between Logos and Verb reflects the circular relationship of father and daughter, of king and people, of power and authority. This relationship governs the laws, whose type and enforcement designates the just king, the 'real' father and master of the Verb.

The ancient privileged relationship between maternal uncle and nephew which still existed in the twelfth century was challenged by the new importance given to paternity. Generally sons were sent to be educated by their mother's brother. In this connection the family of Lambert de Wattrelos is often given as an example. Lambert outlines these relationships in the introduction to his *Annales Cameracenses* (1152–70): he himself bears the name of his mother's brother; another of his maternal uncles, the abbot of Mont Saint-Eloi, takes him into his monastery and guides him in his career, as he also does for three sons of his other sisters; Lambert's eldest brother, a soldier by profession, seems also to have followed the adventurous life of one of his mother's brothers.[14] The importance of the relationship between maternal uncle and nephew is particularly apparent in the courtly romances and the world of epic, so much so that in the *Chansons de geste*, the designation son + genitive of the father's name appears only for recently-created heroes such as the 'fils Aimeri' in the Guillaume Cycle or the 'quatre fils Aimon' for Renaud de Montauban and his three brothers.[15]

Françoise Le Saux, in her study of the *Historia Regum Britanniae* written by Geoffrey of Monmouth in 1137, thinks that the positive relationship between a maternal uncle and his nephews stems from the importance of the king as father of his subjects, which demands the necessary abolition of the 'identity of the son so that he may be assimilated to a father as soon as the son accedes to the throne'.[16] It is true that in the patrilinear system the son represents a political threat (usurpation is always to be feared) and one has only to recall the terrible wars waged against their father by the sons of King Henry II of England. However the *Historia Regum Britanniae* was written long before the troubles Henry II had with his offspring and many other kings assured their succession by crowning their sons during their own lifetime without having to suffer the quarrels which seem peculiar to the Angevins. The succession of this dynasty on the throne of England in the twelfth century is interesting. Henry I died in 1138 without a male heir (his only son was drowned in the shipwreck of the *Blanche Nef*); in spite of the fact that he had designated his daughter Mathilda as his successor, it was his nephew Stephen de Blois (the son of his sister Adèle) who assumed the crown. However Stephen was vigorously opposed by Mathilda, who wanted the crown to pass to her own son, Henry Plantagenêt, the future Henry II. The war which split the kingdom throughout this period is in my opinion a struggle of principle between the new priority of the grandson and that of the nephew in the order of succession.

If, in the light of these reflections, one examines the nature of kings' affection for their sisters' sons in the literature of the period, one perceives that it is often explained and at the same time discredited by the suggestion that the nephews are the result of an incestuous love between brother and sister, and that therefore the order of succession from uncle to nephew is thereby subverted. It is well known that the reference to a very grave sin by Charlemagne, who did not dare to confess it to St Giles, goes back to the *Vita Aegidii* which dates from the tenth century. The legend of the incestuous origin of Roland was so widespread at the end of the twelfth century that Rita Lejeune thinks that the *Chanson de Roland* bears the stamp of Charlemagne's guilt: 'by his martyrdom Roland sought to redeem a shameful origin which was at the source of his redoutable spirit of immoderation, while Charlemagne would redeem the sin of his youth by tears and repentance, after wars in the service of the faith'.[17]

Let us now turn to the Arthurian romances. The love of King Arthur for Gauvain, 'the sun of chivalry', is well known; Arthur's son, Loholt, although sometimes referred to, plays a practically non-existent role,[18] because the essential point of the Arthurian romances is not so much filiation (although the ultimate cause of the collapse of this universe will be the treason of Mordred, nephew and son through incest of Arthur) as paternity which expresses itself through the story and kingship which is merited rather than inherited.

From the beginning of *Erec et Enide*, the first romance of Chretien de Troyes, who was writing between 1170 and 1190, the royal function of paternity appears in the creation of 'adventure'. By deciding to hunt the White Stag and restoring the custom of kissing the most beautiful lady, Arthur opens the story, launches the 'adventure' and gives the future hero the opportunity to distinguish himself. When Perceval in the *Conte del Graal* describes Arthur as 'the king who makes knights' (lines 492 and 838–9), he expresses in his innocence a truth which goes beyond the simple ceremony of dubbing. As for the adventure of Erec, whose meeting with Enide, difficult period of early marriage and ultimate coronation by Arthur are related by Chretien, this is the story of a slow and painful ascension to the life of coupledom and to royalty as if the two were connected, although Erec was born the son and heir of King Lac. Royalty must be merited even if one receives it by birth.

In *Le Chevalier au Lion*, Chretien de Troyes shows Calogrenant recounting his misadventures at the fountain of Broceliande while the tired king is taking a siesta. This incites his cousin Yvain to go there in turn, followed shortly afterwards by Arthur and his court, so that the adventure story and the adventure of the knights are closely knitted together and stimulated by the king.[19] Subtly therefore the movement of the knights' adventures is given in parallel to the creative activity of the story-teller, inviting us to ask ourselves how Chretien saw his function.

In his various prologues, he shows clearly that he has a strong awareness of his authority. Whereas in *Cligès*, his second romance, he sets forth the works that he has already written, he defines his function as a writer in the prologue to his first, *Erec et Enide*. He not only names himself but declares that he is the composer of a well-organised and well-structured story taken from a tale that professional story-tellers used to spoil in the course of telling. Of his own story he says that it will never be forgotten as long as Christianity remains on earth, and he finishes by stating 'this is Chretien's boast'. It can be seen that on the one hand Chretien diminishes the importance of his source, a story from the past to which he gives no weight of authority, and on the other that he emphasises his own part in the composition of this new work, which, he boasts, will be unforgettable. Respect for the source is not important for him, what matters is only the new work which in its coherence generates its own truth.

In *Le Chevalier de la Charrete* he attributes the subject and main idea to Marie de Champagne (line 26), but once again claims for himself all the credit for having written and given structure to it (lines 28–9). Similarly, in *Le Conte del Graal* he refers to a mysterious book as a source of his work and, from the beginning of the prologue, presents himself as the one who has sown the seed:

> *Crestïens seime et fait semence*
> *D'un romanz qu'il encommence*
>
> (lines 7–8)

[Chretien sows and lays the seed of a romance that he begins]

In all his prologues, Chretien attempts to transfer the authority of the past and of his sources to himself, the creator of the new work, while at the same time telling, through the romantic adventures of his heroes, his own adventures as a writer.[20]

La Mort le Roi Artu, written in 1230, the last romance of the huge literary monument which is the *Lancelot en Prose*, tells of the collapse of the Arthurian world and ends with the story of how Mordred usurps the throne of his uncle and father, King Arthur, attemps to steal his queen, and meets his death at the king's hand while mortally wounding him.[21] Incest has created chaos by breaking down the order of filiation and relationship. The crime of the father is manifested in the person of the son and, thrown into confrontation, each kills the other as if caught in a trap or a mirror reflecting their own crime. No continuation is possible: with the sons of Mordred exterminated by Lancelot and all those who have not been killed in the final battles ending their days in hermitages, the Arthurian world closes in upon itself. This same closure is found in the game which turns the creation of fiction upon itself. Neither King Henry, who asked for a sequel to the *Queste del Saint Graal*, nor Gautier Map, who wrote the story, was the real patron and author of the work.[22] Through them, the writer introduces the function of creative writing, which is a game played between reality and fiction to the extent that the border between the two disappears.[23] Although the act of writing is illustrated by the interaction of *potestas* (Gautier Map) in the service of *auctoritas* (King Henry), the source of the story is no longer a work from the past but only the royal desire of the one who directs and holds the pen.

The study of these few texts from the twelfth to the beginning of the fourteenth centuries has shown that the overevaluation of paternity – which incest represents – is perceived as an obstacle on the level of both speech (which becomes forbidden) and action (dominated by failure) and always results in the absence of the desired successor. The fact remains that to engender sons in the permitted framework of exogamy, to give daughters in marriage but also to engender heroes, adventures and stories, is the fulfilment of the paternal and royal function. The authors, who did not yet see themselves in this light, either make their works the echo of the Verb, the mirror of truth that tradition guarantees or, conscious of their talents, point out their role and function or hide themselves behind glamorous names subtly indicating that desire is the primordial source of writing.

Notes

1. See Georges Duby, 'Structures de parenté et noblesse dans la France du Nord aux XIe et XIIe siècles', in *Hommes et Structures au Moyen Age* (Paris: Mouton, 1973) pp. 267–85, 'Structures familiales dans le Moyen Age occidental' in Duby, *Mâle Moyen Age* (Paris: Flammarion, 1988) pp. 129–38, and 'Structures familiales et aristocratiques en France du XIe siècle en rapport avec les structures de l'Etat', in *ibid.*, pp. 139–46; see also K.F. Werner, 'Liens de parenté et noms de personne' in Duby and J. Le Goff (eds), *Famille et parenté dans l'Occident Médiéval* (Rome: Ecole Française de Rome, 1977) pp. 13–40.
2. A. Guerreau-Jalbert, 'Sur les structures de parenté dans l'Europe médiévale', *Annales*, E.S.C., 36 (1981), pp. 1028–49, particularly p. 1031; see also Marc Bloch, *La Société féodale* (Paris: Albin Michel, 1939) pp. 201–2.
3. Paul Zumthor, *Essai de poétique médiévale* (Paris: Seuil, 1972) pp. 64–82.
4. Duby, *Le Chevalier, la femme et le prêtre* (Paris: Hachette, 1981) pp. 47 and 111–13.
5. J. Rychner (ed.), *Les Lais de Marie de France*, CFMA 93 (Paris: Champion, 1968).
6. See my article 'Woman and the weight of sovereignty', *Shadow* (Edinburgh), 1991 vol. 8., pp. 12–22.
7. M. Zink (ed. and trans.), *Le Roman d'Apollonius de Tyr* (Paris: Union Générale d'édition, 1982); J.R. Scheidegger, 'Pères et Filles dans *Apollonius de Tyr*', in *Les Relations de parenté dans le monde médiéval, Senefiance* 26 (1989) pp. 259–71.

8. Claude Lévi-Strauss, *Structures élémentaires de la parenté* (Paris: Mouton, 1968) p. 565.
9. Zink, *op. cit.*, p. 29.
10. Scheidegger, *op. cit.*, p. 268.
11. Zink, *op. cit.*, p. 22 and Scheidegger, *op. cit.*, p. 268.
12. Scheidegger, *op. cit.*, p. 269.
13. Scheidegger (*op. cit.*, p. 270) notes that in this sequence – bleeding, life-story telling alias sexual act, tears alias orgasm – one can see again the same passage from the carnal to discourse which occurred in the brothel.
14. Duby, 'Structure de parenté', in *Hommes et structures du Moyen Age*, pp. 275–6; see also F. Vercauteren, 'Une parentèle de la France du Nord aux XIe et XIIes', *Le Moyen Age* 1, xix (1963) pp. 223–44, which gives the full story of the family of Lambert de Wattrelos.
15. R.R. Bezzola, 'Les Neveux' in *Mélanges J. Frappier* (Geneva: Droz, 1970) pp. 89–114. See also W.O. Farnsworth, *Uncle and Nephew in the old French Chansons de Geste* (New York: Ams Press, 1966; 1st ed. 1913); Lévi-Strauss, *op. cit.*; Claude Masset 'Préhistoire de la Famille' in *Histoire de la Famille* I, pp. 79–97.
16. F. Le Saux, 'Relations familiales et autorité royale: de L'*Historia Regum Britanniae* au *Brut* de Layamon' in *Les Relations de parenté dans le monde médiéval, Senefiance* 26 (1989), pp. 215–31, particularly p. 218.
17. Bezzola, *op. cit.*, pp. 101–8, citation p. 104, my translation; he refers to the following: B. de Gaiffer, 'La Légende de Charlemagne, le péché de l'empereur et son pardon', in *Recueil de travaux offerts à Clovis Brunel* I (Paris: Société de l'Ecole des Chartes, 1955) pp. 490–503; R. Le Jeune, 'Le péché de Charlemagne et la Chanson de Roland' in *Studia philologica. Homenaje offrecido a Damaso Alonso* II (Madrid: Gredos, 1961) pp. 339–71 and R. Le Jeune and J. Stiennon, *La Légende de Roland dans l'art du Moyen Age* (Bruxelles: Arcade, 1961) I, pp. 145–52, tables 4 and 18; II, tables 127b and 152. See also A. Demoulin, 'Charlemagne, la légende de son péché et le choix de Ganelon pour l'ambassade', *Marche Romane* XXV (1975) pp. 105–26.
18. K. Busby, 'The Enigma of Loholt' in K. Varty (ed.), *Arthurian Tapestry: Essays in Memory of Lewis Thorpe* (Glasgow: University of Glasgow, 1981) pp. 28–36.
19. See my article 'Le roi Arthur dans les romans de Chrétien de Troyes' in J.-L. Cabanèsond U.-G. Duboish (eds.) *Images européennes du pouvoir* (Toulouse: Université de Toulouse-le-Mirail, 1995) pp. 67–79.
20. See Michel Zink, *La Subjectivité littéraire* (Paris: PUF, 1985) particularly pp. 38–42.
21. J. Frappier (ed.), *Textes littéraires français*, 2nd ed. (Genève: Droz, 1956).
22. Courtier of Henry II, archdeacon of Oxford, author of *De Nugis Curialum*, Gautier Map died in 1210 while Henry II died in 1189. He could not have been the author of *Lancelot en Prose*, which was written between 1215 and 1230.
23. Their names must also have been used to give a source of authority to, and therefore to ensure the fame of, the new work.

7

Père and *Mère*: Unequals in Language

Philippe Bolusset

My main concern here is to look at the French lexical item *père* ('father') from a purely linguistic point of view, with reference to other terms referring to kinship relations such as *mère* ('mother'), *fille* ('daughter') or *fils* ('son').

Grammatical tradition has long accustomed us to consider vocabulary and grammar as two separate categories and, within the lexical component, to make a clear distinction between what are frequently called 'content words', referring strictly to notional concepts, and so-called 'function words', marking essentially logical relations. Such distinctions seem to ignore the fact that in numerous languages some lexical terms can combine both functions, referring to objects or notions and at the same time marking grammatical relations.[1] One need only consider the way that the French words *pas* or *point* have now often become the sole markers of negation in contemporary spoken French[2] or how such verbs as *faire* ('to make', 'to do') or *venir* ('to come') can, depending on context, function either as full content words or as verbal auxiliaries of modality or aspect.

Some linguists go so far as to suggest that there might be no such clear-cut dividing lines in language and that the traditional categories and distinctions currently in use in grammar and linguistics, such as those between vocabulary and grammar, nouns and verbs or semantics and syntax, tend to blur our perception of language and may conceal the operations of intricate rules far more subtle than we had imagined.[3] We may now have to change our position to adopt a radically different approach to language, considering it from a more unifying perspective that transcends such categories, where the received dividing lines will eventually fade away to reveal an order far more fluctuating and adaptable than appearances tend to suggest, an order with a dynamic of its own which one might compare to the laws at work in any living organism or even to the workings of the brain.[4]

This makes sense, especially when it becomes more and more evident that vocabulary and grammar, semantics and morpho-syntax are constantly interdependent and interactive in the construction of meaning.

In this light the object of the present analysis, which is however far from exhaustive, is to demonstrate that, despite their apparent symmetry, simple words referring to kinship relations, such as *père, mère, fils* and *fille*, can be found to have imperceptible dissimilarities where their semantic values or syntactic properties are concerned. Furthermore, when these terms are used figuratively in association with an inanimate grammatical subject, their occurrences seem to be highly sensitive to context. The fact that they are subject to contextual constraints may imply that they have inherent properties which prevent or restrict their occurrence in certain contexts. I am not of course referring here to the gender rules – whether semantic or grammatical – governing the use of these words in French.

A comparison of the word *paternité* ('paternity'/'fatherhood') with the word *maternité* ('maternity'/'motherhood') reveals that these two terms, both nominalised predicates, do not refer to exactly the same concept. Not that they should of course, but they should at least refer to symmetrical notions. On the contrary however, the contexts in which they may occur vary considerably.

Although the definition of these two words given by various dictionaries is symmetrical – *L'état ou qualité de père [ou de mère]* ('the state or quality of being a father [or mother]') – as soon as one triggers their referential value by inserting them into a particular context, the disparity between the two appears. Thus according to *Le Robert*, the word *paternité* can mean a feeling, a legal bond or, metaphorically, the fact of being the author or creator of a piece of work or the instigator of an action. This is not the case with the word *maternité*, which refers only to the biological process of giving birth to a child and, by metonymy, to the ward of a hospital or clinic where this process usually takes place. There seems to be no mention, curiously enough, of any figurative use of this word in the dictionaries. It is true that, like *paternité*, the word *maternité* can also refer to the maternal feeling but, according to Robert, this particular meaning is extremely rare.

From a purely semantic and lexical point of view, the distribution of the four terms referring to the closest kinship relations – *père, mère, fils, fille* – operates along a biological gender divide and a parent/child relation, which, according to componential semantics, features the presence or absence of semantic traits such as [+ male] [+ female]

[+ parent] [+ child]. However, in French, the polarised symmetry of these four lexical items is somehow altered by the fact that the word *fille* is also part of another paradigmatic class when opposed to *garçon*. On a syntactic level, all these terms are substantives, but *père* and *mère* may also function as predicates, unlike *fils* and *fille*: one can say of someone *il est père* ('he is a father') or *elle est mère* ('she is a mother'), but not *il est fils* ('he is a son') or *elle est fille* ('she is a daughter'), which could only be a tautology. According to our ontological postulates, the properties of being a daughter or a son are inherent to all human beings and therefore do not need to be predicated, whereas *être-père* ('being a father') and *être-mère* ('being a mother') are contingent properties.

When it comes to the figurative use of these terms, a distinction should be made as to whether they are associated with animate or inanimate nouns. Their metaphorical use with inanimate nouns can be found in many languages, but it is not universal. In Russian for instance, such use is impossible.[5] It should be stressed that the term 'metaphorical use' refers here only to what are known as lexicalised metaphors or 'dead metaphors', in other words metaphors that are already part of the linguistic code as opposed to genuine innovative metaphors produced freely by an individual speaker.

There are many examples of figurative use of the lexical item *père* in association with an animate subject, where the term acquires the meaning of creator, inventor or instigator, such as *Eschyle père de la tragédie* ('Aeschylus, the father of tragedy'), *Proudhon père de l'anarchisme* ('Proudhon, the father of anarchism') or *l'auteur père de ses écrits* ('the author, father of his works'), whereas examples with the figurative use of the word *mère* seem far less common and in any case acquire a totally different meaning value. The only example to be found was mentioned by Larousse: *être la mère des pauvres et des orphelins* ('to be the mother of the poor and orphaned'), where the word *mère* conveys the different meaning of protector. Could Simone de Beauvoir be described as *la mère du féminisme* ('the mother of feminism')? It is very unlikely, although not impossible. She may be called *la grand-mère du féminisme* ('the grandmother of feminism'), but this implies the slightly different meaning of 'forerunner' or 'precursor', with the emphasis on the generation gap. It is precisely these differences and disparities between the referential values of such words as *paternité* and *maternité* or *père* and *mère* which were the starting point of this study.

All four kinship terms may express a relation of cause (*père/mère*) or consequence (*fils/fille*) when used metaphorically with inanimate nouns (for example, *le travail est souvent le* **père** *du plaisir* ('work is often the **father** of pleasure'), *l'oisiveté est* **mère** *de tous les vices* ('idleness is the **mother** of all vice'), *l'admiration est* ***fille*** *de l'ignorance* (admiration is the **daughter** of ignorance), *des vers* ***fils*** *de l'amour* (poetry that is the **son** of love), but they do not seem to be equally productive. In French however, *père, mère* and *fille* are much more frequently used metaphorically than *fils*, of which only one example was found, with the lexical item *mère* undoubtedly the most productive and most frequently used since, unlike the word *père*, it has the added characteristic of functioning as a noun determiner by simple affixation (for example, *une maison-mère* (parent company)).

When used metaphorically with inanimate nouns, both *père* and *mère* acquire the meaning of cause, source, origin, and obviously their distribution in French is governed by the grammatical gender of the inanimate noun to which they apply. However the fact that, in association with an animate subject, the word *père*, unlike its counterpart *mère*, can acquire the meaning of 'author' or 'instigator', suggests that it features a strong agentive property which still seems to be active when it is used in relation to an inanimate subject. It should be understood that I am using a definition of the word 'agent' which is far more limited than the one the term is usually given in traditional grammar: traditionally the grammatical subject of an action is referred to as the 'agent' of the action, whereas the grammatical subject will be considered here as properly the 'agent' of an action when and only when that subject is seen as the active source consciously triggering the action, in other words when a degree of intentionality on the part of the subject is entailed. Thus Mary in 'Mary broke the glass' can only be considered as the agent of the action if the process was intentional and not accidental.

Proving that the agentive property is fundamental and inherent to the lexical item *père* in contrast to *mère* seems a rather difficult task, since in French the choice of *mère* or *père*, though both apparently synonymous in their metaphorical meaning of 'cause', will clearly depend on the grammatical gender of the inanimate noun to which the term applies. I shall therefore refer to examples in English, where there is a similar metaphorical use, but one which is not subject to constraints of grammatical gender.

If we compare examples in English and French, we find that in both languages the use of *père* or 'father' in relation to an inanimate noun is far less frequent than with *mère* or 'mother'. This could be precisely because the strong agentive property of the former pair, which does not seem to feature in the words *mère* or 'mother', considerably restricts their association with inanimate nouns. If we then examine the examples from our corpus – although it is by no means exhaustive – in those cases where both pairs are used metaphorically with an inanimate noun, we notice that, in examples using the word *père* or 'father', the consequences resulting from the cause (the inanimate grammatical subject) can in most cases be interpreted as ontologically positive or beneficial (for example, *le besoin est* ***père de l'industrie*** ('need is the **father of industry**'), *le travail est* ***père des bonnes moeurs*** ('work is the **father of good manners**'), *le temps est* ***père de la verité*** 'Time is the **father of truth**'), whereas in those featuring the word *mère* or 'mother', the consequences can be either detrimental or beneficial (for example, *l'ignorance est la* ***mère de tous les crimes*** ('ignorance is the **mother of all crimes**'), *la chasteté est la* ***mère des vertus*** ('chastity is the **mother of virtue**'), *l'indécison est la* ***mère de l'échec*** ('indecision is the **mother of failure**'), *l'assiduité est la* ***mère du succès*** ('diligence is the **mother of success**').

J.J. Franckel has suggested that beneficial and detrimental properties are deeply linked to the presence or absence of intentionality on the part of the subject, in other words to whether the grammatical subject is truly the agent of the process.[6] According to him, any action which entails a certain degree of intentionality on the part of the subject will be generally perceived as beneficial for that subject, whereas an action over which the subject appears to have no control will most probably be interpreted as detrimental to the subject. This makes sense: why should one willingly cause harm to oneself?

In the case under consideration here, it is obvious that an inanimate grammatical subject cannot have 'agentive' features, since intentional properties are essentially restricted to humans. However, I would suggest that inherent in the lexical item *père* is a strong 'agentive' value, which may be weakened in a metaphorical context with an inanimate noun, but yet remains strong enough to prevent the possibility of the word's occurring in a context where the grammatical subject is the origin of what may be perceived as detrimental or negative. This does not mean that *père* is never used figuratively in association with something detrimental; however the constraint of the word's agentive value must limit such occurrences considerably. By contrast, if the word *mère* lacks inherent agentive properties, then such constraints will not apply, allowing the grammatical subject to be the cause of something either beneficial or detrimental.

These ideas seem entirely contradicted by the following maxim by the French seventeenth-century author La Bruyère in *Les Caractères*: '*Si la pauvreté est la mère du crime, le manque d'esprit en est le père*'. For here the word *crime*, which refers to a notion generally perceived as negative and detrimental, occurs in association with the word *père*. I shall return to this point later, demonstrating that, in this case, the context itself requires such an association, but first we need to determine whether there is a difference of meaning between *père* and *mère*, despite their apparent synonymy, and to show that the choice of *père* rather than *mère* was not made entirely on the basis of style or grammatical gender, since *la stupidité* and *le dénuement* could easily be substituted for *le manque d'esprit* and *la pauvreté* to accommodate gender agreement.

La Bruyère's maxim uses what in grammar are called concessive clauses, whose logical structure is, 'if P of x, then Q of x'. In concessive clauses we infer from clause P the opposite of clause Q.[7] In this case, what is contrasted is not just *la pauvreté* and *le manque d'esprit*, but the whole predicate *être la mère de* and *être le père de*, despite the fact that *mère* and *père* are both synonymous of origin. Therefore *père* and *mère* cannot have exactly the same meaning value or the formal concessive structure of this sentence would be irrelevant. It is true that symmetrical and mirror structures are common features of La Bruyère's style in *Les Caractères* and that *père* and *mère* are relational opposites; however the concessive interpretation of the sentence can hardly be justified solely on grounds of style. How could such a sentence be interpreted if we substituted the word 'cause' for both *père* and *mère*?

I would suggest that the word *mère* is inherently devoid of agentive property and intentionality, having thus a purely instrumental property – although it may acquire agentive values contextually when referring to an animate subject. By contrast, the lexical item *père*, which entails some degree of intentionality, is assigned a more active role when used figuratively with an inanimate noun. Therefore the meaning of *père* and *mère* in La Bruyère's maxim differs slightly and could be paraphrased as 'if poverty is the root of crime, stupidity is what triggers it'. Such an interpretation is justified by our social and cultural presuppositions, for we know that poverty is linked to crime, but it does not always lead to crime, whereas a lack of discernment can only lead us to make choices which are necessarily detrimental to ourselves. For it is inevitable that something as detrimental as an inability to make a proper judgement has negative consequences. Culturally, both poverty and stupidity have negative connotations and are perceived as detrimental, but unlike stupidity, poverty can also be positively valued.

It is my view that this is the reason why the word *père* is used in association with a consequence considered as detrimental, and also that it contrasts the passive role of poverty with the more active role of stupidity, in relation to crime. The English translation of the sentence, 'If poverty is the mother of crime, stupidity is its father', is more likely to be given such an interpretation, since the question of grammatical gender is neutralised and seems to confirm our intuition that the figurative use of 'father' and 'mother' do not have exactly the same meaning value.

Of course one could argue that 'father' and 'mother' are strictly synonymous of origin and that the sentence should be interpreted as: 'poverty alone does not lead to crime, but the combination of poverty and stupidity does'. In that case, the grammatical subjects of each clause should be interchangeable and the interpretation of the sentence should not be affected whether we say: 'if poverty is the mother of crime, stupidity is its father' or 'if stupidity is the mother of crime, poverty is its father'. Here though, the latter sentence contradicts the logic of the concessive clause structure 'if P, then Q', which entails that P, both for the speaker and the co-speaker, has already been validated independently, in other words that P is a postulate considered to be true and does not need to be verified. For while the link between poverty and crime is indeed generally accepted and does not need to be demonstrated, the idea of crime as the corollary of stupidity is, on the other hand, totally subjective in the sense that it is not part of our cultural preconceptions and involves La Bruyère alone.

We know that in Canadian French and in Creole the words *père* and *mère* can also express a superlative or intensive value and that – even more interestingly – in French the word *mère* can mean the model or prototype: *ce chef-d'oeuvre a servi de mère pour de nombreuses copies* ('this masterpiece provided the model for numerous copies'). As in French and English, in Arabic *oum* ('mother') and *âab* ('father') are used metaphorically to express the cause or origin, but with an added superlative meaning. The famous speech by Saddam Hussein on the eve of the Gulf War, in which he used the expression 'the mother of all battles', and where incidentally 'mother' does not mean the origin but 'the greatest of all', has led to numerous adaptations in the English language. In a particularly relevant example from an American sitcom shown recently on television, a man who is seeking reassurance from his wife about his ability to be a good father is told: 'You are the mother of all fathers'. In this case it is not the superlative value which predominates, but the meaning of prototype, model.

This particular value leads us to think that the lexical item 'mother', whether in English, French or Arabic, has the property of centring an occurrence of the notion it determines on the prototypical value of the notion; for instance, in our example 'the mother of all fathers' does not refer to any particular occurrence of father that would match the definition of father, including fathers who are not 'good', but to a father who is truly a father, the highest degree of father. However it must be said that the meaning values of origin and prototype are very close.

To conclude, I have tried to show that lexical items such as 'mother' and 'father', apparently synonymous when used metaphorically, in fact feature slightly different meaning values and I suggest that these differences are linked to underlying properties inherent to the terms. It then becomes necessary to determine whether these properties derive from deep-rooted socio-cultural preconceptions which define the role of fathers as truly creative while the mother's role is perceived as merely reproductive or instrumental. After all, the word 'matter' in Greek comes directly from the word 'mother'.

In any case, this analysis does not claim to be exhaustive, nor conclusive. It simply suggests that, underlying the apparent instability and profusion of values emanating from them, lexical items, like grammatical markers, may have stable properties which, in combination, themselves provide the space in which such a profusion and flexibility of values can be generated.

Notes

1. See Stéphane Robert's analysis of the word 'ginnaw' in Wolof: '"Puisque" et "le dos" en Wolof: une tempête dans le signifié', *Le Gré des langues*, I (1990) 82–92.
2. The original role of these two words in negative phrases was as simple intensifiers of the word *ne*, which alone conveyed the negative.
3. Notably the 'Groupe de recherche URA 1028: Invariants langagiers', Université de Paris 7. See J.J. Franckel, D. Lebaud, D. Paillard, S. de Vogüe, *La Théorie d'Antoine Culioli: ouvertures et incidences* (Paris: OPHRYS, 1992).
4. On the development of brain cells, Gerald Edelman's theory of 'neural Darwinism' seems to point in that direction. See also G. Bernard,

'Formalisation dynamique des relations prédicatives', *La Théorie d'Antoine Culioli: ouvertures et incidences*, pp. 163–81.

5. V.G. Gak, 'On the problem of general semantic laws', *Linguistics* 182 (1976) pp. 39–52.
6. See J.J. Franckel, 'Du Dommage engendré par les marqueurs grammaticaux', *La Notion de prédicat*, URA 642 (Paris: Laboratoire de linguistique formelle, Université de Paris VII, 1989) pp. 161–84.
7. See S. de Vogüe, 'Inférence sous inférence', *Le Gré des langues* 1 (1990) 20–1 and S. de Vogüe, 'Si, la syntaxe et le point de vue des opérations', *La Théorie d'Antoine Culioli: ouvertures et incidences*, pp. 107–21.

(Translated by Trista Selous)

II
Absent Fathers

8

Life without Father: Revisions of Paternity in Women's Writing in France

Jennifer Birkett

> My father died, leaving traces
> everywhere. (Hélène Cixous)[1]

The first effect of the father's absence is to make more visible to his heirs the marks of his presence everywhere in their landscape. The second is to give them the space to assess his legacy and choose to assume or reject it. In the matter of choosing, the most interesting case studies come from moments when generational conflict expresses itself in the larger political conflicts of revolutionary social change. The interest increases when the focus is on daughters, whose relatively marginalised position in the public domain has often offered them options for transforming the inheritance which are more open and more radical than those of sons. Consideration of the work of three women writers, selected from three points of France's evolution from monarchy to democratic republic (abandoning the King, father of his people, for the brotherhood of the citizen-State), shows three very different ways of coming to terms with the authority of the father, through challenge, compromise or outright collusion. The three are Anne-Louise-Germaine de Staël (1766–1817), arguably the most important writer of the Revolution of 1789 and its Napoleonic aftermath, George Sand (pseudonym of Aurore Dupin, 1804–76), whose most interesting work falls between the revolutions of 1830 and 1848, and the *fin-de-siècle* novelist Rachilde (Marguerite Eymery, 1860–1953), writing after the repression of the Commune in 1871 and against the socialist fervour which swept France and Europe in the 1880s and 90s.

Rethinking the father is a central issue for 1990s feminism. The first half of the decade has seen a reassessment of the irreconcilable opposition assumed to exist between father and mother and masculine and feminine, which formed the starting-point of much feminist thinking in the 1980s. At that time feminist academics tended to cast the relationship of the feminine to the father in terms of the antagonisms identified by Lacanian psychoanalysis, with its presentation of paternal law and discourse as the gateway to existence as a subject within Western European culture, its insistence that the child's entry into culture involved a renunciation of identification with the maternal body, its natural starting-point, and its declaration that the feminine cannot exist as an autonomous subject within the discourse of culture. Lacanian language performed a helpful function for feminist political organisation in the 1980s by focusing attention on the rhetorics which construct the feminine as the mirror-opposite of the masculine: darkness as opposed to light, nature to culture, feeling and silence to intellect, creativity and speech, passive to active, desired to desiring, sources of chaos rather than agents of order. These oppositions are discursive constructs, not matters of transhistorical fact. Nevertheless, renewed at the threshold of the twentieth century in the formulations of reactionary decadence, they were and still are strongly enough lodged in the Western European mind to sustain the allocation of women to subordinate social roles.

Changes of direction in the 1990s emphasise instead the link between gender relations in the family and relations within society at large, and revise the politics of the Oedipal triad as a base for the revision of social hierarchies. Most recently, feminist theorists have taken fresh interest in the work of Julia Kristeva and its categorical refusal of simple oppositions of mother- and father-functions and their respective allocations to realms of nature and culture.[2] Kristeva's account of the semiotic (*La Révolution du langage poétique*, 1974) presented the mother as primary mediator of culture to the child in the womb, transmitting the body-rhythms which are the foundations of the rhythms of syntax. In *Des Chinoises* (1974), she presented the mother-figure in Chinese tradition as not just a reproductive function but also an independent agent in the public domain.[3] In *Histoires d'amour* (1983), considering the constituting structures of narcissism, she spoke of Freud's argument that knowledge of the father is mediated through the mother and the child's primary identification is with 'the father-mother conglomerate':[4] not a passive maternal body but a loving father, through a pre-Oedipal mother who is not passive but herself both speaking and desiring. With such a reconstructed model of parentage, Kristeva argued, different social relations can be conceived, based not on hierarchical oppositions and exclusions but on inclusive and collaborative forms.

Revising the paternal inheritance in these particular terms is not of course a question for the writers who are the subject of this essay. Yet there is a striking and persistent structural likeness between the analyses and solutions offered at their different historical moments and the preoccupations of our own present. 'Traditional' oppositions of masculine and feminine capacities and attributes are contested by Staël and Sand in their own terms, especially as they refer to women's allocation to nature rather than culture and the denial of women's capacity for creativity, speech and active desire. All three writers confront the subordination of mother to father. Most important, all three recognise the wider social ramifications of rethinking sexual hierarchy: then as now, daughters imagining resistance to the constraints of the father's desire must come to terms with the parallel desire of the brother-clan to overthrow the father. The fatherless heroine of Cixous's *Dedans* turns immediately for speech to her brother; the warrior-women of Monique Wittig's *Les Guérillères* (1969) stand around the father's grave with the generation of revolutionary sons; and for Sand, Staël and Rachilde the same question arises: what might brother and sister make together of a father-free world?

GERMAINE DE STAËL: REMAKING THE TRACES

The most enquiring mind of her generation, a co-forger of the European mind, and perhaps the most influential proponent of the transformation of Enlightenment into Romantic culture, Germaine de Staël constantly acknowledges in her work her debt to her father, Louis XVI's Finance Minister, Necker, who died in 1804.[5] Less often acknowledged but also a potent influence was her mother, Suzanne Cruchod, essayist and salon hostess, advocate of women's education and a celebrated participant in the debate on divorce. In Staël's novel, *Corinne ou l'Italie* (1807), the father-figure is both present and absent: absent in death, but present in the traces of meaning that remain for negotiation.[6] The novel establishes a textual space where biological fathers no longer exert direct authority and sons and daughters can test the limits of their inherited roles and explore their capacity to invent new relational structures in the private and the public domain. In the absence of the father, Corinne makes herself the author of a new cultural generation.

The story of the love-affair between the Anglo-Scot Oswald, Lord Nelvil, and the Anglo-Italian Corinne raises issues of gender and generational politics on individual, national and international levels, offering a Utopian account of how social and cultural change might be forged within and between peoples in a nascent Europe. In one sense, the attempted union of the two lovers figures the possible destiny of an Italy which, when the novel was being written, had just fallen under Napoleonic rule. Oswald is the representative of a patriarchal state, founded on social hierarchy and military discipline, where the stability of public life is felt to depend on the confinement of women to the domestic sphere. Corinne is the favourite child of a country which is a conglomerate of territories and kingdoms, its military past forgotten, renowned now for its creative imagination, where women play central roles in public culture. Staël hoped that Napoleonic order might marry with the liberal but decadent culture of Italy to engender a new and invigorating sense of nationhood. In a more general sense, the dilemma of Oswald, torn between loyalty to his dead father and life with Corinne, articulates the challenge confronting post-Revolutionary Europe, showing the fear of freedom ingrained in individuals shaped by the limits and hierarchies of authoritarian order. Out of the traces left by the absent father, the son forges his own chains.

The absent father – or rather, two absent fathers – is the founding condition of the narrative. One is Corinne's own, the 'good' father who died when she was a child. The other is the 'bad' authoritarian father mourned by Oswald. The splitting of the father-figure is a deliberate device, involving for example the attribution to Oswald's father of authoritarian statements produced originally by Necker (*Discours sur la mort* and *Discours sur le devoir des enfants envers leurs pères*).[7] The device makes it possible to incorporate aspects of the paternal figure into a model of a more open and liberated order, echoing in fiction the ambitions for liberal constitutional change which Staël nourished in the political domain.

Oswald sails into harbour in Italy, nursing his guilt at having once rebelled against his father to make a freer life of his own. Deadlocked in this double persona of authoritarian father and rebel son, he has his chance for release in his fortuitous meeting with Corinne. She too is by inheritance a double and contradictory figure: she is both maternal body, identified with others, and innovative artist. The narrative is driven by the attempted resolution of these contradictions, in which all depends on Corinne's ability to resist the father without rejecting him.

From the beginning, the text is crammed with male figures from all orders in Italy and all nations of Europe, each competing to claim Corinne as his own and trying to remake her in the image of his own desire. Corinne refuses these limiting options, as she refuses to be tied to one nation. She improvises her own genealogy, which involves a larger imperative to remake cultural patrimonies. The love story narrows her choice to two apparently opposite inheritances. Oswald is the advocate of an Ossianic tradition frozen in the cult of dead values. Corinne is drawn to Mediterranean culture. She inscribes herself in the line of the 'feminine' Italians, Dante, Michelangelo, the builders of Ancient and Christian Rome, who were eager to modify inherited forms to serve the needs of new generations and tried to incorporate changing discourses and perspectives into the living social landscape. Through her own journey of desire over the terrain of Italy and England, seeking both Oswald and herself, through the paternal traces, she finally creates a language of renewal and reconciliation.

The text closes on a constellation of sequences predicting a future where the deadly thrall of the father is turned into a source of life through the desiring feminine voice. On the public stage, Corinne's swansong, delivered by a young female singer to the admiring audiences of republican Florence, appeals to coming generations in the name of the great artists of the past. In the private domain of the family, she invents a new amalgam of mother and father figures, drawing together herself, Oswald and her sister Lucile, Oswald's wife, as biological and cultural parents of Julie, a new kind of daughter. The experience involves too much personal disappointment to establish a brother-sister clan which has sunk all its differences, but the ground has been cleared for change. Most telling are the final throwaway lines which refuse to close the narrative in any return to previous order. Instead, they enact syntactically and semantically the perpetual negotiation between closure and openness which has been the subject of Staël's whole text, invoking a father-figure who can be both the determining centre of a discourse and a matter of utter indifference, subject in his own right and object of the confident and open discourse of a female narrative voice.

GEORGE SAND: FAILURES OF REVISION

For George Sand too, the father's absence provides an opportunity to review issues of authority and change. Her reconstructions are never as radical as Staël's and her work recognises more clearly the pull of familiar hierarchy which in the last analysis reinstates the Oedipal father. Like the sons of her Romantic generation, her desire for change carries within it the anticipation of failure and loss. Her fictions oscillate between Utopian optimism and a sense of despair, in which the desiring, speaking feminine struggles unsuccessfully to emerge from the paternal shadow into her own place. In parallel, the new structures for social relationships to which Sand aspires cannot be convincingly formulated.

Sand's own father, Maurice Dupin, died in 1808, when his daughter was four. The absent Maurice takes up a great deal of space in the first two volumes of Sand's *Histoire de ma vie*, which she began writing in 1847,[8] and provides essential elements of the image she constructs of herself. Sand is, she says, modelled on her father (I, p. 312). But equally, she models her father on herself; the feminised portrait she presents of him in the second volume is symptomatic (II, p. 159). To reverse Cixous's famous phrase, the father's body is the blank page on which Sand writes herself into history, attributing to him the characteristics and virtues she wants to identify in herself. In particular, the aristocratic inheritance represented by Maurice is important for her, balancing the inheritance of the relatively poor Parisian mother whom he married in 1804, shortly before his daughter was born.

Sand's personal project – using the father to establish herself – is offered in her autobiography as a model to be adopted by a society committed, she hopes, to orderly change. The people, just like the nobility, must understand their own genealogy. They must know themselves both as generated by their own works, actors in the present, and as children of the past, dependent on a parental succession. In this succession, she indicates, almost as an afterthought, mothers count as much as fathers: 'Thus it is very true that every man is the son of his works; but it is equally true that every man is the son of his fathers, of his ancestors, *patres et matres* '(I, p. 56).

The consequences for individuals and societies of such attempts to remodel the patriarchal inheritance are explored in Sand's historical novels. Two in particular are worth close study as exemplifying the contradictory extremes in which her thought becomes embroiled: *Mauprat* (1837) and the second version of *Lélia* (1839), both written as Sand came under the influence of the socialist and feminist Pierre Leroux.

Mauprat, the Gothic historical novel serialised in the *Revue des deux mondes* April–June 1837,[9] rewrites the conflicts of social orders, generation and gender in the 1770s and 80s as a relatively bloodless movement towards change. Its aim is clearly to advocate a similar outcome for the pre-revolutionary moment in which Sand was writing. As its patronymic title suggests, the text starts and ends with the name of the father and the concept of the importance of the family line. The voice that marks out the ground of this history is a masculine one – in fact, doubly so. A young man of the post-Revolutionary generation, describing his visit to the Mauprat estate, sets up the narrative frame in which Bernard Mauprat, the patriarch of the new age, tells the tale of his own re-education and the transformation of the Mauprat fortunes. The Gothic scenario conveys both the horror and the fascination of the world of feudal fathers. Bernard himself still embodies its potential for cruel violence, which is the other face of its capacity to maintain order and discipline.

Sand likewise splits the father-inheritance into two. The evil father, responsible for the worst excesses of feudal aristocracy, is represented by the degenerate elder line of the Mauprats, set against the cadet branch which still preserves the values of its chivalrous origins, and in which father has handed on to son the benefits of enlightened education. Bernard, son of the elder line, is adopted into the younger by its last representative, Hubert, and through his love for his cousin Edmée, Hubert's daughter, is himself educated into the values of enlightened society. Edmée, like Bernard, is a figure who bridges two worlds. Bernard's desire for her is expressed in traditional terms: he sees her face configured in the beauties of the night landscape of the Mauprat estate, and identifies his longing to possess her with his longing for the land. Edmée's acceptance of desire couched in these terms is the means by which she tames and transforms Bernard. She is however for herself a creature not of nature but of culture, steeped in Rousseau, whose revolutionary enthusiasm she mediates to Bernard. She declares herself a Mauprat, in her determination to resolve the problem of Bernard in the way she chooses. She declares her fraternal solidarity with Bernard, and her sense of responsibility for him, in the name of the father: 'He is my cousin, he is a Mauprat, he is almost a brother' (p. 194). Bernard comes to see Edmée no longer as simply an object of desire but a chivalrous comrade: 'She was no longer the beautiful girl whose presence troubled my senses; she was a young man of my own age... capable of that sublime friendship that created brothers in arms' (p. 197). This reconceptualisation of the relations between the couple makes it possible to reforge links between aristocracy and peasantry. Edmée, Bernard and the peasant sage, Patience, the voice of revolution, constitute a new family triad with Bernard as its undisputed head, and history is set on course for Utopia. But beyond the rhetoric of brotherhood two points stand clear: the father is back in command, and his recuperation has been at the expense of the would-be liberated and liberating daughter. Well before the end of the text, Edmée has fallen into silence, lauded to the last by Bernard, described, quoted and paraphrased by him, but still existing only in terms of his voice, which finally closes the narrative.

Lélia, in the second version of 1839, was presented by Sand as an act of faith in God, progress and humanity, written in a spirit of optimism intended to form a sharp contrast with the despairing scepticism of the first version of 1833.[10] The difference is not always easy to see. In this text, the absence of the father is written as a metaphysical question, in the language of Romantic frustration. Having assumed responsibility for their own destinies, the children of this generation find their merits unrewarded and unwanted. Whether God is deemed dead or, as Lélia finally fideistically declares, simply silent, the situation is the same. Lélia and Valmarina/Trenmor, her revolutionary brother, are both doomed to wretchedness and failure.

The narrative of *Lélia*, starting in the name of the feminine, is concerned with establishing the voice of the autonomous desiring feminine subject – the heroine determined to father herself. Lélia can find no sufficient object for her desire, which she calls God and which Valmarina says, accurately, is her own pride. He sums her up: she vacillates between Promethean ambition and the uncertainty that comes of women's subordinate situation. She identifies two ways out of her dilemma. Either she can join the Cardinal in his attempted reform of the father-clan of Catholic hierarchy, or she can throw in her lot with Valmarina and the revolutionary brother-clan. The risks of the latter are too great and she has no confidence in her own generation. She chooses the Church, despite Valmarina's warning that its power is dead.

Lélia proclaims her enthusiasm for the social good, and uses the familial language of solidarity: 'I should like to embrace the universe with an outpouring of daughterly and brotherly love' (p. 538), but ultimately she is self-interested. She may speak of pitting her own values against those of patriarchy, but her values are as competitive and hierarchical as those she claims to oppose. The narrative charts her downfall. Valmarina meets her one stormy night on the mountaintop, stumbling over the rocks, and listens to her delirious confession of impotent desire. In an evocation of her frustrated ambitions, she casts herself in a Luciferan role, sitting in the place of the absent father, contemplating from her rocky pinnacle the forms emerging from chaos and writing herself as the source and origin of an order which she declares can never be achieved. As she reaches the recognition that the absolute truth she has been seeking is only the echo of her own desire, she falls dead from her height. Her voice echoes into silence, and the revolutionary brother-companion buries her and continues his pilgrimage alone. The last words in this version, as in the version of 1833, are his, declaring the duty to continue the struggle.

RACHILDE: REVIVING THE DEAD

In the world of Rachilde's writing, alliance with the revolutionary brother is never an option, though the traces of the dead hands of the fathers and their deleterious effects were everywhere visible in the France in which she wrote – in demographic decline, economic failure, the ten per cent unemployment of the 1880s that was as much due to laissez-faire policies as European recession, and the loss of international prestige to the emerging nationalist powers of Italy and Germany and the capitalist democracy of the United States. For Rachilde, the revolutionary brother was associated with the terrain of a much-detested mother, whose father had edited the radical anti-Bonapartist newspaper from which all the family money came, and who did her best to discourage her daughter from becoming a writer. Rachilde was devoted to her father, an illegitimate aristocrat, who had commanded the cavalry regiment which covered Bazaine's retreat in 1870. This heroic failure, however, would have preferred a son.

Rachilde's second novel, *La Marquise de Sade* (1887),[11] invoking in its title the authority of another deposed patriarch, sets out the anguish of the present-day daughter who perceives, too late, that the father she idolises has no time for her and nothing of substance to give. In his absence, after his death, she turns disillusionment into a marketable commodity by ironic support for the shreds of power that still cling to paternal prestige. Mary, the sadist, jeers at the old men who desire her youth, stands by while the little brother who threatens her position is accidentally smothered by his nurse and bleeds to death by pinpricks the young men who cannot match her own ambition. Energy, she notes, is with the workers who stand at the edge of her world, but it is not matched by social power.

The shifts of power post 1870–1 that drove the elites of France into a state of siege are registered by Rachilde and the avant-garde Parisian circles to which she belonged as problems with no solutions. Anarchist and anti-establishment gesture are part of her writing and her lifestyle, but the decaying house against which she rails is too comfortable to leave. Rachilde and her coevals celebrate the absent father, while resenting his inability to keep out the gathering dark. In the short dialogue 'The Crystal Spider', son and mother are locked together in the darkening house of the absent patriarch, confined by his dereliction and their own panic to the space he has built. The mother, unintentionally, kills her son, sending him out into the dark to look for a lamp for them both.

Rachilde's writing, exploring the nightmares of repression, maintains and glamorises traditional Oedipal patterns while denouncing the Oedipal figures. The father is the determining figure in the triad, a once-powerful authority declining into senescence (the Emperor of the short story 'The Death of Antinous') or the ironically-conceived wax model made by a German craftsman for the heroine of her first novel *Monsieur Vénus*,[12] whose thighs open symbolically at the touch of a button in his equally symbolic mouth. The mother is a devouring monster and the child – the future – is the object of the murderous resentments of both parents. For Rachilde the father's absence leads to the end of generations.

This is writing marked by the perverted pleasure of recognising that all are devoured by the desire of the dying father. In the short story 'The Grape Harvest of Sodom' (1894), the female outcast is crushed in the grape-vat while the old men sodomise the boy-child, and a bloody sun sets on a desert landscape of desiccated patriarchs. In the novel *The Jongleuse* (1900),[13] where father and husband are both absent, the central concern of the text is to reconstitute the patriarch. The tale-spinner and word-juggler of the title, the marquise Eliante, orphaned in the Franco-Prussian war, acknowledges to her young lover that her dead husband has shaped her, by what he has taught her of perverse sexual desire and what he has given her of position and wealth, stolen from the colonies. Even the tales she tells are reproductions of the forms of his desire. Eliante has chosen to remake the absent patriarch in herself and she embodies not only his power but his weakness. Her rage at her own supersession destroys her as it blights the lives of generations to come.

Between the positions taken by the son in Staël's *Corinne*, Sand's Lélia and the daughters in Rachilde's fictions, the wheel comes full circle. The traces left by the father in the terrain of history, available for fresh constructions of gender and social relationships, are instead reinforced by a self-interest which finds more immediate (masochistic) gratification in keeping things as 'nature' intended. The powers embodied in inherited landscape can appear overwhelming. Oswald, seeing in the blackened slopes of Vesuvius the image of his own devastation by guilt, loses himself in ecstasies of terror. His collapse into powerlessness, like Lélia's recognition of her impossible ambition, has its parallel in the fate of the woman in 'The Grape Harvest of Sodom', drawn by her own desire out of the patriarchal landscape, only to be crushed by the massed strength of the old men. Sons and daughters who collude with paternal power are drawn to destruction: the force of established order pulling to inertia and decay is near-irresistible.

In sharp contrast is the stance taken by the daughter of Enlightenment culture to the same inherited landscape. Corinne, faced with the black violence of the paternal past, looks away in search of something different. What she sees instead is a vast and various social domain, still marked with the traces of the fathers who made it but capable, in its diversity, of being remade. As in the new writers of our own generation, reason picks itself out of Oedipal intimidations and, in the name of community, moves on:

> A profound silence reigned around Oswald and Corinne... nothing could be heard but the whistle of the quivering flame. One sound from the town did however reach that place; the peal of bells rang out through the air: were they tolling for the dead? were they announcing a birth? No matter, they provoked a tender feeling in the travellers. 'Dear Oswald,' said Corinne, 'let us leave this desert, let us go back down to the living... here I feel only anguish and fear: it seems to me that nature is being treated like a criminal, condemned, like some depraved being, never again to feel its Creator's benevolent breath. This is surely no place for the good; let us go.' (II, p. 63)

Notes

1. Hélène Cixous, *Dedans* (Paris: Des Femmes, 1986), p. 14.
2. This issue has been interestingly discussed in Kelly Oliver, *Womanising Nietzsche: Philosophy's Relation to the Feminine* (New York/London: Routledge, 1995) with reference to the work of Kristeva and also that of Luce Irigaray. See especially Chapter 6, 'Save the Mother'.
3. Julia Kristeva, *La Révolution du langage poétique: L'avant-garde à la fin du XIXe siècle: Lautréamont et Mallarmé* (Paris: Le Seuil, 1974), and *Des Chinoises* (Paris: Des Femmes, 1974).
4. Julia Kristeva, *Histoires d'amour* (Paris: Denoël. 1983), p. 56.
5. See for example Simone Balayé, *Madame de Staël: Lumières et liberté*, Chapter 2, 'Madame de Staël et la Révolution' (Paris: Editions Klincksieck, 1979); Marie-Claire Vallois, *Fictions féminines: Mme de Staël et les voix de la Sibylle* (Saratoga, California: ANMA Libri, 1987); Béatrice Didier, *Ecrire la révolution (1789–99)*, Chapter 6, 'Sensibilité et Histoire: *Les Considérations* de Mme de Staël' (Paris: PUF, 1989).
6. Madame de Staël, *Corinne ou l'Italie*, 2 vols. (Paris: H. Nicolle, 1807). Page references are to the edition by Claudine Herrmann (Paris: Des Femmes, 1979).
7. See Vallois, *op.cit.*, p. 119.
8. George Sand, *Histoire de ma vie*, 10 vols. (Paris: Victor Lecou, 1854–5). Page references in this essay are to the two volumes published with Introduction by Denise Brahimi and Christian Pirot (Saint-Cyr-sur-Loire: Christian Pirot, 1993).
9. George Sand, *Mauprat*, 2 vols. (Paris: Félix Bonnaire, 1837). Page references in the present essay are to the edition by Jean-Pierre Lacassagne (Paris: Gallimard, 1981). The first formulation of the work was in 1835, as a short love story of which only a manuscript fragment exists.
10. George Sand, *Lélia*, 2 vols. (Paris: Dupuy-Tenré, 1833), new edition 3 vols. (Paris: Félix Bonnaire, 1839). Page references are to the edition by Pierre Reboul (Paris: Garnier, 1960).
11. Rachilde, *La Marquise de Sade* (Paris: Monnier, 1887).
12. Rachilde, *Monsieur Vénus* (Brussels: Auguste Brancart, 1884).
13. Rachilde, *La Jongleuse* (Paris: Mercure de France, 1900).

9

Absent Fathers across the Spectrum of Local Colour in the Short Stories of Kate Chopin

Janet Beer

Kate Chopin, born in St Louis, Missouri in 1850, was a Southerner. Despite the fact that Missouri did not secede and was therefore on the side of the Union, everyone around Kate O'Flaherty, as she then was, supported the Confederacy, and her own exploits, like tearing down a Union flag from her mother's porch, earned her the name of St Louis's 'littlest rebel'.[1] Rather than dwelling on her almost inevitable support – in view of her French and Irish family history – for the Southern states in the conflict, I want to use this aspect of her background to point to the word 'rebel', not confederacy. Kate Chopin was always rebellious; if the fiction she wrote to support her six children after the premature death of her husband has a consistent theme, it is rebellion. Her work is always in dialogue with the nature of authority, whether this authority derives from secular or religious law, or from both, as in the case of marriage.

The majority of her stories are set in the state of Louisiana, the narrative landscapes which predominate are New Orleans and Natchitoches Parish, the scenes of her short married life. It was in the deep South that Chopin found the location for her fiction, in its particular and highly-regulated combination of Creoles, French Acadians and Blacks. These were the inhabitants of a landscape which offered itself to her as a distinct topography which both reflected the complications of long association with another culture, in this instance that of France, and also offered its own specifically local variation on an American theme.

I intend to explore here the way in which Chopin uses the regional in her work in order to defuse the potentially explosive nature of her subject – and that subject is the nature of authority. I will argue that the popularity of the genre of local colour in the post-Reconstruction period enabled her to gain access to an audience which would otherwise have shied away from the potentially controversial themes and structure of her writing. Stories which are apparently straightforward and unchallenging, like 'Athénaïse', published in 1896, are susceptible to readings which offer devastating critiques of the social organisation.

Chopin was controversial because she challenged authority and this authority is chiefly that of the father, whether God the father, the patriarch in the system of slavery, or the leisure class father, going about his business. These fathers are absent – in all but name – in gradations of colour, local and otherwise; according to their colour they are either forcibly absent, as is the case with the sold-away slave father of La Belle Zoraïde's child, or morally absent, as with the father of Miss McEnders in the story that bears her name.

Chopin's work is not polemic, hers is a view that privileges the individual in spite of gender or class, but she takes every advantage of the cover that writing as a local colourist gives her to tell the stories of those who, like Athénaïse, suffer the 'realization of the futility of rebellion against a social and sacred institution'.[2] The reading audience expected Louisiana whimsy and folklore, and she often gave it to them in her sketches and yarns, but she also gave them Louisiana prejudice and tragedy.

Kate Chopin's writing career – from 1888 until her death in 1904 – was coincident with the most productive years in the literary careers of the best known amongst the American writers usually described as local colourists. Chopin, indeed, is generally featured amongst this number and in recent years a good deal has been made of the uses to which she puts regionalism in both the subject and structure of her fiction. In his recent book *Cultures of Letters: Scenes of Reading and Writing in Nineteenth Century America*, Richard Brodhead says:

> Regionalism became a dominant genre in America at the moment when local-cultural economies felt strong pressure from new social forces, from a growingly powerful social model that overrode previously autonomous systems and incorporated them into translocal agglomerations. This genre's great public flowering began with the Northern victory in the Civil War, in other words with the forcible repression of sectional autonomy in favor of national union and the legal supplanting of the locally variant by national norms of

> citizenly rights. Regionalism's heyday was in the years of corporate-capitalist industrial development in America, with its reinsertion of agrarian and artisanal orders into a new web of national market relations.[3]

Chopin would, under this formulation, be constructed as one of the writers thus working quite deliberately up against the grain of corporatism in America, her pictures of a rural, backward community providing some kind of refuge for the reader from the relentless trend in the larger culture towards an industrialised homogeneity. Indeed, in the majority of her fiction Chopin does take us back to a pre-Civil War Louisiana, thus reinforcing even more emphatically the alien qualities of the social organisation depicted therein to the turn of the century reader.

However, local colour is not, either in Brodhead's construction or Chopin's use, simply a refuge from the reality of the post-war world. It is a means of entry into the kind of writing that found a ready audience in the new leisured classes – those readers equipped with the aesthetic sensibilities of the practised vacationer in both exotic and familiar landscapes.[4] Within the safe haven of the genre of local colour Chopin could write about the enduring, immutable and, above all, topographically undetermined aspects of human nature. As she says in her review of Hamlin Garland's *Crumbling Idols*: 'Human impulses do not change and can not so long as men and women continue to stand in the relation to one another which they have occupied since our knowledge of their existence began'.[5]

So, the use of local colour – in terms of settings, dialect, customs, the comic or the sentimental – is the method for Chopin not the substance of her writing. It is the marketing ploy as well as the means by which, in Sandra Gilbert's formulation in her Introduction to *The Awakening and Selected Stories*, Chopin could conceal her purpose and 'tell what would ordinarily be rather shocking or even melodramatic tales in an unmelodramatic way, and without fear of moral outrage'.[6]

Here is Kate Chopin herself on the matter of regionalism: reporting on 'The Western Association of Writers', in an article published in *Critic* on 7 July 1894:

> Provincialism in the best sense of the word stamps the character of this association of writers, who gather chiefly from the State of Indiana and meet annually at Spring Fountain Park. It is an ideally beautiful spot, a veritable garden of Eden in which the disturbing

> fruit of the tree of knowledge still hangs unplucked. The cry of the dying century has not reached this body of workers, or else it has not been comprehended. There is no doubt in their souls, no unrest: apparently an abiding faith in God as he manifests himself through the sectional church, and an overmastering love of their soil and institutions.
>
> Most of them are singers. Their native streams, trees, bushes and birds, the lovely country life about them, form the chief burden of their often too sentimental songs. Occasionally the voice of one of them reaches out across the prairies and is heard by the world beyond. For this is the soil, these are the conditions, and the Western Association of Writers are the typical human group which have given us James Whitcomb Riley, Mrs Catherwood and Lew Wallace.
>
> Among these people are to be found an earnestness in the acquirement and dissemination of book-learning, a clinging to past and conventional standards, an almost Creolean sensitiveness to criticism and a singular ignorance of, or disregard for, the value of the highest art forms.
>
> There is a very, very big world lying not wholly in Northern Indiana, not does it lie at the Antipodes either. It is human existence in its subtle, complex, true meaning, stripped of the veil with which ethical and conventional standards have draped it. When the Western Association of Writers with their earnestness of purpose and poetic insights shall have developed into students of true life and true art, who knows but that they may produce a genius such as America has not yet known.[7]

This is Chopin's version of the critique of the parochial which Sinclair Lewis offers us at the opening of *Main Street* (1920); like Lewis she condemns with faint praise before condemning with a loud roar, empowered as she is by the inheritance of the whole of human civilisation. Local colour for Chopin was the way she obtained an audience for pieces like 'The Story of an Hour' – refused initially as too outrageous by *Vogue* and subsequently turned down by *The Century, Short Stories* and *The Chap-Book*. This story was eventually published by *Vogue* only after Chopin achieved great success with *Bayou Folk*, a collection of short stories firmly rooted in Natchitoches Parish in rural Louisiana. In this volume she satisfied an audience hungry for stories about the denizens of Louisiana, in the words of Houghton Mifflin's advertisement for the book, her subjects were 'semi-aliens' as far as the rest of the United States was concerned.[8]

Kate Chopin's writing is in many ways the perfect illustration of Brodhead's formulation of regional writing, purveying, as it does, a world both strange and familiar, distant and yet local. Writing for an audience outside Louisiana she communicates the culture of that State to an America predicated as a foreign country within the fiction. In the story, 'La Belle Zoraïde', published in *Vogue* in 1894, the narrative is framed by the acknowledgement that the tellers and the tale should really be expressed in a foreign tongue – foreign, that is, not only to the Yankee but to anyone outside the French-speaking diaspora. The narrative is written in the standard English expected by its trans-American audience but it has Louisiana parentheses around it. We are given to understand at the outset that the story is translated for us from 'the soft Creole patois, whose music and charm no English words can convey',[9] and the story closes with a taste of the real thing: 'but this is the way Madame Delisle and Manna-Loulou really talked to each other: – "Vou pré droumi, Ma'zélle Titite?" "Non, pa pré droumi; mo yapré zongler. Ah, la pauv' piti, Man Loulou. La pauv' piti! Mieux li mouri!"'.[10]

Here Louisiana is a nation unto itself as le beau Mézor is 'sold away into Georgia, or the Carolinas, or one of those distant countries far away, where he would no longer hear his Creole tongue spoken, nor dance Calinda, nor hold la belle Zoraïde in his arms',[11] having fathered a child in spite of the wishes of La Belle Zoraïde's mistress. Having contradicted the desire of the slave-holders to control the colour of the offspring of their slaves, neither father nor mother are allowed to perform the basic human function of parent in the life of their child. The little 'griffe' girl, who is brought back to the house to remind Zoraïde of the baby she produced and to restore her poor shattered psyche, is rejected as having less reality than the bundle of rags the deprived mother now clings to: 'Nor could she ever be induced to let her own child approach her; and finally the little one was sent back to the plantation, where she was never to know the love of mother or father'.[12] Local colour here is indeed local – the ruling class seek to manage the enslaved in order to produce the exact tint that will please them aesthetically whilst leaving unchallenged their right, as unmixed, to rule.

The story 'La Belle Zoraïde' also provides an opportunity to elucidate the relationship between local colour and the nature of authority in the stories that deal with the tragedy of the absent father in the culture of slavery. The role of heavenly as well as earthly father has been usurped by the ruling class here: Madame Delarivière expects to be able to control Zoraïde in terms of who she loves and to deprive her of her right to be a mother. Such hubris will always result in tragedy, however, as Chopin says: '...there was a more powerful will than Madame's at work – the will of the good God, who had already designed that Zoraïde should grieve with a sorrow that was never more to be lifted in this world'.[13] This is the small world of Louisiana, where slavery apparently has a gentler aspect than in other parts of the slave-holding South:

> No wonder Zoraïde was as charming and as dainty as the finest lady of la rue Royale: from a toddling thing she had been brought up at her mistress's side; her fingers had never done rougher work than sewing a fine muslin seam; and she even had her own little black servant to wait upon her. Madame, who was her godmother as well as her mistress, would often say to her:– 'Remember, Zoraïde, when you are ready to marry, it must be in a way to do honour to your bringing up. It will be at the Cathedral. Your wedding gown, your *corbeille*, all will be of the best; I shall see to that myself.'[14]

This small world is shown, in spite of all Zoraïde's privileges, to be no less a state of tyranny because it makes pets of some of its slaves. Zoraïde is powerless to choose a husband or a father for her child, even to mother her own child and, ultimately, to keep her own sanity. Here, and in 'Désirée's Baby', published in *Vogue* in 1893, Chopin critiques the absolute power held over the life and death of people in their ordinary human relations as they are affected by the existence of slavery. We never know whether Désirée is black or white, we do know, however, that her husband is, by Louisianan terms of reference, black, and yet responsible for maintaining white supremacy. Like his counterpart, Valet de Chambre, in Mark Twain's 1894 novel, *Puddn'head Wilson*, Armand Aubigny masquerades as racially pure because of an act of secrecy perpetrated by his mother in defiance not only of the cultural mores but the law of the land.

At the beginning of *Puddn'head Wilson*, at the point where the author introduces us to all of his most important characters he takes care to mention the total irrelevance to the narrative of one Colonel Cecil Burleigh Essex, the biological father of Valet de Chambre, latterly Tom Driscoll. Aside from acknowledging his pedigree and dignified status in the community we are plainly told: 'with him we have no concern'.[15] He is simply the supplier of superior semen to Roxy, the one-sixteenth part black slave, enabling her to produce the one-thirty-second part slave, Tom, who will, by virtue of being created in his father's image, usurp the master's place in the social hierarchy for as long as the one-thirty-second part of his body which enslaves him remains undiscovered.

The white father as the quintessentially absent father in nineteenth-century Southern writing is familiar to us from Twain's story and others. Kate Chopin takes that absence and converts it into a different form. She does not engage in satire here at the expense of those like Twain's pretentious denizens of Dawson's Landing with their pseudo-English names and their well-defended status as First Families of Virginia. In Chopin's fiction the business of paternity has fallen into such disuse that, once believing Désirée to be responsible for having borne him a son of mixed race, Armand simply 'no longer loved her, because of the unconscious injury she had brought upon his home and his name'.[16] Disuse, however, does not mean inaction as it did in Dawson's Landing. The civilisation of Armand's parents and particularly his mother – the Frenchwoman who had 'loved her own land too well ever to leave it'[17] – goes up in flames at the end of the story:

> Some weeks later there was a curious scene enacted at L'Abri. In the centre of the smoothly swept back yard was a great bonfire. Armand Aubigny sat in the wide hallway that commanded a view of the spectacle; and it was he who dealt out to a half a dozen negroes the material which kept this fire ablaze.
>
> A graceful cradle of willow, with all its dainty furbishings, was laid upon the pyre, which had already been fed with the richness of a priceless *layette*. Then there were silk gowns, and velvet and satin ones added to these; laces, too, and embroideries; bonnets and gloves; for the *corbeille* had been of rare quality.[18]

The letter from his mother to his father which reveals her to have been of 'the race that is cursed with the brand of slavery'[19] lies still undiscovered as Armand burns all evidence that he was ever willing to fulfil the role of father. Sitting in isolated splendour the tyrant Armand watches the remnants of his family burn along with what remains of a life which owed a debt to an older and perhaps more tolerant society.

It is in scenes such as these that Chopin twists the real limitation of local colour back upon itself to expose the true horrors of the parochial. Where local colour enabled her to entrance the audience that earned her a living, it also enabled her to show the destructive power of the time, the place, the customs, the practices of a distinct and xenophobic culture such as pre-bellum Louisiana. That parochialism which Twain turned into satire is here exposed as unrelieved tragedy.

Tom Driscoll in Twain's novel, revealed as immune from prosecution for the murder of the great white father because as a slave he is above – or below – the law, is sold down the river. Armand watches unmoved as Désirée walks into the Bayou, drowning in the role of the tragic mulatta – a role of a sudden forced upon her in complete indifference to her colour or lack of it. All – black, white and indifferent – are the victims of the divide of colour. Armand does not give her a second glance, so entirely is his identity embedded in the maintenance of the divide; whether this means the maintenance of separation from his own wife and son is irrelevant to him. His feelings are contingent upon his family's ability to sustain him in his role as Master, if doubt is once cast upon his capacity to distinguish black from white then his means of authentication is lost. The implication within the story is that he fathers children indiscriminately upon one of his slaves – 'La Blanche'. Désirée reports to her adoptive mother on the strength of her baby's lungs: 'Armand heard him the other day as far away as La Blanche's cabin'[20] and it is her own child's likeness to one of La Blanche's 'quadroon' boys that finally alerts Désirée to the truth about him. However, the name of 'Father' means absolutely nothing to Armand – it is Master that moves him. The story begins with an abnegation of parental responsibility as Désirée is abandoned, probably by a party of Texans, in true fairy tale fashion – she is the infant found asleep at the gates of the great house. Her own baby, however, is not so fortunate. He leaves the house into which he is born – ironically named L'Abri ('The Shelter') – in his mother's arms as she takes him away to die; there is no shelter for those who are denied a father in the system of slavery.

Chopin's Louisiana is a more complicated location than Twain's Dawson's Landing in terms of its inter-ethnic boundaries. It is the American, not just the Yankee, who is alien here and paternity is thus interrogated in terms of its role in the religious culture of a state closer to France than to New York and still in a post-colonial relationship with Europe. Where Chopin deals with the leisure class in the urban environment, as she does in *The Awakening* and 'Miss McEnders', the absent father is the businessman, the provider of the daily bread for the woman whose leisure and its daily inconsequence becomes the driving force behind the narrative. The abnegation of the father/husband of responsibility for the diurnal reality or the moral condition of the life of the family is contiguous with the void at the heart of the life of the woman.

In the case of Edna Pontellier in *The Awakening*, her husband, Léonce, walks in and out of the domestic setting as work or leisure variously appeal to him. He is acknowledged within the mores of his culture as a good and thoughtful provider of both treats and necessities but he is nevertheless impervious to the independent sentient existence of his wife and to her discontents. Her leisure, her extended holiday on Grande Isle with the children and nursemaid, is the 'serviceable evidence'[21] – in Thorstein Veblen's words – that he can afford to keep his family in both luxury and idleness; it is adequate demonstration of his efficacy in the position of father as assigned to him in the culture.

The particularly local conditions of Léonce Pontellier's assumptions about the sufficiency of the way in which he conducts his family life are, however, dislocated and changed by the fact that his wife is a Kentucky Presbyterian and, as such, does not know what to do with the feelings and emotions which have been aroused in her by her exposure to both the warm, heady atmosphere of the South and the free and frank treatment of matters physical in Creole society. Edna is overcome by wave after wave of physical sensation, connected to her learning to swim in the warm waters of the gulf, to her courting by Robert Lebrun, to her taking possession of herself in terms of recognising a sensuous being with needs beyond those of the mother-women who surround her. Her awakening is expressed through the intellectual as well as the physical, it incorporates the effects of her upbringing upon her adulthood and involves the shedding of fealty to both father and husband, although not her dependence upon men for fulfilment.

Elsewhere in her fiction – and specifically in the story 'Two Portraits' or 'The Nun and the Wanton' – Chopin depicts this dependence upon male authority as reflected in the paternalistic structures which dictate both sexual and spiritual expression for women. The interchangeable nature of this dependence is here made literal, and so literal that Chopin never found a publisher who would take it. 'Two Portraits' is a diptych which shows the same woman exposed to two dramatically different types of upbringing, one by a whore and the other by a 'holy woman', but the total absorption in the 'God-Man, the Man-God'[22] is exactly the same in both cases and results in a destructive self-abnegation in the adult woman.

Chopin is not a moralist. Her stories may often look homiletic, especially the very brief tales, but they are rarely simple enough to draw a single conclusion from, unless that conclusion leads towards a general plea for tolerance and a greater plea for scepticism about the nature of authority. 'Miss McEnders' is such a story. Mr McEnders, Georgie McEnders' father in the story, is represented only by a photograph upon her desk, in the vulgar excesses of his 'too-sumptuous'[23] front door and in the rumours of the street and Mademoiselle Salambre's sewing room. Here, however, the figures of the father and the lover of Miss Georgie McEnders become blurred into one as both are revealed as leading secret lives of deception and decadence. Whilst Georgie is described as 'white-souled'[24] and absorbed in the propagation and maintenance of morality amongst the deserving poor, to the extent that she will not allow her trousseau to be sewn by a woman with an illegitimate child, the source of wealth which allows her purity to remain unsullied is shown to be generated on the wrong side of the law. Georgie spends her time 'in Christian endeavour'[25] and remains separate from the real business of living; she is confined to the desperate imitation of the business world of her father and her fiancé:

> 'Two o'clock – look up M. Salambre,' said the list. 'Three-thirty – read paper before Women's Ref.[orm] Club. Four-thirty – ' and here followed cabalistic abbreviations which meant: 'Join committee of ladies to investigate moral conditions of St. Louis factory-girls. Six o'clock – dine with papa. Eight o'clock – hear Henry George's lecture on Single Tax.'[26]

In delivering her sermon to Mademoiselle Salambre: 'You must be made to understand, madam, that there is a right way to live, and that there is a wrong way,'[27] Georgie attempts to make herself a professional moralist but, in her total ignorance of the origin of the funds which shore up her moral high ground, she is doomed to fall as the seamstress delivers insinuation after insinuation about the men who stand in authority in her life. It is hinted that the absent father of Mademoiselle Salambre's child may be Mr Meredith Holt, Georgie's fiancé, the man who the seamstress describes as 'not fit to be the husband of a self-respecting bar-maid'.[28] Her father's wealth is denounced as stolen by the merest and most ignorant street urchin and Georgie is left with her dependence, her romantic life and her daughterhood sullied and ruined: 'Upon the table there she found a box of exquisite white spring blossoms that a messenger had brought from Meredith Holt, during her absence. Without an instant's hesitation, Georgie cast the spotless things into the wide, sooty fire-place. Then she sank into a chair and wept bitterly.'[29]

The father with whom she thought she stood in intimate relation has been taken away from her by the knowledge that other people have of him. Her ignorance of the separation of public and private in the masculine sphere of operation destroys the foundation upon which she has built her life. Chopin's work is often concerned with those who are victims of their own certainties. The Louisiana of her fiction is a place rife with such certainties; even in the post-bellum Creole world there is no movement toward the Union, quite the opposite, the local culture seems to endow its inhabitants with renewed confidence and conviction of purpose and ideology. A definition of the local which offers its people immunity from the changing world, from the influences of the art and culture of the nation as a whole, is, as discussed earlier, a creed which was abjured and scorned by Kate Chopin. Local colour was the genre in which she made her name, but it was also the means by which she allowed her readers to challenge the idea of the comfortable, the old-fashioned or the static as an adequate aesthetic.

Notes

1. E. Toth, *Kate Chopin*, (London: Century, 1991), pp. 63–4.
2. Kate Chopin, *The Complete Works of Kate Chopin*, ed. P. Seyersted, (Baton Rouge: Louisiana State University Press, 1969) p. 432.
3. Richard Brodhead, *Cultures of Letters: Scenes of Reading and Writing in Nineteenth Century America* (Chicago: University of Chicago Press, 1993) pp. 119–20.
4. See Brodhead, *op. cit.*, 'The Reading of Regions', for a detailed discussion of the role of the upper-class vacation in the context of late nineteenth century literary production.
5. Chopin, *op. cit.*, p. 693.
6. Kate Chopin, *The Awakening and Selected Stories*, ed. Sandra Gilbert (New York: Penguin Books, 1984) p. 16.
7. *The Complete Works of Kate Chopin*, pp. 691–2.
8. Toth, *op. cit.*, p. 223.
9. *The Complete Works of Kate Chopin*, p. 304.
10. *Ibid.*, p. 308.
11. *Ibid.*, p. 306.
12. *Ibid.*, p. 307.

13. *Ibid.*, p. 306.
14. *Ibid.*, p. 304.
15. Mark Twain, *Pudd'nhead Wilson* (1894) (London: Penguin Books, 1969) p. 58.
16. *The Complete Works of Kate Chopin*, p. 244.
17. *Ibid.*, p. 241.
18. *Ibid.*, p. 244.
19. *Ibid.*, p. 245.
20. *Ibid.*, p. 241.
21. Thorstein Veblen, 'Conspicuous Leisure' in *The Theory of the Leisure Class: An Economic Study of Institutions* (1899) (New York: Random House, 1961).
22. *The Complete Works of Kate Chopin*, p. 464–5.
23. *Ibid.*, p. 204.
24. *Ibid.*, p. 205.
25. *Ibid.*, p. 211.
26. *Ibid.*, p. 204.
27. *Ibid.*, p. 208.
28. *Ibid.*, p. 209.
29. *Ibid.*, p. 211.

10

Death of the Father and Birth of Idolatry: from Mme de Sévigné to her Daughter

Angela Cozea

From Mme de Grignan, Moulceau, 28 April 1696.

So total and irreparable a loss does not lead one to seek consolation beyond the bitterness of tears and groans. I do not have the strength to raise my eyes high enough to find the place from which help should come; as yet I can only look around me, where I no longer see that person who bestowed countless blessings on me, whose only concern was to give me each day some new proof of her tender affection, with the pleasure of her company. It is quite true, sir, it takes a superhuman strength to bear so cruel a separation and so much deprivation. I was far from prepared for it: the perfect health which she visibly enjoyed and a year of illness during which I was in danger of my life a hundred times took from me all thought that nature might take its course in my case. I flattered myself, flattered myself that I would never suffer so great a misfortune; I am suffering it now, and I feel it in all its harshness.[1]

A KNOT [IN] DURATION, AS THOUGH THE TIME THAT THE I ENDURES WERE CONTINUING INTO EXCESS

I am beautiful, I'm not at all weepy as in this scribble. Anyway my dear, I am not to be pitied for my portrait, but because I'm so far from you, because I can only be with you *metaphysically*, because I'm losing such precious time.[2]

'From her marriage at the age of eighteen to Henri de Sévigné, a good-looking young orphan,' says Roger Duchêne in his 'Notice' to the

Lettres choisies, Madame de Sévigné 'had two children and lands to manage in Britanny following his death in a duel…over another woman. He was unfaithful to her, but they had a happy enough life together.'[3]

The dates 4 February 1651 and 4 February 1671 fell immediately before Mme de Sévigné's twenty-fifth and forty-fifth birthdays respectively. In 1651 Henri de Sévigné fought a duel against Moissens, the Chevalier d'Albret, over his mistress Mme de Gondran. He died the following day. In 1671 Mme de Sévigné's daughter, Mme de Grignan, left her mother's house in Paris to join her husband in Provence.

Emmanuel Levinas uses the term 'deference' to refer to our relationship with death.[4] 'This deference to death' he says, 'is not sense, nor can it be situated, localised or objectified.' The very unicity of the *I*, or what Levinas calls the intrigue of this unicity, has its origins in the *I*'s deference to the non-sense of death.[5]

I shall seek to describe the perspective of Mme de Sévigné's letters, the questioning that they conceal, according to what I see as their determining principle, namely 'the death of the father'. My aim is to understand the way that, having suffered the death of her husband, Mme de Sévigné undertook to maintain her relationship with her daughter without ever forgetting her own deference to death. The perspective of these letters interests me insofar as it establishes a rapport with the infinite. By this I do not mean a spatial infinity, such as that apprehended by consciousness, but rather a temporal infinity, a duration of which any person can know only a fragment. This perspective is the equivalent of what Levinas calls 'the knot' tied in duration by the death of another. How does this deference manifest itself when awakened by the unbearable fact of death, to which feminine sensibility reacts? 'In the *Phaedo*, Socrates, called upon to affirm the all-powerfulness of being, is the only one who is perfectly content,' says Levinas. That the spectacle of death is bearable only to the masculine sensibility 'emphasises the devastating nature of another person's death'.[6]

My hypothesis was suggested by the coincidence of '4 February', date of both the daughter's departure and the duel which killed M. de Sévigné. This coincidence occurs at a formal level, with no obvious content: it is an anniversary unmentioned in any letter; however this is not to say that it lacks significance.

In her book on the image of motherhood in Sévigné's writings, Michèle Longino Farell speaks of the 'moment of separation'.[7] The 'reasonedness' of her commentary, its coldness and banalising effect arise from the fact that Farrell's reading of Mme de Sévigné's correspondence considers the events in terms of the information they contain: 'Although the marriage was reported as far from idyllic and is hardly mentioned by Sévigné herself in any of her writings,' the death of her husband 'surely…must have been a blow, minimally to her sense of security'. For Farell these are facts belonging to the realm of 'information' and judged important only to the extent that they support her argument: 'And her own birthday was 5 February (1626). Although it generally went uncelebrated, Sévigné occasionally mentioned it in her letters, so that it was not altogether unmarked.' The intentionality of this commentary is reflected at the formal level in the way that it shows no trace of sensibility – since sensibility is no longer required for the analysis of discourse – and, at the conceptual level, in the reduction of the relationship between Mme de Sévigné and her daughter to a relationship of subject/object, in other words to a relationship in which feelings and events become elements in an 'epistemological' system, a system which can be identified in the theories of subjectivity with which we are concerned today:

> She specifically *contextualized* her birthday as of significance because it coincided yearly with the anniversary of her daughter's departure. All of the feelings of abandonment that a widow (a *husbandless woman*) might have on the anniversary of the spouse's death and on her birthday are stirred up by the new blow of her daughter's departure as she experiences for the first time being a *childless mother*.[8]

We should note that the dates and events under discussion here are considered from the point of view of an '*I*' – that of Sévigné – who can only be defined in opposition to 'the world': in its relation to the *I* the world either grants or denies, gratifies or punishes. Farell's aim is to reconstruct the way that 'Sévigné seeks and finds formulas to translate her own experience'. This, says Farell, necessarily involves the aggression basic to any search – the action through which one seeks and finds – and consequently a translation of pre-established elements belonging to a world organised by and exclusively for masculine thought and action: 'Filtering herself through this "other" construction of the world produces a grammatically enforced self-alienation. Although such intertextuality will anchor and ornament her writing, it will repeatedly vitiate attempts at self-apprehension and expression and point to the constructed nature of her assumed identity.'[9]

Farell is referring here to Mme de Sévigné's quotation, on her birthday in 1674, of a poem by Marot, 'which she recycles . . . intact, recognisable, apparently ignoring the gender difference'.[10] Sévigné's translation of her sources is necessarily destined to fail, thinks Farell, because Sévigné gives barely a thought to that which, in her, should speak of her feminine *I* in a particular way.

Yet the silence which surrounds the death of her daughter's father in these letters does not necessarily signify that a gap or absence has taken its place or that this death should be understood as an absence unrelated to the living. Rather than closely linking it to her being through what Farell, following a well-rooted tradition, sees as the inevitable manifestation of her self-interest – 'a blow, minimally to her sense of security' – this fateful day is the reminder and prefiguration of the *separation* which henceforward threatens mother and daughter. It is also doubtless a link to her own death, a reminder of death received by Mme de Sévigné twenty years to the day after the infamous duel. According to Levinas:

> That which language calls 'death' – what is regarded as the end of someone, is also an eventuality transferable onto oneself. This transfer is not merely mechanical: it belongs to the plot or to the plotting of the *I* and cuts the cord of my own duration, or *weaves a knot into that duration, as though the time that the I endures were continuing into excess*.[11]

We need to ask in what sense does the plot of the *I*'s unicity unravel? For through this plot Mme de Sévigné manages to give a face – *eidôlon* – to the 'otherness' that came into being with the death of the father. This sense of otherness is actually the call of death, which the daughter's departure seems to answer.

The relationship between mother and daughter is one of responsibility for each other. First there is the question of bodily well-being, in other words health and money.[12] Mme de Sévigné clearly differs from her son-in-law the Comte de Grignan, the other father-figure in this story. After the birth of her daughter's third child, Mme de Sévigné becomes so worried that she asks her son-in-law to moderate his haste to perpetuate the family line: 'I am even beginning to think it is time to remind M. de Grignan of his promise. Just think, this is the third time that you are giving birth in November; it will be in September next time if you do not control him.' Her daughter's health was terribly threatened by these yearly confinements: 'You have suffered more than if you'd been broken on the wheel, that's for sure. Shouldn't he be driven to despair, if he loves you, at causing you such torture every year? Isn't he afraid of losing you?'[13]

The *I* must know nothing of death in order to take on responsibility for the other in all passivity. This is 'an unknowingness which in real experience translates into our ignorance of the day of our death, an ignorance in virtue of which the *I* writes bouncing cheques as though it had eternity at its disposal'.[14] I have chosen to call 'otherness' the mother's idolatry of her daughter. This idolatry is a peculiarity of their relationship and marks the twenty-five years of their life 'together' from 4 February 1671 onwards. 'My pain would be mediocre if I could depict it to you; I shall not undertake to do so...I beg you, my dear daughter, to take care of your health. Preserve it out of love for me...'[15]

What is the meaning of this emotionality and these tears? Roger Duchêne tells us that 'On 6 February 1671, when the marquise writes to her daughter, who has left two days earlier to rejoin her husband in Provence, it is the day after her forty-fifth birthday. She knows,' he goes on, 'that her letter will be the first of a series which will continue as long as her daughter's absence, but she does not know how long that absence will last, nor that there will be many others, more or less until her death: eight years' worth spread over twenty-five years. She knows that she is an unhappy mother.'[16]

She knows and does not know: following Levinas we can say that Mme de Sévigné's love for her daughter is determined by 'the duration of time as a relation with the infinite'. At the heart of the differentness, actual or anticipated, which her daughter becomes through her distance, 'diachronicity is like the "*within*" in the phrase "the-other-*within*-the-same", except that the Other cannot penetrate the Same'.[17]

A TOUCH OF NON-SENSE

'Once she was with her daughter, she had probably nothing to say to her', put in Mme de Villeparisis.

'Most certainly she had: if it was only what she calls "things so slight that nobody else would notice them but you and I." And anyhow she was with her... Mme de Sévigné was after all less to be

> pitied than most of us. She spent a great part of her life with the person whom she loved.'
>
> 'You forget that wasn't "love" in her case, since it was her daughter.' 'But what matters in life is not whom or what one loves,' [M. de Charlus] went on, in a judicial, peremptory, almost cutting tone, 'it is the fact of loving. What Mme de Sévigné felt for her daughter has a far better claim to rank with the passion that Racine described in *Andromaque* or *Phèdre* than the commonplace relations young Sévigné had with his mistresses. It's the same with a mystic's love for his God. The hard and fast lines with which we circumscribe love arise solely from our complete ignorance of life.'[18]

Mme de Villeparisis is unconvinced by Mme de Sévigné, finding her 'constant anxiety about her daughter' exaggerated: 'She refers to it too often to be really sincere. She's not very natural.' Mme de Villeparisis 'could not help feeling that there was something rather "literary" about that lady's distress at being parted from "that tiresome Mme de Grignan"'. Here we see the arbitrary – in the sense of unique, extraordinary, never-sufficiently-motivated – aspect of Mme de Sévigné's love. In other words, the mother's response goes far beyond the qualities in her daughter that might warrant it. But Charlus briskly corrects Mme de Villeparisis: he knows that nothing is more true than Mme de Sévigné's love. If there is to be passion, such as the mother felt for her daughter, something of the order of the non-sense of death itself must manifest itself in love.

Mme de Sévigné's love does have an apparently 'arbitrary' aspect, originating perhaps in the fact of their separation. However this 'arbitrary' aspect is very strictly governed by the inviolable laws which shaped the correspondence as time went by: the counting of days, respect for deadlines, the delays and lost letters, real or imaginary, all discussed in the greatest detail. In their strict regularity down the years, fulfilling the promise to write without fail is the first and most religiously observed duty. What mattered for these two women was that each worried about the other, as manifested in their letters and thus in the representations they gave each other of their respective states when they were apart and in the care they gave each other when they were together.[19]

To explain how this non-sense – which accompanies the relation to death and is translated in the passion for her daughter – can be spoken of as a 'sense which is not already understood in the *conatus*', we must remember that Mme de Sévigné's patience cannot itself be understood as a 'status' which has a value in an exchange of knowledge, or in what Levinas calls an 'institution'.[20] Proust characterises the family as institution through the words of Mme de Villeparisis for whom, on the one hand, the husband's death is the end of his being, a passage into nothingness, while on the other, the marriage and departure of Mme de Grignan mark the end of a non-arbitrary relationship between mother and daughter and the beginning of another phase, which should also be based on worth.

From the moment that they are separated, mother and daughter are no longer in equivalent, interchangeable positions: 'I don't want you to say that I was a curtain that hid you. It's just as well if I did hide you; you are even more lovable when the curtain has been drawn'. While, for the daughter, being uncovered – being without her mother, being independent – may throw a full light on her own qualities, for the mother, being far from the daughter means being stripped: 'you must be exposed to show your perfection;... As for me, I feel totally naked, as though I've been stripped of everything that made me lovable'.[21] Her daughter's presence is the only thing that can make her 'lovable'. The mother does not demand 'reciprocity'; she does not insist on receiving what she gives. For the mother the daughter's independence is the necessary condition of her 'perfection', so that theirs is necessarily a heteronomous, unequal relationship.[22]

In speaking of what lies beyond institutional justice, including the so-called 'natural' family norms as understood by Mme de Villeparisis and all the critics of Mme de Sévigné that she represents (Farell's interpretation is a contemporary example), Levinas reminds us of Plato's words: beyond the visible and the invisible, beyond appearance, there is the beyond of the dead who judge the dead, 'as if the justice of the living could not pass through human clothing, in other words could not penetrate the attributes which, in other people, are offered to knowledge, attributes which reveal, but also conceal them'.[23]

When her daughter is far away, Mme de Sévigné is stripped – as only the dead can be – and her judgement is just. The true judgement, whose merit Plato describes and which Mme de Villeparisis does not recognise, is this 'each-for-the-other', 'the end of the prestige of appearance'. In the absence of her daughter Mme de Sévigné recognises a non-sense which is that of death. She cannot think of God because death itself, in the form of her daughter's absence, gets in the way: 'I pretend to be alone. I make myself a little Trappist monastery; I want to pray to God here, to have a thousand thoughts. I plan to ... yearn for the love of God. But, my dearest, what I shall do much better than all of that is to think of you ... It is a great weakness, but for myself I do not know how to resist a tenderness that is so just and natural.' [24]

IDOLATRY COMES FROM THIS SPATIAL TRANSCENDANCE TRAVERSED BY VISION

My initial question was: how, in the relationship between these two women, does the death of the father manifest itself? Clearly the answer to this must touch on what has been called Mme de Sévigné's idolatry and which she calls her weakness, her inability to place God before her daughter.[25] 'Although I am not *insensitive* to what matters to me, I am blessed with a health so perfect that, as I have told you, it amazes me ... Nevertheless I do have these most salutary thoughts that every person ought to have ... and without a dear one whom one cannot but love too much, it would be hard to understand why one should leave so convenient a life, so well suited to doing the thing that *in all justice* ought to occupy us.'[26] But this is not idolatry in the sense of a weakness. It is not an idolatry which, instead of attaching itself to the kind of truth that manifests itself only as truth beyond the corporeal world, concentrates on the things of this world and imagines that the world ends with one's being-in-the-world (as the philosophers, or the theologians, would have it). Rather this is idolatry in the sense of love as a responsibility beyond equity, or the meeting of responsibility. It is what Levinas calls a stain in the world that cannot be erased.[27]

In Levinas's definition, idolatry is the crossing of space without the hand's participation, without the 'eye leaving its socket'. We should remember that by 'masculine sensibility' I mean the sensibility thought out, if not dictated, by philosophy, where suffering and death are not unbearable. For the father who conceives of death as the end of being and passage into nothingness the fear of death is a fear of the annihilation of one's own *I*. Here the *I*'s understanding of the other involves assimilating, drawing the other to itself in a death governed by the same principles that govern being. While 'heaven calls for a gaze which is different from that of a vision which has already been identified, springs from need and becomes a hunt for things'.[28]

For feminine sensibility, the spectacle of death is unbearable:

> This irreducibility of the emotional is revealed even in the Socratic effort of the *Phaedo*... Even here, the approach of the dying Socrates does not lose its emotional resonance, although the recognition, in dying, of this annunciation of being (Socrates will at last be visible in death) purports to be a rational learned discourse or theory. This is the intention of the *Phaedo*: theory is stronger than the anguish of death. Yet even in this dialogue there is an *excess* of emotion: *Apollodorus weeps more than the others, he weeps immoderately – and the women have to be sent out.*[29]

For Apollodorus, who weeps immoderately, as for the women who must be sent out because their emotion is excessive, responsibility for the other does not end with death. To define this relationship, or this deference 'for what has been and is no longer', we can use the word 'substitution'. This does not mean transubstantiation, there is no question of 'entering' another substance: 'it remains a relationship with another, and as such it is discontinuity, in diachrony, with no coincidence'.[30] In idolising her daughter, the mother does the exact opposite of that which she is accused of. Far from forgetting the salvation of her soul, she dedicates herself to it, though not as to an onto-theological idea.[31] Instead she dedicates herself to the idea of a relationship with death and with time beyond all knowledge. Hence the need to go beyond the platonic conception of theory which is stronger than the anguish of death and the christian idea of death as manifestation of truth.

In the final analysis what counts for Mme de Sévigné is that the natural order should be respected and that she should die before her daughter or rather, that her daughter should not die before her. This is what she means when she defines her excessive love for Mme de Grignan as 'natural'. She does not, of course, use the word in the sense that we understand it today, in opposition to the transcendent, metaphysical order. Mme de Sévigné's idolatry says: 'I pretend to be alone', but I am not. I pretend to concern myself with the salvation of my soul, but I am not interested in myself, except insofar as such concern addresses the well-being – that is, the health – of my daughter.

> I beg you, my dear, let us not give absence the credit for having restored a perfect understanding between us... Let us look back with longing to a time when I saw you every day, you who are the charm of my life and my eyes, when I used to listen to you, whose wit touched me more finely than anything that I ever found

> agreeable. Let us not separate the lovely sight of you from your friendship.[32]

This idolatry which, according to Levinas, is 'a break in transcendence', leads to the 'birth of thought at the price of a shrinking that gathers the volume of the human body to a single point, which no longer casts a shadow. It is as though the eyes no longer retained their place in the sockets, but became instead the unity of a concept placed in the very spot that the concept embraces.'[33] If perspective is an embracing of the world as if it were merely a space, we might ask, still with Levinas, whether the secularisation of idolatry as it becomes ontology (the intelligibility of the cosmos, with representation and presence measuring up to each other) does not coincide with practical human common-sense.[34] 'All practical relations with the world are representation, and the represented world is economic.' It is here that we can begin to learn, with Mme de Sévigné, to 'think of God from the starting point of ethics'. Such an ethics requires Mme de Sévigné to become the 'subject who bears everything, who submits to everything, obeying with an obedience that precedes any understanding, any attention to the command'.[35] It is after her experience of the death of her husband, reproduced twenty years later by the departure of her daughter, that the reversal of heteronomy into autonomy occurs in Mme de Sévigné, in receiving from 'I know not where' that of which 'I am the author', in conceiving her daughter for a second time, as an idol.

Notes

1. Madame de Sévigné, *Correspondance III* (Paris: Gallimard, Bibliothèque de la Pléiade, 1972).
2. Mme de Sévigné, *Lettres choisies*, Roger Duchêne (ed.) (Paris: Gallimard, 1988) p. 212. Abbreviation *Lettres*. I have chosen this edition as the basis for my discussion of the relationship between Mme de Sévigné and her daughter, Mme de Grignan, since 'it offers only authentic letters, from known manuscripts, while the fictitious or approximate Sévigné has proliferated since the first edition of the Marchioness's letters in 1725'. (Note on the cover.)
3. *Lettres*, p. 304.
4. Emmanuel Levinas, *Dieu, la mort et le temps* (Paris: Grasset, 1993) p. 30. Abbreviation: *Dieu*.
5. 'Rather than allowing itself to be described in its actual ocurrence, death concerns us through its non-sense. The mark that it seems to

make in our time (= our relation to the infinite) is a pure question mark: an opening on to that to which no response is possible. A questioning which is already a modality of the relation with the beyond of being'. (*Ibid.*, p. 30).

6. *Ibid.*, p. 23.
7. Michèle Longino Farell, *Performing Motherhood. The Sévigné Correspondence*, (Hanover and London: University Press of New England) 1991, pp. 88–90.
8. Farell, *op. cit.*, pp. 88–90. My emphasis.
9. *Ibid.*, p. 89.
10. *Ibid.*
11. *Dieu*, p. 28. My emphasis.
12. For example, the letter 'Paris, [Monday] 4 April 1689' (*Correspondance III*, p. 567) clearly shows how Mme de Sévigné's worries about her daughter's physical and financial health go together. But there was a time when she did not know, or want to know, how closely the two could be linked: 'To Bussy-Rabutin ... I have to tell you some news which will doubtless make you happy. It is that at last the prettiest girl in France is marrying, not the prettiest boy but one of the most decent men in the kingdom, M de Grignan, whom you have known for a long time. All his wives have died to make space for your cousin, and even his father and son, by some extraordinary good fortune, so that being richer than ever before and, moreover, in his birth, his property and his good qualities being everything we could wish for, we are not bargaining at all as people usually do; we are happy to trust the two families who have passed before us.' (Paris, this [Tuesday] 4 December 1668, *Correspondance I*, p. 105). Her cousin's answer is not enough to put her on her guard and 'Bussy did not hesitate to recall the joke on 13 December 1677, at a time when the third Mme de Grignan was ill' (p. 946): 'From Bussy-Rabutin ... There is only one thing that causes me concern for the prettiest girl in France: Grignan, who is not old, is already on his third wife; he goes through almost as many wives as clothes, or at least carriages. Apart from that, my cousin seems very happy.' (Chaseu, this [Saturday] 8 December 1668, pp. 106–7).
13. *Correspondance I*, p. 386.
14. *Dieu*, p. 30.
15. *Correspondance I*, pp. 149–51.
16. *Lettres*, p. 305.
17. *Dieu*, p. 28.
18. Marcel Proust, *Within a Budding Grove*, *Remembrance of Things Past I*, trans. C.K. Scott Moncrieff and Terence Kilmartin, (London: Penguin, 1981) p. 819.
19. Care following which Mme de Sévigné was, moreover, to contract her last illness, from which she died.
20. 'The *I* – or me in my singularity – is someone who escapes their concept. The *I* only appears in its unicity by responding to other people in a responsibility which cannot be avoided, in a responsibility which I cannot discharge. The self is the identity of oneself which forms

through the impossibility of being replaced – a duty which goes beyond any debt – and thus a patience whose passivity cannot be belied by any assumption of responsibility... If patience has a meaning as an unavoidable obligation, this meaning becomes inadequacy and institution if there is not a little bit of non-sense underlying it.' (*Dieu*, p. 29).

21. *Correspondance I*, pp. 155–6.
22. Levinas would say: 'There is a heteronomy in this relation with other people in which I myself am torn from my beginning in me, from my equality with me. This heteronomy, the true meaning of otherness, is an alteration which is not alienation, nor slavery, nor loss of unicity – since precisely no one can replace me, since I have been chosen.' (*Dieu*, p. 222).
23. Levinas, 'Idéologie et idéalisme', *De Dieu qui vient à l'idée* (Paris: Vrin, 1992) p. 28.
24. *Correspondance I*, pp. 199–200.
25. 'Believe me, my dear, the only feeling I can have for you is one of unequalled tenderness, perfect appreciation and a natural liking which will end only with me. In Livry I am trying to learn what I should do to turn from these ideas. My difficulty lies in the fact that I have no ideas which have nothing to do with you, and I don't know where to get new ones from;... So, my dear, we must hope that time will make them less bitter. A little devotion and love of God would calm my spirit; you should give way only to that.' (*Correspondance I*, pp. 717–18).
26. *Correspondance III*, pp. 896–7.
27. '... eyes turned to heaven separate in some way from their body. In this separation the complicity between hand and eye, a complicity older than the distinction between knowing and doing, is shunned. The gaze raised to heaven reaches the untouchable, the sacred... The distance thus covered by the gaze is transcendance. The gaze is deference and not an upward movement... Idolatry comes from this spatial transcendance traversed by vision.' (*Dieu*, p. 188).
28. *Ibid*. p. 188
29. *Ibid*., p. 22, my emphasis.
30. *Ibid*., p. 214.
31. On this subject see Pascal's reflections on idolatry in, for example, 'Letter from Pascal and his sister Jacqueline to their sister, Mme Perrier' (1 April 1648), 'Letter on the death of Pascal Senior, written by Pascal to his older sister Mme Perrier, and to her husband' (17 October 1651), *Pensées et opuscules*, ed. Léon Brunschvicg (Paris: Hachette) 1978, pp. 87–9; 95–107.
32. *Correspondance I*, p. 243.
33. *Dieu*, p. 189.
34. 'Is Western knowledge not then the secularisation of idolatry?' (*ibid*.).
35. *Ibid*., p. 229.

(Translated by Trista Selous)

11

The Father Effect: Rimbaud, Pessoa

Jean-Jacques Hamm

Sooner or later when talking about the father one has to bring in elements from myths or family romances, including those of neurotics.[1] While we can find a father-creator of the Garden of Eden, a '*dolce Padre*',[2] to borrow Dante's designation of Virgil, or the father Victor Hugo describes as a 'hero with such a sweet smile',[3] the cultural figures that accompany us are often more threatening. They are called Ouranos, Kronos, Yahwe, Abraham, Agamemnon, Laius or Wotan and their functions are linked to tales of violence in which the father's will appears as a desire to kill his offspring. Jean-Paul Sartre sums up this type of situation ironically in *Words*:

> The rule is that there are no good fathers; it is not the men who are at fault but the paternal bond, which is rotten. There is nothing better than to produce children, but what a sin to *have* some! If he had lived, my father would have lain down on me and crushed me. Fortunately, he died young.

And he adds that thus: 'I have no superego'.[4]

Thus we have here a primary cultural configuration linking fatherhood to murder that lies at the root of sacrificial acts and later of tragedy.

The other side of this configuration is reflected in acts of rebellion against the real or symbolic father, who is negated in either word or deed. A few examples of such acts would be Kronos the son castrating his father Ouranos to be supplanted in turn by his own son Zeus, Oedipus killing his father with the well-known results, the brothers Karamazov attacking their father, who has become an anti-model, or William Blake vehemently denouncing 'Nobodaddy ... Father of Jealousy'.[5]

In the field of the theory of influence, Harold Bloom uses an oedipal model to show how necessary it is for the spiritual survival of would-be poets that they distance themselves from their great literary ancestors.[6] It would be possible to discern in the theory and practice of parody a body of symbolic assassinations which are necessary to the birth and flowering of new works and to the renewal of forms.

Another culturally established pattern of fatherhood is that of *Eli, Eli, lema sabachtani*, the god who abandons his son at the moment of crucifixion, the god who is not, or is no longer there and who, in the version of Jean-Paul Richter's *Dream* revealed to them by Mme de Staël's translation, fascinated Romantics such as Vigny and Nerval.[7] We should also not forget the initial message of Nietzsche's *Zarathustra* on the death of God.

In this essay I should like to analyse a different kind of relation to the father. This is the case of the father as non-reference point, as non-object and thus as void, something that is invisible but whose effects are felt and to which I am not even sure I can give the name of father. It is an effect linked to an absence, a diffuse, perverse effect which is yet not ephemeral since it engulfs and modifies a life. It is the trace of something which is only an origin insofar as it is absent, whose absence is experienced as both constraint and freedom, disaster and energy. Through an interplay of patterns I am thus seeking here to reconstitute the elements of a scotomisation, a missing constellation, or continent linked to what I have to call, for want of a better term, the father. My aim is to define the clues, attitudes, actions or obligations that lead us to assume a father effect, a significant non-reference point.

I have chosen to approach this question by looking in parallel at the work of two poets, Arthur Rimbaud (1854–91) and Fernando Pessoa (1888–1935), proposing a double reading of two texts together in order to reveal the appearances and disappearances of the father effect. Our reading is based essentially, but not exclusively, on two prose texts: Rimbaud's *Correspondance* with his family after 1875, that is, after he stopped writing poetry, and Pessoa's *Book of Disquiet*, started in 1913 and unfinished at the author's death. These are then, on the one hand, a non-work and on the other a 'work in progress or in ruins'.[8]

Rimbaud describes the hell of Cyprus, Aden or Abyssinia. Pessoa's book is a 'message from Limbo'.[9] It is 'the book of the non-life of Bernardo Soares',[10] one of the author's pseudonyms. 'In reality, the whole of the *Book of Disquiet* is death writing... more than death writing, this book, the blackest of our entire literature, is also the death of Writing.'[11] This book describes the opposite of rest, of tranquillity: the

Book of Disquiet is the book of un-quiet, of un-tranquillity. It is the state of mind that Alain Borer attributes to Rimbaud: 'In Abyssinia, Rimbaud is always *unquiet* in the English sense of restless, from the Latin *inquietus* – without rest.'[12]

There are some important differences – to which we shall return – between Rimbaud's undertaking and that of Pessoa. The latter, 'unsuited to life',[13] produces, as Antonio Tabucchi has said, a work reminiscent of Rilke's *Malte Laurids Brigge*, of Jules Laforgue's *Complaintes* and T.S. Eliot's 'place of disaffection'.[14] This is a far cry from Rimbaud's wonders. However, Rimbaud's wonders disappeared when he renounced *écriture* and his writing was banalised into *écrivance* following a deliberate amnesia.

However I shall start parenthetically with a few biographical elements, starting with the father's absence. Rimbaud's father, a soldier whose offspring recurred with his periods of leave, disappeared from the family in 1860, and became, in its terms, a non-person. Arthur was six. Pessoa's father died when Fernando was five. Rimbaud's father is absent from his son's poetry, as from his correspondence. Jean-Louis Cornille notes that: 'This is not a case of a father symbolising the law or censure, so much as a Name of the Father, leaving Non-Father behind him as a kind of residue.'[15] In Pessoa's case, the mother's destiny is laid over that of the father and obliterates it. Twice the poet gives a biographical untruth: 'My mother died very young; I never knew her' (*BD*, p. 9); 'I don't remember my mother. She died when I was only one year old' (*BD*, p. 135). In fact Pessoa was thirty-seven when his mother died. He also gives a false date for the death of his father: 'My father, who lived a long way from us, killed himself when I was three and I never knew him. I still don't know why he lived far away. I have never particularly wanted to know' (*BD*, p. 135).

The material quality of life of both poets was poor: Rimbaud sought the fortune that would have given him a private income; Pessoa was a low-level employee in Lisbon who wished 'To be a retired major, that's the ideal state in my eyes. What a pity not to have been, eternally a retired major' (*LDI*, II, p. 252). Both share a similar feeling of a life on the rocks, of uselessness. One would be killed by syphilis, the other by alcohol. Pessoa describes himself as 'the integral Passer-by' (*LDI*, I, p. 124), an expression which could apply equally well to Rimbaud. One can also see, though to a lesser extent in Pessoa, a lack of interest in publication. While Rimbaud eventually saw his productions as 'dishwater! they were nothing but dishwater' (*OV*, p. 901), Pessoa saw literature as cowardice (*LDI*, I, p. 98). This was of course a phenomenon of the times; one need only think of the attitude of Stéphane Mallarmé, Germain Nouveau's hostility to publication or the silence of Paul Valéry.[16] And perhaps, as Cornille says, 'One can only reach the Unknown by remaining completely unknown oneself.'[17]

Some of Pessoa's statements read like Rimbaldian echoes: 'To live is to be other' (*BD*, p. 48); 'I continually feel that I was someone else, that I felt and thought as another' (*BD*, p. 229); 'Living is like crochet patterns to someone else's design' (*BD*, p. 24); or this quotation from Oscar Wilde: 'Most people are other people' (*LDI*, II, p. 232).

Both are so-called accursed poets because poetry, the essential activity, involves and modifies the relation to the world. The curse, and here I refer to Benjamin Fondane's book *Rimbaud le voyou*,[18] also originated in the passage from a poetry of celebration to a poetry of knowledge.

On 14 March 1916 at the port of Lisbon, Pessoa noted: 'There are boats that will call at many ports, but not one will call at the port where life no longer causes suffering and there is no quayside where one can forget' (*LDI*, I, p. 23).

On 20 May 1891 the *Amazone* entered the port of Marseille. On board was a dead man temporarily reprieved, a defeated man. End of biographical parenthesis.

I shall examine the father effect from three different angles: in the relationship of the two poets to humanity, to space-time and, lastly, to form and writing. Differences will become apparent which will help to define the suggested effect.

As T.S. Eliot reminds us, 'This is a place of disaffection'. The relation to others is hell. They are nobodies. Like Pessoa, Rimbaud constantly condemns the mediocrity of the world, of 'those bands of savages or imbeciles' (*OV*, p. 589), those 'stupid shop employees' (*OV*, p. 589). Pessoa, surrounded by 'characters of no interest' (*LDI*, I, p. 29), is 'irritated by the happiness of all those people who do not know that they are unhappy' (*LDI*, I, p. 49). The words 'those people' are also to be found from Rimbaud's pen, to refer to the bosses he despises: 'those people are misers and rogues' (*OV*, p. 521). 'Slavery,' writes Pessoa, 'is the only law of life, there is no other ... The cowardly love we all have of freedom ... is the irrefutable proof of how our slavery weighs upon us' (*BD*, p. 10). Throughout Rimbaud's writing, whether he is in Cyprus, Aden or Abyssinia, we find as a constant leitmotif the feeling of being a prisoner, the need to stay in one place in order to amass the money to go somewhere else where he will feel less of a slave: 'I'm staying here, and I have to stay here, because it's far too far away from everywhere' (*OV*, p. 482).

Both men look at the world from an alienating outside. In Pessoa's texts the motif of the foreigner constantly returns: 'I've always been considered by everyone to be an intruder or, at the least a stranger ... an outsider' (*BD*, p. 154); 'I belong ... to that species of man that is always on the edge of the thing they belong to' (*BD*, p. 207); 'Though I walked amongst them a stranger, no-one noticed' (*BD*, p. 13).

These words are echoed in Rimbaud's cry: 'What a desolate existence I lead in these absurd climates and insane conditions' (*OV*, p. 582). And Pessoa wrote: 'Unknowingly, I have been a witness to the gradual wasting away of my life, to the slow shipwreck of everything I ever wanted to be' (*BD*, p. 137).

Their worlds are made of rejections. One example is the rejection of politics. To admit the importance of politics is to accept the social comedy and its absurdity. Rimbaud writes to his family: 'You tell me the political news. If you only knew how little I care about it! I haven't touched a newspaper in more than two years! All these debates are incomprehensible to me now' (*OV*, p. 548). Pessoa says: 'The supreme honour to which a superior being can aspire is not even to know the name of the Head of State of his own country, better still not to know whether he lives in a monarchy or a republic' (*LDI*, II, p. 141). This deliberate ignorance of politics springs from Pessoa's profound anarchism:[19]

> To subordinate oneself to nothing – be it another human being, someone we love, or an idea – to maintain that aloof independence that consists in not believing in the truth nor, were such a thing to exist, in the usefulness of knowing it: that, it seems to me, is the proper condition of the intellectual life of thinkers.... To be is to be free ... As free from ourselves as we are from others, contemplatives without ecstasy, thinkers without conclusions, the liberated slaves of God, we all live out the brief interlude that the absentmindedness of our executioners commutes into a temporary stay of execution. Tomorrow we face the guillotine, or if not tomorrow, the day after. (*BD*, p. 217)

Neither God nor master. The important thing is to preserve one's independence, one's freedom. Rimbaud, who describes himself as a deserter from his father's regiment (*OV*, p. 464), though in fact he was never in it, constantly claims the right to freedom, flight and nomadism. He had already announced in *A Season in Hell*, 'One day perhaps he will marvellously disappear' (*OV*, p. 426).

Faced with the world both men respond with silence. The silence of Rimbaud's letters is enormous. The words destined for others remain on the surface in an exchange without depth: 'nothing here', 'look after my business', 'buy me some books', 'send me some objects', 'invest my money well', 'don't waste time moaning'. The only feeling is in the salutations. A wall is being erected between Rimbaud and the others, which is hardly broken until the letters to Isabelle, from Marseille, when sickness has taken hold of him. 'Happy are those who entrust their lives to nobody' writes Pessoa (*LDI*, II, p. 222).

The generalised, omnipresent and somewhat wearisome 'I' of Rimbaud's letters, like Pessoa's 'I', appear as kernels of independence in the face of a threatening world. It is in the folds of the self, in the self-image, that expansion is possible. 'My soul' writes Pessoa, 'is a hidden orchestra ... All I hear is the symphony' (*BD*, p. 8). We might recall Rimbaud's words 'I am becoming a fantastic opera' (*OV*, p. 434), with which he describes the delirium of *The Alchemy of the Word*. But the rare appearances of a positive self-image, aristocratic for Pessoa and solar for Rimbaud, contrast with the threats of what Pessoa calls the abjection of the orphans of fortune (*LDI*, II, p. 146). 'One needs', he writes, 'a certain intellectual courage to recognise unflinchingly that one is no more than a scrap of humanity' (*BD*, p. 153). Facing him stands 'the bothersome child, the very stupid beast', the 'Monts-Rocheux cat' (*OV*, p. 287) that gave off a terrible smell, the ass, animal of desire and abjection, omnipresent in the writings of Rimbaud,[20] who expresses a profound horror of himself, for example when he says: 'I live in a very *assinine* (*'bête'*) and *beastly* (*'embêtant'*) way' (*OV*, p. 497).

Both men's worlds are filled with an immense boredom, which Pessoa defines as malaise, fatigue, a blasé disgust with the world, or a physical sensation of chaos and above all as an 'absence of mythology' (*LDI*, I, p. 169). He writes: 'Sometimes when I raise my heavy head from the books in which I keep track of other people's accounts and of the absence of a life of my own, I feel a physical nausea. It may come from sitting so bent over but it goes beyond a mere question of numbers and disillusion. Life sickens me like a dose of bad medicine' (*BD*, p. 56). And Rimbaud writes from El Harar: 'I don't care at all about life ... and it's a good thing this life is the only one, and that that is obvious, since one can't imagine another life with greater boredom than this' (*OV*, p. 501).

Both feel themselves to be caught in a world of nothingness. 'Nothing [one might say, quoting another artist of the void] will have taken place but the place'.[21] Pessoa says: 'I belong to nothing, desire nothing, am nothing' (*LDI*, I, p. 125). Such phrases constantly return in his prose and poems, such as 'Lisbon Revisited' or 'Tobacconists', which begins:

> I am nothing,
> Never shall be anything.
> Cannot will to be anything.
> This apart, I have in me all the dreams of the world.[22]

Rimbaud lives each day as a void: 'Here nothing, nothing at all' (*OV*, p. 463); 'Here, in Aden, there's nothing' (*OV*, p. 531); 'Nothing very interesting for the moment' (*OV*, p. 499); 'Don't be surprised that I seldom write: the main reason is that I never find anything interesting to say' (*OV*, p. 766). Pessoa writes: 'I'm nobody, absolutely nobody' (*BD*, p. 8). Thus are defined nothingness, reality and an availability without employment.

Can these attitudes – horror of others as of oneself, a certain sense of abjection, the feeling that bad luck is round the corner – be seen as manifestations of the father effect, the effect of an absence that governs behaviour? Certainly, if we remember another type of relationship to reality, to the void, which Clément Rosset calls a lightness of thought, implying clairvoyance and freedom.[23] In the cases of Rimbaud and Pessoa, an absence, a point of non-reference that generates meaning, produces an ethos that is sometimes raging, sometimes tormented and generally pessimistic.

Does the father effect express itself in the choice of a certain kind of space or landscape? Pessoa is a city-dweller, Rimbaud a nomad. Their daily lives are made of very different landscapes: for the former the city, for the latter the wide-open spaces. A similar sensitivity to the nudity of the physical world is at work in the writings of both poets:

> Wide are the deserts, and all is desert.
> It takes more than a few tons of stones or standing tiles
> to disguise the earth, this earth which is truth.
> Wide are the deserts, deserted and wide the souls,
> deserted because none cross them but themselves,
> wide because in them all is visible, and all is dead.[24]

Pessoa returns to this desert landscape, from a poem dated 4 October 1930, many times in his prose: 'I love impossible landscapes, and the vast stretches of desert plateaux where I shall never go' (*LDI*, I, p. 41); 'I seem... to be nothing but a dried up autumn on the desert wastes' (*LDI*, I, p. 188). And, in this context, he states that: 'Landscapes are repetitions' (*LDI*, I, p. 202). In their symbolism these statements echo Rimbaud's harsh realities of 'deserts... without roads, without mail, without travellers' (*OV*, p. 502), of 'countries totally unexplored by Europeans' (*OV*, p. 502). Here is his description of Aden: 'You can't imagine the place at all. There is not a tree here, not even dried up, not a blade of grass, not a parcel of earth, not a drop of fresh water... There is absolutely nothing to see and touch but lava and sand which can't produce the most minimal vegetal life. All around is a desert of sand which is absolutely arid' (*OV*, p. 601). Or again, from Larnaca in Cyprus: 'There's nothing here but a chaos of rocks, the river and the sea. There are no houses. No earth, no gardens, not a single tree. In the summer it's eighty degrees. At the moment it's often fifty' (*OV*, 473). One is reminded of T.S. Eliot's lines in *The Waste Land*:

> Here is no water but only rock
> Rock and no water and the sandy road.[25]

The father effect makes way for a different tense: that of the present. The elimination of the father is the elimination of the past. Thus Pessoa can write: 'I live always in the present. I know nothing of the future and no longer have the past. The former weighs me down with a thousand possibilities, the latter with the reality of nothingness' (*BD*, p. 61). Rimbaud's letters establish the present as narrative tense. Writing a long letter to his family from Genoa, in which he tells the story of his journey, he says of experiences he has had that are now past:

> This morning I arrive in Genoa, and receive your letters. A passage to Egypt costs a fortune... It is coming to the end of the month... At Amsteg... the road begins to climb... we do nothing but overlook precipices... we pass a place of remarkable horror... At the sound of the bell an unsavoury young man receives you; you go up to a low, dirty room... You see big yellow dogs whose story is well-known... In the evening there are about thirty of us. (*OV*, pp. 465–7)

This is a timeless journey. Moreover Rimbaud spatialises time with a combination of present tense, deictics and the use of 'there is/are':

'He told me to wait here... There's no work here at present... life here is outrageously expensive...' (*OV*, p. 582); 'It's summer for you and it's winter here, that is to say it's quite hot, but it often rains. This will last a few months' (*OV*, p. 500); 'It's winter for you now, and it's summer for me. The rains have stopped; it is very sunny and quite hot. The coffee is ripening' (*OV*, p. 509); '... this country. It's the bottom of a volcano, with no plants' (*OV*, p. 537); 'I'm still well, and I hope that you are the same... Nothing new here' (*OV*, p. 578); 'I've moved back here, for a long time. I'm setting up a French trading post' (*OV*, p. 698). As Alain Borer notes, 'Rimbaud's place is both somewhere and nowhere'.[26] It is a present, a presence and an absence. 'We are not in the world,' he wrote in *A Season in Hell* (*OV*, p. 422). 'Good-bye to here, anywhere' (*OV*, p. 373).

Rimbaud's here-and-now can be read in his 'there is/are', in his enumerations and also in photography, that art effacing all temporal dimension other than that of the instant that fixes and kills. Rimbaud refuses narrative in his letters because he prefers observation, a writing based on observation, fatherless writing. Absence enables a literature of minute-taking, of report in the administrative sense. Without a goal one can only take notes, make lists. In *Rapport sur Ogadine* he says: 'Here is the reported information... Ogadine is the name for a meeting of tribes... There are two roads... The Ogadines... are very tall' (*OV*, pp. 571–3). Can a link be made in this case between the geography of the journey and the father's absence? Can the journey's geography be seen as an anti-hierarchy, a non-aborescence, a rhizome?

What is the relation between the father effect and form? Does the father effect lead to particular forms? The demiurgical creator completes his works. The alpha–omega of the divine, the journey from the beginning of the story to its end and the resolution or closure make ripples to which theocratic or patriarchal language traces its origin. Is there an atheist writing, an a-fatherly, *a-pater* writing? Let us put forward a few hypotheses: writing without God, or without the father, to the extent that it does not cheat, can doubtless only be fragmentary and incomplete. A body of work such as that of Mallarmé bears witness to the co-presence of two types of writing and the issues embodied in each. On the one hand, *Le Tombeau d'Edgar Poe*, a hieratical hommage to a peer and a father, places the poet on the side of the finitude of identity and of found and created continuity. On the other, *Pour un tombeau d'Anatole*, a long and incomplete cry of pain, sketches out the evanescence of the son, the progressive invasion of the void.[27]

There is another genre which shows the two sides of the father effect: on the one hand the resolution of the mystery and establishment of a reassuring rationality, and on the other doubt about the nature of experience. One is reminded here of the fantastic as defined by Tzvetan Todorov[28] and of Roland Barthes' writable text.[29] To complete is to enter a simulacrum of the order of God or of the gods. Incompleteness, when it is deliberately chosen, thus remains one of the supreme acts of negation of God and his successors. Completeness is his, or their, glory.[30]

Pessoa gets the wrong genre when he states that he 'tells with indifference [his] autobiography without deeds, [his] story without life' (*LDI*, I, p. 31). What he is establishing is in reality a self-portrait, that genre *par excellence* of the negation of the father, in its effacing of genealogical narrative. 'The self-portrait' writes Michel Beaujour, 'addresses itself, since it cannot call on God.'[31] This genre of the here and now is a garden of ruins, a collection of effigies, of *vignettes*. 'I am myself the substance of my book.'[32] 'On the father, I have nothing to say because I am an anti-history. I am what crosses the specular space. I am a memory reconstituted on the way across a space: Don Juan and the commander, Lucrezia, Judith, the Medusa's raft.'[33] Here we recognise the title of Michel Leiris's fragments. From the father's ashes, from the effect of his absence, something can be born which is neither narrative nor poem but, to advance a different hypothesis, a prose poem, an illumination of the instant, a wild parade.

But here is the moment of divergence. Rimbaud and Pessoa follow very different courses. The former is a man of action who does not spare his energies; the latter refuses to act at all, constantly claiming his right to dream, stating that 'In me the habit of dreaming and the ability to dream are primordial' (*BD*, p. 202) and that 'Action is a disease of thought, a cancer of the imagination' (*BD*, p. 256). Pessoa is a man of procrastination: 'Put everything off. One should never do today what one can equally well neglect to do tomorrow' (*LDI*, I, p. 251). Dreaming is a second life for him and, 'Why shouldn't we – men, gods and world – be someone's dreams, someone's thoughts, marooned forever outside existence?' (*BD*, p. 162). Rimbaud does not dream; he acts, tirelessly.

Pessoa is a man without a project, without a future. Rimbaud looks towards the future, towards new departures, new voyages, new faraway places. He is a nomad who tells his family he cannot come back to live with them. He has plans, he wants to read, he writes reports, he makes responsibilities for himself, he invites them (*OV*, p. 691). While both have 'the apocalyptic feeling of life' (*LDI*, II, p. 101) to use Pessoa's expression, Rimbaud works with an eye to the future. Pessoa says he has no future.

But Pessoa is in literature, in writing. Pessoa does not burn his texts, does not disown them, he stores them all in a trunk for posthumous reading. He is in limbo, in the space of the unborn. Rimbaud, without realising it, far from the Parisian stage, is in the process of leaving limbo. Rimbaud the African, the geographer, traces an epic of conquest – derisory doubtless – as had his father.[34]

Does the father effect exist? We are faced with a methodological difficulty arising from diachrony. The Rimbaud of the *Correspondance* and the Pessoa of the *Book of Disquiet* have reached the particularly pessimistic end-points of a more complex process. There are many Rimbauds as there are many Pessoas and it would be wrong to claim otherwise.

The father effect, if it exists, can only be a perverse, diffuse effect, both destructive and demiurgic. An obsessive fear returns: 'on the father there is doubtless little to say' but much to do, with and against. Goethe was no doubt right to state that in the beginning was not the Logos, the word, but the act. Cronos displaces Ouranos, Zeus displaces Cronos. The death of the father, his absence, is the son's breath of life, the possibility for him to exist, even if it is only the terrible existence of an adventurer or drunken poet.

Notes

1. Sigmund Freud, 'Family Romances' in *Standard Edition* IX, pp. 235–45.
2. Dante, *Purgatorio*, IV, 44.
3. Victor Hugo, 'Après la bataille' in *La Légende des siècles.*
4. Jean-Paul Sartre, *Words*, Irene Clephane trans. (Harmondsworth: Penguin, 1967) pp. 14–15.
5. William Blake, *Complete Works*, (Oxford: Oxford University Press, 1976) p. 171.
6. Harold Bloom, *The Anxiety of Influence A Theory of Poetry* (Oxford: Oxford University Press, 1973).
7. Mme de Staël, *De L'Allemagne* III (Paris: Hachette, 1959) pp. 284–90.
8. The abreviations of the texts referred to are as follows:
   OV: Arthur Rimbaud, *Oeuvre-Vie* (Paris: Arléa, 1991)
   BD: Fernando Pessoa, *The Book of Disquiet*, Maria José de Lancastre (ed.), Margaret Jull Costa trans. (London: Serpent's Tail, 1991)
   LDI: Fernando Pessoa, *Le Livre de l'intranquillité*, (Paris: Christian Bourgeois, 1988, 1992)
   The quotation is from Robert Bréchon in *LDI*, p. 15.

9. Eduardo Lourenço, *LDI*, I, p. 8.
10. *Ibid.*, p. 10.
11. *Ibid.*, p. 12.
12. Alain Borer, *Un sieur Rimbaud: La Terre et les pierres* (Paris: LP, biblio/essais, 1991) p. 51.
13. *BD*, p. 261.
14. *The Complete Poems and Plays of T.S. Eliot* (London: Faber & Faber, 1969), p. 173.
15. Jean-Louis Cornille, *Rimbaud nègre de Dieu* (Lille: Presses Universitaires, 1989) p. 18.
16. We should like to note in particular the case of Germain Nouveau (1851–1920): 'On his death in 1920, almost all his poetic work remained unpublished by his own wish. He had always resisted publication, not hesitating to sue those who had taken steps in this direction', Claude Jeancolas, *Le Dictionnaire de Rimbaud* (Paris: Balland, 1991) p. 194.
17. Cornille, *op. cit.*, p. 105.
18. Benjamin Fondane, *Rimbaud le voyou* (Paris: Complexe, 1990) pp. 91–2.
19. See *Le Banquier anarchiste* (Paris: La Différence, 1988).
20. Cornille, *op. cit.*, pp. 118–31.
21. Stéphane Mallarmé, *Oeuvres complètes* (Paris: Gallimard Pléiade, 1945) pp. 474–5.
22. *Selected Poems*, Jonathan Griffin trans. (Harmondsworth: Penguin, 1982) p. 111.
23. Clément Rosset, *Le Réel traité de l'idiotie* (Paris: Minuit, 1977) p. 77 and ff.
24. Fernando Pessoa, *Alvaro de Campos* in *Oeuvres Complètes* (Paris : La Diffiérence, 1968).
25. Eliot, *op. cit.*, p. 72.
26. Borer, *op. cit.*, p. 55.
27. *Pour un tombeau d'Anatole* (Paris: Le Seuil, 1961) p. 288: 'father... I feel the void invade me'.
28. Tzvetan Todorov, *Introduction à la littérature fantastique* (Paris: Le Seuil, 1970) p. 28 and ff.
29. Roland Barthes, *S/Z*, Richard Miller trans. (London: Cape, 1975).
30. Dante, *Paradiso*, XXXIII, 85–90.
31. Michel Beaujour, *Miroirs d'encre* (Paris: Le Seuil, 1980) p. 14.
32. Michel de Montaigne, *Essais* (Paris: Gallimard (Pléiade), 1950) p. 25.
33. Michel Leiris, *L'Age d'homme* (Paris: Gallimard, 1946).
34. See Charles H.L. Bodenham, *Rimbaud et son père. Les clés d'une énigme* (Paris: Les Belles Lettres, 1992).

(Translated by Trista Selous)

III
Reinventing Father

12

Fatherhood in the Works of George Sand

Anna Szabó

The work of George Sand is both deeply marked by the period in which it was written and deeply reflective of that period's chief characteristics, formed, deformed and filtered through the author's experiences and subconscious fantasies. This is particularly true where the notion of paternity is concerned. One need only read the first books of *Histoire de ma vie* to understand how much her father's early death affected young Aurore. If, in the autobiography, the writer lingers so long on the father she scarcely knew, it is in order to overcome a sense of loss which she still felt keenly, even in her forties. In creating the myth of the father, Sand was seeking above all to resuscitate his word in order to give herself at least the illusion of possessing a spiritual father. While for so many others the problem is finding a way to escape paternal oppression, the problem for Sand, as Philippe Berthier has pointed out, 'was exactly the opposite: not that she had too much father in her life but that she didn't have enough'.[1]

The father's absence was all the more painful in that the child experienced it within a family racked by the conflicts of early nineteenth century France. Thus the traumas of the outside world quickly became lived experience for her, giving rise to the 'unanimiste'[2] dream in which Aurore created a full-blown myth organised around an androgynous, conciliatory character who was a projection of her own desires to love and be loved in a real, complete family. The Corambé myth of union underpins the whole Sandian universe and as such is highly pertinent to the series of problems under discussion here.

Sand's novels deal with the period from the fall of the ancien régime to the beginning of the Third Republic, a period when paternity faced perhaps its greatest crisis as the very foundations of its power were undermined. The career of George Sand coincides with the period of the Civil Code, which ultimately restored the father to a position of power. We know however that in reality nothing could halt the tide of change in matters of social behaviour, nor the gradual waning of paternal authority. Indeed this state of exploded fatherhood, with its metamorphoses and consequences, its crises and conflicts between the generations, has left its imprint on the novels of the period in which fathers almost invariably play an important role, whether as central or secondary characters. Quite naturally the novels also express the very deep private aspirations of their author in that they also describe that other reality which is the world of desire: an ideal world peopled with fathers who carry out their paternal duties with love and devotion. It is not difficult to discern the influence of Rousseau in this image of the 'new father', which reflects to a certain extent the spirit of the Revolutionary period's jurisprudence, especially in its emphasis on the material interests of the child, born in or out of wedlock, and on voluntary fatherhood. For Sand, as for the legislators of the Revolutionary period, the latter notion meant the victory of the social over the biological. It marks the victory of a free acceptance of father's role over the mere passive recognition that children have been engendered. For fatherhood is not simply a physical matter; it is also, and perhaps primarily, a spiritual matter.[3]

The whole question of fatherhood revolves around similitude and difference, fidelity and independence, according to whether or not it is viewed from the father's point of view or that of the child. In the pre-1848 novels, the figure of the father is more often than not associated with negativity and doubts, but the perspectives opened up by fatherhood, in harmony with the main lines of Sand's thinking, tend rather towards portraying the father as a conciliatory figure, that is to say towards establishing an equilibrium.

ABSENT FATHERS (LIVING OR DEAD)

The reader who is familiar with the author's family history on the one hand and on the other the history of the period, with its very high number of illegitimate births[4] and all the ravages of war, will not be surprised to find in Sand's novels, especially of the 1830s and 1840s, a marked absence of fathers which seems to border on the obsessive.[5] But this absence indicates a certain presence: the presence of the problem posed by fatherhood itself, whether good or bad. For, apart from certain cases in which nothing is known about the father, children's experience of this absence is a painful one which often leads them into all sorts of waywardness. Thus Indiana, brought up by an authoritarian father, is simply 'changing master' and 'changing prison'[6] when she marries. Others have to put up with the tyrannical behaviour of guardians, like the protagonist of *Mauprat*, ill-treated by a fearsome and corrupt grandfather, or Gabriel(le) who is prevented by her grandfather from ever knowing even to which sex (s)he belongs. This grandfather, who incarnates paternal omnipotence in all its feudal glory, despises the vulgar obligations and childish concerns of bourgeois fathers and is driven by the overweening ambitions implicit in the patrician view of fatherhood to the point of having his granddaughter murdered.[7]

By way of compensation, the bastards and foundlings who are so numerous in these novels often enjoy some exceptional ability or faculty which raises them above the common run of legitimate children. In Sand's novels, it would appear that the child of obscure origins is not simply a more or less clever reworking of a well-used theme. The fatherless child is by definition a being free of prejudices and constraints and as such is perfectly integrated into the Sandian system, allowing a range of social and moral issues to be articulated. It is for this category of characters that the father is least problematic: the very necessity of fatherhood itself is placed between parentheses. From among the many possible examples we might consider Consuelo, a great singer and Goddess of Poverty who, completely ignorant of everything relating to her father, has 'never even thought to ask herself whether she has one'.[8] It is only through seeing the whole of humanity as her family that she is able to fulfil the duty and live out the destiny imposed upon her by the sole name she bears: Consuelo. In no way does she feel frustrated by this: 'I have no other name,' she says to her friend, 'society has not burdened me with the honour of a family name to uphold.'[9]

PRESENT FATHERS

Authoritarian fathers

This moral and social type, the despot who cruelly mistreats his child, is far more common in the novels written before 1848[10] and one consequence is that father/child relationships are far more antagonistic here than in subsequent novels, where the antithetical character type, the ideal father,[11] is far more commonplace. This restructuring of the paternal model would seem to reflect the novelist's own private vision of the world. For in the 1830s and 1840s socialism enabled her to establish her distance from and opposition to the preceding generation far more than the conciliatory, albeit critical, thinking of the older years could have done.

The children's revolt more often than not takes the form of flight. Those characters who remain behind have no real depth. Such is the case of André (1834), who is capable of no more than an outburst of fury, an abortive attempt at murder, and is condemned to vegetate in the shadow of a terrifying father, himself a highly colourful character.[12] Moreover, reactionary views, a lack of respect for women and the absence of any true culture – indeed mere outright vulgarity – are all characteristics which define the authoritarian father as distinct from the new father who loves and protects his child.[13]

Loving fathers

These tender and indulgent fathers also fulfil the maternal function with regard to their offspring. They care for them 'more than befits a man'[14] and if they are in control it is only 'through the power of love'.[15] It goes without saying that in such cases, fatherhood is essentially a matter of love and duty – there is little if any talk of rights.[16]

Since the spirit of the Enlightenment also allowed for a freer expression of feelings, these fathers dare to exhibit a more tender side, although affection is far more readily expressed between fathers and daughters, between whom these novels present something resembling an idyllic relationship. According to contemporary accounts this was very often the case in middle class families, but such a happy pairing (a warm-hearted, open-minded father and an intelligent, virtuous and adoring daughter) was not unknown in noble circles in Sand's work. It is nevertheless significant that noble fathers, who are also considered as of 'incomparable goodness',[17] are never quite up to the mark of bourgeois fathers. This is because the bourgeois fathers are in harmony with the times whereas the noble fathers already belong to the past.[18]

What does all this mean if not that, in order to be a good father, love and devotion are simply not sufficient. Fatherhood is also, if not primarily, a spiritual matter and the man who is not on the side of progress can never properly fulfil the role of educator in the child's best interests, which are necessarily orientated towards the future.

SUBSTITUTE FATHERS

In a fictional universe where the vast majority of characters come from incomplete families, usually because of the absence of the father, it is quite natural that there should be a variety of father substitutes: their presence is a necessary element in the internal logic of the stories themselves. Adopted fathers, godfathers or paternal friends all replace the missing father and try to make up for and/or correct the deficiencies and inadequacies of the child's education. Above all, they offer a model of fatherhood which corresponds very neatly to the fantasies of those characters suffering from fatherlessness. This model is in no way inferior to the biological model, quite the contrary. Indeed it is this category of characters, sometimes merging with the category of spiritual fathers, which shows voluntary fatherhood in its most positive light. [19]

It should be noted here that rather than simply accepting voluntary fatherhood, these fathers actively lay claim to it. One of the characters in *Horace*, Paul Arsène, is a case in point. He loudly claims and proclaims his paternity of the child born to the woman he loves. Another clearly symbolic example is to be found in the socialist novel *Le Meunier d'Angibault*, where a small boy, the son of an aristocrat, has two adopted fathers: the one an educated bourgeois and the other an honest workman. 'Why shouldn't he be an educated man as well as a hard-working labourer?' inquires one of these voluntary fathers who, in the closing scene of the novel, lifts the child high above his head. This action of raising a child at arm's length above one's head, a fairly common iconographic and literary device, is above all a way of laying claim to fatherhood. The direction of the movement suggests the father's strength, a gesture of faith and hope for the future.

In certain situations in the novels, the role of the father is taken on by a lover or husband. Such characters accept responsibility for the moral education of a young woman and believe they are acting in the best interests of their protégée. Jacques, for example, undertakes to educate his wife in order to make her a free and happy woman, almost in spite of society. This superhuman man is doomed to meet with failure, however, as his young wife is unable to follow him to the heights to which he would like to take her; she suffers at not being treated as an equal; she regards Jacques less as a husband than as a father who inspires her with fear as much as love.[20] In this instance the Oedipus complex is working in reverse. But Jacques, ever the sublime father, knows how to forgive: he leaves in order to allow his daughter/wife to live happily, following her own heart.

SPIRITUAL FATHERS

Spiritual fathers, mentors of various kinds, all fulfil their educational role with the utmost seriousness.[21] They are the lay priests of a humanitarian religion, the more or less belated sons of that form of social romanticism which, enjoyed an extraordinary extension of life in Sand's work, despite a certain re-organisation of values. In the complete works, the proportion of these characters is very uneven: we find only five before 1848, whereas after this date there are at least a dozen who are much more actively involved in the plot (usually as *destinateurs*). This distribution is in itself significant: it tells us firstly that in the novels of Sand's maturity, truth is not the preserve of young revolutionaries or ecstatic artists but may also be found in mature characters who have experience of life and are responsible fathers. (A consequence of age? In part, naturally). The weighty presence of spiritual fathers in the Second Empire novels also tells us that social (or humanitarian) aspirations and faith in the power of the word (albeit somewhat less ardent than before) have outlived all the doubts and disappointments.

The first and most powerful figure in the series, in both his ardent passion and tragic grandeur, is Father Alexis, 'the most learned of all the monks', in *Spiridion* (1838).[22] This ideal master bequeaths to his spiritual child the most precious of legacies: a spiritual inheritance. Alexis dies fulfilled, since his life has not been without purpose: 'I know that I shall not drop like a sterile fruit from the tree', he says to his disciple. 'The seed of life has impregnated your soul. I have a son, a child more precious than my own flesh and blood; I have a son born of my own intelligence.'[23]

In this mystical novel, which sets before the reader an uninterrupted succession of masters and disciples, the organisation of the characters suggests that the search for truth must be the task of successive generations. This is one of the key ideas of Sand's work and it also explains why, in the final analysis, the fathers in her novels can never be treated lightly.

But the status of spiritual father is not the preserve of learned men alone. There are others, such as the almost illiterate 'rustic philosopher' in *Mauprat* (1837), who is an incarnation of that mystical abstraction 'the People' and becomes one of those responsible for the education of an ignorant and unrestrained young nobleman. In a novel published in 1845, *Le Péché de Monsieur Antoine*, it is an old Marquis with communist convictions who takes the place of a tyrannical father interested only in money. He becomes the 'real father' of a young bourgeois in order to initiate him into the world of a sort of mystical socialism.[24]

What marks a change in the post-1848 novels is, firstly, that the spiritual fathers are now all well-educated bourgeois and indeed learned men or nobles who are already living as bourgeois and secondly, that these characters are also good, responsible fathers. One of these emblematic characters is presented as 'the messenger of hope and of life', the 'antithesis of the sceptical poet'[25], possessing a certain wisdom 'of which he believes himself to be the depositary and not the inventor or the master'.[26] Another of his colleagues, a rich bourgeois philosopher, vigorously combats all forms of intolerance, particularly religious intolerance. He saves several characters from perdition and creates happiness all around him. The greatest ambition of his son Emile(!) is to be worthy of him for, as he says, 'he is my father, my master, my friend'.[27] The end of the story is marked by the apotheosis of the father; his is the victory of open-minded enquiry over obscurantism. In most of the novels of this period, fathers and sons are allies in the struggle they wage together in the name of freedom of thought and certain moral and spiritual values which they consider threatened by the spirit of utilitarianism.[28]

The protagonist of *La Tour de Percemont*, the last avatar of this type of father, combines the functions of biological father, substitute father and spiritual father. In addition, he is something very rare in this fictional universe, the head of a happy and unbroken family. He is a lawyer, a 'good and happy bourgeois'[29] and, through his profession, depositary of numerous secrets. He represents humanity idealised and has all the attributes of Providence itself since it is he who controls every aspect of the plot. Loved and respected by all, he is at one and the same time the master of ceremonies and the judge who dispenses justice.

The father in these later novels is strongly identified with a whole range of positive values. He is essentially conservative in so far as he defends the order and the values of the past, but he is presented as being open to all those forces likely to foster the perfectibility of man, the basis of all moral and social progress. On the one hand these glorified fathers exhibit all the masculine stereotypes: they have both physical and moral strength; but on the other, their unquestionable authority is softened by a tenderness traditionally considered as a feminine characteristic. These more or less androgynous characters embody a desire for harmony in much the same way as the heroines, whose force of character displays exactly the same mix of masculine and feminine attributes.[30]

Throughout the nineteenth century France lived through the consequences of its collective parricide,[31] a liberating act which was not unproblematic: the undoing of the father increased the insecurities of the sons.[32] Thanks to her personal experiences, George Sand was able to understand this better than anyone. In her later novels especially, as if in an attempt to return to the most acute desire of her childhood, she imagines a fictional world in which one can feel safe, thanks above all to the presence of fathers.[33]

It could be argued therefore that the 1860s and 1870s mark the 'Period of Fathers'[34] in Sand's career. This reign of the fathers happens to coincide with the advent of the learned men, with the omnipresence of bourgeois values and with the morality of common sense over passion. A change in the way young people are represented is also discernible. They are less able to defend themselves in their own right than were the young characters in the early novels, who still had sufficient resources of their own to succeed. Hence the increased importance accorded to the mentors, spiritual fathers and exemplary heads of families who surround the young. It should be pointed out that in these novels it is always a group of individuals which triumphs: a family surrounded by friends. This is the expression of the myth of union, a key vector in Sand's view of the world.

In 1833 a character in *Lélia* could still remark, 'What are these ties of blood which carry such weight in the eyes of common mortals, compared to the ties which heaven forges for us in the treasury of its mysterious affinities?'[35] Ties of blood, which are never assigned an absolute value nor even really seriously called into question in Sand's work, seem to be tied rather more tightly in the later novels: here, more often than not, biological fathers and spiritual fathers are the same person. But this represents only a minor modification of Sand's established value system, since the essential position remains unaltered: paternity is above all a moral and intellectual matter.

In the 'Republic' of the later novels therefore the Father has the status of first among equals; he is an idealised character in the system, an expression of the need for equilibrium and the desire that antagonistic forces be reconciled. His authority cannot be called into question because anyone wishing to do so would themselves need to have authority. On the other hand Sand's work always challenges paternal authority in its legal sense. In Sand's novels, paternal authority seems to be desirable because it is in fact necessary; but it is an authority derived from moral values and founded on intellectual qualities and above all on love. The Father, in this instance, is a utopian version of the father who hides some of the modern father's characteristics behind his traditional mask. While he remains the master, he has no desire to be exclusive: he is open to all sorts of influences and is capable of change and adaptation since he believes, along with his creator, that all human contact must be based on exchange.

Notes

1. 'Notes sur le roman familial' in P. Berthier, *Figures de fantasme* (Toulouse: Presses Universitaires du Mirail, 1992) p. 190. On this point, see also the prefaces by Denise Brahimi and Anna Szabó in Vols II and III of *Histoire de ma vie* (Saint-Cyr-sur-Loire: Pirot, 1994).
2. P. Berthier, 'Corambé: Interprétation d'un mythe' in P. Berthier *op. cit.*, p. 185.
3. Cf. *Histoire des pères et de la paternité*, Jean Delumeau and Daniel Roche (eds.) (Paris: Larousse, 1990) p. 283.
4. And, as a result, a very high number of children, both legitimate and illegitimate, who were abandoned for one reason or another. In 1831 31,000 abandoned children were recorded in Paris alone. Cf. *ibid.* p. 341.
5. Fifty-one absent fathers before 1848, as against 30 after that date. Alongside the 51 absent fathers in the novels of the pre-1848 period, there are only 22 fathers who are present and in 'good health'.
6. *Indiana*, Pierre Salomon (ed.) (Paris: Garnier, 1983) p. 68. Other characters appear to be the victims of a bad mother who is sometimes narrow-minded and selfish, sometimes bad-tempered and possessive and sometimes weak and over-loving. See Valentine, Pauline, Alezia (*La dernière Aldini*), Karol (*Lucrezia Floriani*).
7. *Gabriel*, Janis Glasgow (ed.) (Paris: Des Femmes, 1988) p. 50.
8. *Consuelo*, vol. I, Simone Vierne and René Bourgeois (eds.) (Meylan: Aurore, 1983) p. 235.
9. *Ibid.* vol. II, p. 307. In connection with the fatherless or illegitimate child, see also: *Simon*, *Teverino*, *La Petite Fadette*, *François le Champi*, *La Filleule*, *Elle et lui*, *Malgrétout*, *Le Piccinino*, *L'Homme de neige* and *Ma Soeur Jeanne*. Nor should we forget Lucrezia Floriani, an independent woman who chooses to bring up her children, born outside wedlock, alone. The case of the Marquis de Villemer is unique: he is the father of an illegitimate child. Here therefore the problem is dealt with from the point of view of a father who is suffering as a result of separation. As soon as possible he acknowledges paternity and shares responsibility for the child's upbringing with his wife, who is not its mother. This is one of the very rare examples of voluntary maternity. One can count also among the dead fathers a number of exemplary fathers whose

memory is religiously honoured as though to reinforce the myth of lost paternal omnipotence. This may be because they have met with an heroic death, like Valentine's father, killed at Waterloo, Simon's father, massacred by the Chouans, Fiamma's father, a hero of Italian Independence or finally the father of Michel-Ange Lavoratori and of the Piccinino, a more ambivalent but clearly similar case since '[he] has done great things for his country'. (*Le Piccinino* II, René Bourgeois (ed.) (Genoble: Glénat, 1994) p. 177.) Alternatively it is because they were already recognisable as the new father dreamed of by Rousseau, instanced by the enlightened nobleman who brought up his son 'in accordance with the religious belief of equality before the law' (*Horace*, Nicole Courrier and Thierry Bodin, eds., Meylan: Aurore, 1982, p. 108). It goes without saying that the memory of these fathers is beneficial since their legacy, in the moral sense, continues to comfort and sustain the children.

10. Twelve cases as against only six in the post-1848 novels.
11. Fifteen ideal (biological) fathers after 1848, only five before that date.
12. Psychological analysis is here linked with social observation, as is almost always the case in the work of Sand. Among the terrible and hateful fathers, who are always associated with negative values, we find representatives from all the social classes, from the nobleman who dispossesses and abandons his younger son (*Nanon*), through the rich bourgeois seeking to dominate everyone and everything, who is 'more powerful than the old lords' and wishes to buy his son's very thoughts (Cardonnet in *Le Péché de Monsieur Antoine*), to the miserable, drunken, vulgar workman who develops 'an unspeakable passion' for his daughter (Marthe's father in *Horace*). See also in this category: Aldine's father in *Monsieur Sylvestre*, the count of Flamarande in *Flamarande* and *Gabriel* where the paternal role is taken by the grandfather, a perfect incarnation of paternal authority.
13. Between these two categories it is also possible to identify weak fathers, fathers who are defective for one reason or another, and those who love their children badly and so make their lives difficult in spite of their efforts: the fathers of Juliette (*Leone Leoni*), Athénaïs (*Valentine*) and Joséphine (*Le Compagnon du Tour de France*). See also *L'Uscoque*, *La Filleule*, *Tamaris*.
14. This at least is what Fernande thinks in *Jacques* (Michel Lévy Frères/ Jules Hetzel, 1857) p. 157.
15. G. Sand, *Mont-Revêche* (Paris: Michel Lévy Frères, 1869) p. 206.
16. Jacques in the eponymous novel, speaks thus at the birth of his children: 'I receive this austere kindness from God in the contemplatively referential spirit of the man who knows where his duty lies.' p. 140.
17. *Mauprat* Claude Sicard (ed.) (Paris: Garnier Flammarion, 1969) p. 102
18. See *Mauprat*, pp. 98 and 157. Another variant is to be found in *Le Compagnon du Tour de France*. The function of father is here taken by the grandfather, 'perhaps the most advanced of all the nobility of the day'. (René Bourgeois, ed., Grenoble: Presses Universitaires de Grenoble, 1979, p. 259.) But we can see how the road which leads from theory to application is a long and arduous one: the idyll

between the count and Yseult comes to an end as soon as the young girl seeks to take advantage of her supposed freedom. For all that he brings up his daughter in the spirit of *Emile* (pp. 260–1 and p. 306), this father is incapable of ridding himself 'of the influences of his earliest education and prejudices he imbibed with his mother's milk'. In addition we see this character change: from 'adjuvant' he becomes 'opposer' to the heroine. Other novels where the good father plays a more or less important role: *Consuelo* (Albert's father), *Le Péché de Monsieur Antoine, Les Maîtres sonneurs, Les Dames vertes, Flavie, Valvèdre, La Famille de Germandre, Césarine Dietrich.*

19. This type of father is a constant element in Sand's fictional world and he appears in more or less equal numbers in the pre- and post-1848 novels. A few examples: *Simon* (Simon's godfather, an excellent lawyer and the personification of probity); *Le Piccinino* (Pier-Angelo, sensitive, a very good artisan and the archetype of the intelligent but unlettered man); *Les Maîtres sonneurs* (Huriel, '*le grand bûcheux*'); *Francia* (an honest bar-owner, austere and patriotic); *Flamarande* and *Les Deux frères* (a peasant bringing up a count's son).
20. This confusion of roles is reciprocal: Jacques too would prefer to remain a father to his wife and feels on occasion that she is his daughter. A similar but slightly different situation is described in *Le Dernier Amour* (1867). See also an early novella, *La Fille d'Albano*, in which a brother acts as father to his own sister. Before becoming Indiana's lover Ralph, first of the christic characters and her protector and liberator, defends and fights for her as a father: 'It is I who brought her up,' he says, 'I consider her my sister and more still my daughter' *(Indiana*, p. 147). Other father substitutes include Porpora and le Chanoine (loving and authoritarian versions) in *Consuelo* and rather sketchy or secondary figures in *L'Homme de neige, Tamaris* and *Flamarande*. The problem of adoption and all its risks is dealt with in *La Filleule*.
21. The only spiritual father not associated with positive values, defeated in fact by a lay person, is a priest, a usurper of the paternal function, Moréali in *Mademoiselle La Quintinie* (1863).
22. This character, inspired by Lamennais and P. Leroux, is in favour of a science based on tolerance and freedom of conscience and is a pro-Revolutionary, for whom the soldiers are no less than 'shining swords in the hand of the Lord of hosts'. *Spiridion*, Georges Lubin (ed.) (Plan de la Tour: Ed. d'Aujourd'hui, 1976) p. 246.
23. *Ibid.*
24. The old marquis, no longer thinking he can act in his own right, designates his successor with the simultaneous bequest of his worldly and spiritual wealth: he chooses a young bourgeois, who is given the task of organising a 'community' in order to realise the marquis' dreams. It goes without saying that this character plays a very active role in the novel's plot: he is the great reconciler who ends up arranging the fate of the young lovers.
25. G. Sand, *Valvèdre* (Paris: Calmann Lévy, 1884) p. 126.
26. *Ibid.* p. 163.

27. *Mademoiselle La Quintinie* (Paris: Calmann-Lévy, no date) p. 74.
28. Incidentally, these characters acknowledge that money has an important role to play in so far as material well-being is necessary for independence. Like Dutertre in *Mont-Revêche* however they regret that the bourgeoisie has become overly realistic and has 'thrown the world of dreams out of the window' (p. 86). A character in *Monsieur Sylvestre* (1865) outlines the same problem from the point of view of young people: 'if it is not against our own parents that we are fighting, it is against our fathers in the general sense of the term, it is against the cult of money which made such inroads during the last reign'. (Simone Vierne, ed., Geneva: Slatkine, 1980, p. 6.)
29. G. Sand, *La Tour de Percemont* (Paris: Calmann-Lévy, 1877) p. 14.
30. Nowhere in Sand's work is the image of paternal authority weakened by the presence of a character quite frequently found in literature, the comical, derisory father, victim of a despotic spouse. There is furthermore only one example of a suffering father, in *Mont-Revêche* (1852). However, although 'nailed to the cross like the Christ of fatherhood', he is not reduced to Old Goriot's fate: his repentant children love and honour him. At the novel's close, he is the 'adored head of a superb family. His forehead, untouched by the lines of age, is marked by divine serenity; but his eyes are those of a martyr who knows the tortures of life.'
31. Did Balzac not write in *Mémoires de deux jeunes mariées* that the Revolution had cut off the head of every single family in France?
32. Cf. Delumeau and Roche *op.cit.*, p. 445.
33. Naturally this is not true for every novel of this period. There are some exceptions, such as *Flamarande* (1875), where the father is disturbingly tyrannical or *Marianne Chevreuse* (1875), in which there are no fathers at all.
34. Simultaneously mothers become much rarer; those there are, in *La Tour de Percemont* for example, are far removed from the earlier glorified image – 'peasant on earth, queen in heaven' – to be found for example in *Simon* (1836). Mme Chantebel is a good woman, rather vain and a little stupid and described with some condescension. Moreover, it should be remembered that, with the exception of a few major figures, the mother is a rather disturbing and not very understanding character.
35. *Lélia*, Pierre Reboul (ed.) (Paris: Garnier, 1960) p. 21.

(Translated by Patrick Corcoran)

13

Politics and Fatherhood in the African Novel: *Le Chercheur d'Afriques* by Henri Lopes

Patrick Corcoran

The theme of fatherhood/paternity is particularly rich and resonant for students of the francophone literature emanating from regions such as sub-Saharan Africa which until relatively recently were under colonial domination. Whatever particular form it may adopt in any given country, the exercise of colonial power inevitably involves what Albert Memmi has called a duo of forces, that is, a special kind of relationship between a dominator and a dominated. The relationship between the colony and the 'mother-country' which colonialisation installs is clearly such a duo, and one for which the child–parent relationship acts as a particularly illuminating metaphor. Perhaps surprisingly an event such as the achieving of political independence has *per se* no particular power to disturb or invalidate the insights such a metaphor provides. In many ways the independent ex-colony has no option but to continue to function within (or against) set structures of thought and patterns of behaviour, and to continue to operate under the influence of socio-cultural role models which ensure that the mother-country goes on exercising an inevitable fascination. Like the child, the colony/ex-colony is a developing entity. As the child is dependent on the parent, so the colony/ex-colony is in a position of subservience with regard to the mother-country, from which emanate legal, linguistic, cultural and economic models. As is the case for the child, the colony/ex-colony is very likely to be seen as having no history of its own, and is likely to find that attempts to relate to the past are channelled through the experiences of the mother-country.

However, the portrayal of the colonising power in terms of a mother-country may evoke the wrong set of connotations. The French expression *mère-patrie* certainly suggests a degree of sexual ambiguity which is neither pertinent nor appropriate. In fact, the 'mother-country' may be a mother to the colonisers but it is more of a father to the colonised. It is probably more accurate to refer to it as a *Vaterland* (a neuter noun in German) and the parent–child relationship is more exactly a father–child relationship. It would certainly be more logical to associate the colonising power with a masculine symbolism to which can be assimilated notions of law-giving, authority, the responsibility for the transmission of certain values and various forms of interdiction, rather than with the feminine symbolism of fecundation and nurture.

In the light of these preliminary considerations, it is not surprising to observe that the novels which have emerged from sub-Saharan Africa in the last forty years have tended to reflect an almost obsessional preoccupation with two chief topics: firstly, political matters in the widest sense (that is matters relating to power and authority – whence power derives, how it is authorised, exercised, legitimised, challenged, transmitted and lost or won) and secondly, with questions relating to personal and/or cultural identity. The two are interrelated of course, and the interrelation pivots around the function, the role and the persona of the father.[1] The axis of power, though by no means to be read exclusively as a series of allusions to the paternal role and function, can never be totally dissociated from these either. Likewise, the axis involving the quest for personal or cultural identity is always ultimately an attempt to identify the authentic paternal persona. Who is my father? Who engendered me and therefore provides the authentic model for my future development?

A brief backward glance over the literary production of sub-Saharan Africa in the last forty years will provide examples of these two axes of reflection. For the first generation of authors from sub-Saharan Africa, writing under colonial domination, the discourse on power naturally tends to focus on the relationship of the Africans with the colonial administration. The works of Ferdinand Oyono, Sembène Ousmane, Mongo Beti and many others, are cases in point. Their novels have a clear political message and they more or less overtly demand the transfer of power from coloniser to colonised. These novels tend to authenticate the claim for political self-determination not by reference to notions of national sovereignty but by reference to an authority which derives from the very distinctiveness of their cultural practices. Interestingly enough, the generalised handover of power that finally occurred in or around 1960 did little to stem the flow of narratives that concern themselves with forms of fictionalised political analysis.[2] In post-independence literature the colonial administration is simply replaced by the head of state, tyrant or despot (conventionally referred to as 'Father of the Nation'), and the uneasy relationship between the people and the wielder of power continues in other forms. The basic problematic does not alter with Independence – an event which in no way proves to be a watershed. Indeed the various 'Fathers of the Nation' struggle to maintain their hold on power, or resort to violence in order to do so, precisely because they are cultural hybrids who may find it expedient to claim descendancy from African traditions but operate according to Western traditions.

Not all 'political' novels from sub-Saharan Africa are so obviously concerned with political events, however. In many novels the ostensibly political content may be minimal, but the preoccupation with power and authority generally remains and is worked out in dramas which have as their setting the workplace, the village or the city, or simply the family. In such circumstances and settings the appeal to tradition and traditional values has the power of law and functions as the ultimate arbiter in human affairs.

The preoccupation with issues relating to identity is not by any means neatly distinct from the preoccupation with power. In a novel like *L'Aventure ambiguë*, for example, the discourse on power is to a large extent depoliticised and expressed in terms of a battle for cultural survival. The coloniser is present in the novel not as the instrument of Western domination but as a symbol of the supremacy of one culture over another. The military battle has been lost long before the events recounted in the novel and the Diallobé people are portrayed as facing a different battle and one which is essentially spiritual in nature. Their cultural distinctiveness is founded on traditional beliefs and practices which define them as a group. Colonisation constitutes a challenge to the worldview upon which these beliefs are predicated and so the ascendancy of newly imported Western values, in part transmitted through the French school (the 'new school'), threatens not so much the physical as the cultural and spiritual survival of the tribe. The great paradox[3] is that the Diallobé, in seeking to preserve their own distinctiveness, have no option but to attempt to better understand the ways of those who know 'how to conquer without being in the right'.[4]

In this particular novel, the two preoccupations (power and identity) fuse into a single concern. But literary genres which at first glance seem worlds away from this politically conscious literature – for example works by writers such as Birago Diop, Bernard Dadié, Camara Laye, Amadou Kourouma and even, perhaps, much of Amadou Hampâté Bâ – by their very attempts to concentrate attention on specifically African cultural characteristics and African realities do so against a background of cultural as well as economic and ideological conquest. It is perhaps because they have gravitated towards the eye of the storm that such writers are able to disregard the whirlwind within which they are forced to operate.[5] Thus, attempts to define the specificity of African culture by harking back to a precolonial past, in many ways smack of attempts to ignore and occult the colonial experience, to deny these new sources of power and influence which contact with the West has introduced onto the scene.

The two preoccupations outlined above figure very prominently in the novel entitled *Le Chercheur d'Afriques* by the Congolese novelist (and erstwhile Prime Minister of that country) Henri Lopes. In *Le Chercheur d'Afriques* the father–son relationship is tremendously complex and not only enriches a reading of the power axis already identified but also focuses upon questions relating to personal, social and cultural identity.

The novel consists of some 97 un-numbered sections which form an account of the efforts made by the protagonist, a young *métis* or 'half-caste', firstly to identify and then to confront his biological father – a white Frenchman who as a young man had served in the colonial administration in the Congo and, having cohabited with a native woman and fathered a son, returns to France leaving his African family behind. The 97 sections or *tableaux* are not arranged according to the actual chronology of events and the setting also skips to and fro between locations in Africa and locations in France, particularly Nantes. In order to make sense of the narrative the reader must not only remain sensitive to chronology (that is, reconstruct the sequence of events recounted in the novel) but also gradually construct a view of the various characters drawing on information originating from different locations (Africa/France) and different historical periods (1930s/1950s). Thus the central quest of the protagonist – that of identifying and confronting his father in the flesh – is paralleled in the task which is delegated to the reader of the novel. Both are involved in deciphering a text and recreating from disparate sources plausible imaginative constructs which are constantly revised in the light of new evidence and tested against what is already known. Indeed, since the absent father has also published texts of his own, commenting on his periods of residence in Africa, the protagonist is not a reader of his own father in a merely metaphorical sense. He also does it literally.

As may be deduced from what has been said so far, the problem of identity clearly looms large in any attempt to comment on this novel. This preoccupation with identity is partly evidenced by the hesitation surrounding the naming of characters. Just as Proust introduces doubts about the sexual orientation of characters through a strategy involving ambivalent names: Gilbert/Gilberte, Albert/Albertine, François/Françoise, so Lopes forces the reader to reflect on the essentially cultural significance of names by ascribing different names to a single character. The protagonist is a case in point. The name given by his father is ostensibly André Leclerc, but his mother and close family have such difficulty in pronouncing the French Christian name that it is transformed into the africanised 'Andélé'. Andélé Leclerc then may be considered a starting point. Subsequently, it transpires that the father actually sends for his son and would have him shipped to Europe. The mother, Ngalaha, does not figure in this plan and so mother and son are forced to flee their village to prevent the possible kidnapping of the boy.[6] Andélé's efforts to understand what is happening forces the Western reader to undertake a comparitive critique of African as against European 'family values'. The boy's relief at the fact that the venerated absent father has finally once more made contact, immediately turns sour as the father becomes the hunter seeking out his progeny rather than the powerful protector seeking to establish a functional family. The reader may be in a position to comprehend if not to understand or accept the implicitly racist nature of the reasoning which underpins this scenario, but for the boy the affair remains shrouded in mystery. One outcome, however, is that his European name becomes dangerous and the condition set for his return from hiding is that he adopt an African name:

> the time had come to leave the hideaway but on the condition that there be no return to the village and no future mention of the names that the father had given to his child.
> Uncle called me and placed his hand on my head.
> – When the pirogue comes to take you downstream, forget your European name....
> – If anyone pronounces it in your presence, even when addressing someone else, act as though you had not heard. If not, beware of the wrath of heaven! If anyone tells you they are called Andélé or

> Leclair, simply nod in reply. Don't shake his hand. Don't make a friend of him ...[7]

And so the boy takes the name Okana.

Names are only problematic where a degree of cultural ambivalence exists. Hence, Andélé's 'brother', whose original name is Mbourangon, is given the name Bangassou when he arrives in the village from the bush. On his arrival in Nantes, where he is a professional footballer, he undergoes another name-change to become Vouragan.[8] Likewise, the name of the father, César Leclerc, is subject to doubt. Difficulties in reproducing the French phonemes by the Africans lead to a corrupt pronunciation of his name. Andélé's mother, for example, refers to him as Suzanne Leclerc.[9] Confusion about names when associated with cultural displacement clearly connect with anxieties as to the identity of the individual within a given cultural setting.[10] When Françoise Hurstel breaks down the concept of paternity into the three terms: function, role and persona, her remarks on function relate specifically to language:

> [Function] belongs to the domain of language and speech, it introduces meaning for a subject in so far as the latter is constituted by what psychoanalysts call the Oedipus complex. It is that which creates meaning in paternity or to borrow the expression used by C. Lévi-Strauss (1958) when referring to shamanic medicine: it belongs to the domain of 'symbolic effectiveness'.[11]

One may wonder to what extent César/Suzanne Leclerc, this confused linguistic construct denoting an absence, effectively functions as a father for young Andélé and what particular form the oedipal drive to confront such a father might take.

Questions of cultural affiliation are raised throughout the novel in other contexts than those relating to names and naming. Not least, for example, in the significance to be ascribed to *métissage* itself. Is it to be associated with positive or negative values, or is it neutral? In so far as the key relationship with the father is concerned, Andélé's status as half-caste is clearly a source of problems. How else to explain his father's abandonment and eventual reclaiming of his son, particularly when read against Joseph's experience? But ultimately, the answer to the question is that it depends on the context and the perspective. As a child in Africa, Andélé is the Commander's son – a status which is a source of pride and a mark of distinction and prestige which sets him apart from others. As an adult in France, his mixed racial origins have the advantage of increasing his appeal for members of the opposite sex, but they simultaneously expose him to the generalised racism encountered by blacks and people of 'exotic' ethnic origins. Neither in Africa nor in France can Andélé consider his ethnicity as unproblematic. In France for example, more often than not he has to argue for the right to be considered black. But in Africa too Andélé experiences difficulties in integrating fully into his native community, a point perhaps best illustrated by his reflections when he learns that his mother is to marry Joseph:

> There seemed to be no place for me in all these considerations. My worries remained. No, I didn't want to change my name yet again. Each new identity had proved traumatic. My friends no longer took me seriously. On each occasion, it was as if I was being asked to be ashamed of my very nature.... Because, apart from the Bagangoulous for whom I was unequivocally the 'son-son', in other words a true son, the rest variously called me 'coffee-coloured', 'the Yuropean', 'white yam' or most vulgar of all, 'half-baked Whiteman'. When things were going well I was a brother, but whenever a discussion started to turn sour I would be the butt of insults just like those madmen at whom children throw stones. As if I were an albino, an ill-bred foreigner, a jackal, a cockroach or a jellyfish.[12]

Andélé's status (in a very neutral sense) as a *métis* does not flow automatically from the fact of having been engendered by a white father. Cultural *métissage* is of necessity a question of identification, in whatever proportions, with the two cultures concerned. The absence of the biological father does not lead to his rejection by the son or by the son's entourage. 'The Commander' lives on to a certain extent in early childhood memories. He also lives on through the mythopoeic powers of his son who happens to chance upon a newspaper account of the military exploits of General Leclerc and for some time afterwards confuses him with his father. He finally lives on in the writings which Andélé eventually tracks down and subjects to a form of exegesis which further contributes to the image he gradually builds up of his father.

The African side to his personality should not be taken for granted either. In the absence of the biological father, substitute fathers are on hand to ensure that the paternal roles[13] of protector, provider and educator are adequately fulfilled. In an African context this is not particularly surprising. The structure of the extended African family, the not infrequent practice of entrusting children to the care of relatives for the duration of their upbringing and the very precariousness of life in Africa would suggest that the absence of the biological father is not a particularly rare occurrence. The Ortigues in their study on psychoanalytical practice in West Africa describe the following scenario:

> In a high proportion of cases, the patient is accompanied not by his father or his mother, but by a 'grandfather', a 'grandmother', a 'big brother', a 'big sister', an 'uncle'.... In the course of the consultation, we often learn that the 'grandfather' is the father of an ex-co-wife of the mother who has some family connection with the paternal grandfather, that the 'grandmother' is a 'sister-same-father' of the maternal grandmother, that the 'big brother' is a distant relative who has been entrusted to the patient's parents so that they can bring him up, or finally that the 'uncle' is a friend of the father who is considered with all the respect due to a real uncle...[14]

In the event, Andélé's acculturation to African values is ensured by Ngantsiala, his 'uncle', although his mother's marriage to Joseph ensures that there are in total at least four father-figures in his life: the absent white biological father, César/Suzanne Leclerc; two black social fathers, firstly Ngantsiala the purveyor of the authentic African tradition, but also perhaps his protective elder 'brother' Vouragan; and finally the *métis* father, Joseph Veloso, who in many ways serves as a model for the peculiarly hybrid set of roles which befall him as a consequence of his mixed blood.

These reflections on names, '*métissage*' and cultural affiliation should go at least some way to illustrating how notions of personal, social and cultural identity are of central importance in the sub-Saharan Africa novel, and in this instance at least are bound up with notions relating directly to paternity. A few complementary details about the eventual development of the narrative are necessary, however, before the analysis of the discourse concerning power relations can be adequately pursued.

Andélé, in the course of two visits to Nantes, eventually tracks down his father, Docteur César Leclerc. On both visits he is looked after in Nantes by his half-brother Vouragan, who ensures his integration into the black community of the city and introduces him to other friends including a girlfriend, Fleur. In a complicated story which unfolds at the mid-Lent carnival and therefore involves deliberately masked identities, Andélé is seduced by a mysterious stranger in Greco-Roman garb. Two days later Fleur tricks Andélé by adopting a disguise and substituting herself for the stranger in a second scene of seduction. The real identity of Fleur only becomes apparent to Andélé once he has left Nantes at the end of this first visit. Her name is in fact Fleur Leclerc and she resides at the address to which he has finally tracked down his father.

Thus, in the atmosphere of license of the carnival Andélé has committed an act of incest with his half-sister. But this act of incest is inscribed in such a complex web of relationships it is difficult to propose a simple reading. Any reading of it must take into account, for example, the classification of Vouragan in the role (but not the function) of father. This would seem to be borne out by two culturally specific sets of references. Firstly, the work of the ethnologist Ariane Deluz among the Gouro tribe of Ivory Coast has identified what might be called a generation 'slippage' which allows a brother to function as a father:

> In Pierre's story we are presented with a case of slippage between generations within a single patrilinear line; a brother situated on the oblique axis has been effectively transformed into a father, and a supplementary generation has thus been created – a fact which echoes a theme expressed in *Oedipe africain* (Ortigues, 1966, p. 57): 'The aggressive confrontation of the father by the son no longer tended to be expressed directly but was horizontally displaced towards the brothers.'[15]

Secondly, throughout Andélé's stay in Nantes, Vouragan plays the role of provider: accommodation, food and even clothing are provided for Andélé. Indeed considerable emphasis is placed upon the loan of fashionable clothes from the best African tailors. This perhaps rather odd detail takes on an interesting meaning when read in conjunction with one of the findings of the Ortigues couple as described in *L'Oedipe africain*:

> To have a father, is to be dressed by him. Custom dictates that it is the father who should buy his children's clothes... When the child is well-dressed and imagines others considering it as being well-dressed, it feels empowered by its father and loved by its father. There is hardly a single case where this aspect is not observable.[16]

Andélé's second visit to Nantes finally involves a meeting with the father. Disguised sufficiently to ensure that access to Dr Leclerc's consultation room is not denied him, Andélé nevertheless reveals himself sufficiently to his father to ensure that he is recognised. This is an occasion for Andélé to make one final transformation of his name: he announces himself as Moïse André Lebrun, the stereotypical name par excellence for the *métis*. The very evening of this visit Dr Leclerc dies.

Andélé's quest to confront his father thus involves an act of incest and brings about the father's death. Both quest and death occur in circumstances which adequately fit the protagonist for the role of sacrificial victim as outlined in René Girard's reading of the Oedipus myth which is proposed in *La Violence et le Sacré*. The carnival, for example, offers a propitious setting for the accomplishment of a sacrificial rite. As Girard writes: 'Properly speaking the "festival" is no more than a preparation for the sacrifice which is at one and the same time its moment of paroxysm and its logical conclusion. Roger Caillois has pointed out that any attempt to theorise the phenomenon of "festival" must be predicated upon a theory of "sacrifice".'[17] But above all, it is Andélé's distinctiveness, physically expressed in his status as *métis*, with all the attendant problems of social integration and exclusion it brings in its train, which eventually marks him out as a fitting sacrificial victim. As is the case with Oedipus, the sacrificial victim functions as a scapegoat upon which are focused all the ills of society. The price both Oedipus and Andélé pay is exile not death and, just as the Oedipus who emerges at Colonus is no longer portrayed in the negative light of Oedipus the King, so at the close of *Le Chercheur d'Afriques*, Andélé's return to Africa is portrayed as a positive event, perhaps even a homecoming.

The two discourses foregrounded in this reading of *Le Chercheur d'Afriques*, the discourse on power and the discourse relating to identity, both ultimately lead to the traumatic confrontation with the father. It is a confrontation which is unavoidable if key questions are to be answered. Whose authority is to be respected? How may substance be given to notions such as respect for law? How may transgressions of the law be identified and dealt with in a context where all differences have been eroded? And the key question of all – the 'who am I?' which triggers the quest for self-knowledge. *Le Chercheur d'Afriques* perhaps reiterates an ancient message: that in order for the subject to constitute itself as subject the death of the father is required.

Notes

1. See F. Hurstel, 'La Fonction paternelle, questions de théorie' in *Le Père, l'espace analytique* (Paris: Denoël, 1989).
2. For example: Sembène Ousmane, *Le Dernier de l'Empire*; Aminata Sow Fall, *L'Ex-Père de la nation*; Henri Lopes, *Le Pleurer-Rire*; Sony Lab'ou Tansi, *La Vie et demie*; Williams Sassine, *Le Jeune Homme de sable*.
3. La Grande Royale summarises this paradox when she says, 'The school towards which I am urging our children will destroy in them those things that today we prize and rightly take care to preserve. Perhaps their memory of us too will be destroyed. There are those who will no longer recognise us when they return from the school. What I am proposing is that we should accept to die in our children and that those who have defeated us should take up all the room that we have left empty.' Cheikh Hamidou Kane, *L'Aventure ambiguë* (Paris: U.G.E, 10/18, 1961) p. 57. (All translations are my own.)
4. 'Comment vaincre sans avoir raison', *ibid*. p. 165.
5. Edward Said captures the spirit of this process in his remarks on nativism and Nationalism as forms of resistance and opposition to colonial values. See *Culture and Imperialism* (London: Vintage, 1993) pp. 276–7. For Wole Soyinka's scathing analysis of the Négritude movement to which Said refers, see his *Myth, Literature and the African World* (Cambridge: Cambridge University Press/Canto, 1978) pp. 126–39.
6. The theme of kidnapping, real or virtual, is echoed by the experience of Joseph Veloso, also a *métis,* who is actually shipped to France by his white father. His education and basic well-being is financed and provided for, but he is isolated from any family contact and ultimately unable to pursue the adventure of acculturation when he is refused entry to a competitive exam on the grounds that he does not have French nationality. It is interesting to note that Joseph too changes name. He is originally named Joseph Velours 'à l'européenne' after his father, le Capitaine Velours, but his name is subsequently africanised to Veloso presumably in order to maintain a sufficient distance between father and son. (Joseph eventually marries Andélé's mother.)
7. Henri Lopes, *Le Chercheur d'Afriques* (Paris: Le Seuil, 1990) p. 176.
8. *Ibid*., pp. 142–3.
9. *Ibid*., p. 15.
10. It also, of course, calls to mind the Lacanian analysis based on the proposition that 'the metaphor of the Name-of-the-Father' rather than 'the real father' acts as the significant element around which is articulated the functioning of the subconcious. See 'D'une question préliminaire à tout traitement possible de la psychose' in J. Lacan, *Ecrits II* (Paris: Le Seuil, 1971) especially pp. 72–3.
11. Hurstel, *op. cit*., p. 244
12. *Le Chercheur d'Afriques*, p. 242.
13. Françoise Hurstel has this to say of the notion of the paternal role: 'We propose a sociological definition: "the totality of those particular

forms of behaviour which are expected either by the family or by society".' (Segalen 1981)...' *op. cit.* p. 244.

14. M.C. and E. Ortigues, *Oedipe africain* (Paris: L'Harmattan, 1984) p. 25.
15. Ariane Deluz, 'Des Pères et des frères' in *Le Père, l'espace analytique* p. 131.
16. M.C. and E. Ortigues, *op. cit.*, p. 103.
17. René Girard, *La Violence et le sacré* (Paris: Grasset, 1972) p. 180.

14

Loys Masson: Father as Text

Michaëla Mongelard

It was through literature that the Mauritian writer Loys Masson sought to create a place, a country for himself in his self-imposed exile.[1] The island, matrix and *prima mater*, structures his work, providing the solid ground, the rich earth from which the writing draws its strength. In his texts, repeated returns to the island reflect the impossibility of forgetting: the door to the past remains wide open and writing itself becomes memory, a testament to the father who was left behind to die and by whose image the son is still seared. The father haunts the son's work, as does the father to whom Kafka writes: 'My writing was all about you; all I did there, after all, was to bemoan what I could not bemoan upon your breast. It was an intentionally long-drawn-out leave-taking from you ...'[2]

The novel becomes a family romance[3] and the writer a child who, discontented with his lot and the parents fate has given him, invents a different life and family for himself. The more fertile the child's imagination, the richer and more prolific his invention; thus in Masson's work we find a rich production of virtual father figures acting as pawns whom the son moves at will on the chessboard of the novel. This discussion will concentrate on three representations of the father figure that appear in the novels *Le Notaire des Noirs* (1961), *Les Noces de la Vanille* (1962) and the short story 'Des bouteilles dans les yeux' (1970): the substitute father, the father as anti-hero and the father who must be killed.

Since the father in Masson's universe is by nature inadequate and incapable of fulfilling his role, he is replaced by another, the *father substitute*. In *Le Notaire des Noirs* we meet André, a puny, sad little creature shadowed by death. The story begins with his arrival at the home of the Galanties, his replacement family. The biological father is absent, as is the mother. The conditions are thus right for the child to find replacements for his inadequate, absent parents or, more precisely to find a substitute father. However André is given not one but several substitute fathers. The candidates are André's uncle Maître

Galantie, his cousin who is training to be a lawyer and Captain Bruckner.

The first candidate, Maître Galantie, has nothing of the kindly relative about him; he has taken André in for fear of the gossips and general opinion rather than out of any real affection. From the moment the boy arrives his uncle displays a lack of sensitivity, complaining openly about the wickedness of André's father in front of the boy and thereby taking the risk of tarnishing the halo of legend which helps to make his nephew's life livable. If Maître Galantie feels a moment's tenderness towards the child he is quick to repress or hide it. The narrator implies that this man who apparently rejects any substitute fatherhood has himself been denied biological fatherhood: 'And did I know that it was the regrets of a lonely man, the face of years and years of disappointments and disasters that Emile Galantie was striking in the child? ... He was rebelling against his thwarted desire to be a father.'[4]

In Maître Galantie we see the first failure of the process of substitution of the father figure. The second candidate, Captain Bruckner, seems more capable of fulfilling the father's role. This old sea-dog has all the attributes required to capture the imagination of a child hungry for dreams and wonders: 'Was Bruckner not the link between himself and his exiled father? He represented voyages and the sea, the long swell of stories ... When the Captain came in, the fantastical would enter with him.'[5]

The Captain can be seen as the writer's double, representing him in the novel. Both use words to invent fables whose function is to act as intermediaries between reality and dreams. The Captain does not scruple to lie in order to gain the child's love. His biggest lie concerns a whale's tooth, which occupies an important place in the narrative: it symbolises the failure of the fantastic. From a magical object (supposedly a tooth pulled from the jaw of a sea-monster by Captain Bruckner) the tooth is transformed into a profane one (a vulgar narwhal's horn bought by the Captain) and this destruction of mystery is a determining event in little André's progress towards death: 'the "Whale's Tooth" ... barred the entry to the harbour that death had been trying to penetrate for God knows how long. It proclaimed that it was possible to get away, to cast off, to escape.'[6]

The Captain's failure to uphold the fantastical and thus to save André from death can be seen as symbolising the failure of the writer who seeks in his text to recreate a familial idyll or, more specifically, to untie the knot formed by the father.

As the revelations concerning the Captain's 'exploits' unfold we witness a process of demystification and indeed of desacralisation of the father substitute. While the father poses a problem it seems equally difficult to find a replacement and this notion is reinforced by the failure of the relationship between André and his cousin, the narrator.

Of all the father-substitutes in *Le Notaire des Noirs* it is the narrator who gets the closest to André. The first time he sees the boy he knows at once that he will love him 'as my child'.[7] Throughout the novel the narrator uses the words 'my child' and 'my son'. But, like the other fathers, this father-substitute disappoints the son and worse, betrays and kills him. Like Peter betraying Christ three times, he betrays André several times. The most important betrayal is centred on another symbol of the marvellous, Flamingo Island. André has heard the cook telling how this island is the whales' graveyard, a magical place where there grow 'flowers that cry out when you touch them'.[8] We should note in passing the sexual symbolism of these magical flowers that cry out on contact with man. It is tempting to link this to the island in Michel Tournier's *Vendredi ou les limbes du Pacifique*.

André goes to Flamingo Island with the narrator and his mistress. Again, the child provides an alibi for the couple's illicit affair. But once on the island, André finds none of what was promised, the island is no sacred place, it is profane. With the desacralisation of the island, the fund of light that André needs to live is even further eroded, bringing him closer to the death that awaits him:

> If Flamingo Island had remained the unreachable paradise for him...–perhaps he would have conquered the drunken thief's face of his father...perhaps once this father had fallen, he would have mentally buried him in the Flamingo Island of glorious resurrections.[9]

The responsibility of the narrator father-substitute in André's death is thus as clear, as he himself confesses: 'If only I had been someone-else, perhaps I would have saved a child long ago.'[10]

From successive father-substitutes each as inadequate as the last, we pass to another inscription of the father figure in the text, that of an anti-hero, which continues the process of demystification or demythification noted above. One of the best examples of an anti-hero is André's father in *Le Notaire des Noirs*. In the structure of heroism defined by Gilbert Durand in *Structures anthropologiques de l'Imaginaire*, we find the following elements: extraordinary circumstances at birth and the hero's 'labours', in other words the obstacles that the hero must overcome and the exploits he has to perform to obtain the object of his quest. The status of 'revolutionary' enables André's father to be seen as a man apart who inhabits a different sphere from that of other men, thus meeting the first condition of the hero's superhuman characteristics. Young André is convinced of the extraordinary, superhuman character of his father: 'It's because my father is a revolutionary that he had to go and live in Madagascar. They were trying to put him in prison... They were, he told me so. He's the black people's friend. He defended them.'[11] Fernand Joliet, André's father, maintains this illusion of a hero father until the very end since, for him, the essential attribute that defines fatherhood is heroism: 'Must he not preserve his father's face? be right – in other words cut a heroic figure – for this innocent [André] whose look must not be dulled?'[12]

But he did not reckon with the destructive work of others. It is from a cousin, Louis Galantie, that André learns the truth, the hard truth, about his father: 'Since the revolution had finally broken out and his father had not been at the meeting place... wasn't that proof that his hero really existed only in the form of the drunkard, the forger exposed by Louis, the wreck?'[13] Driven by one last hope, André goes out into the storm to wait for his father, the father he still longs for against all the odds. For he must disprove to Louis Galantie's words, remove the vile mask of this new father and give him back the only one possible, the only one acceptable, that of the hero: 'He was right at the end of the short jetty with his feet in the water, Captain Bruckner's telescope pointing out to sea. Towards a hypothetical vessel coming from Madagascar... He was looking at nothing and nobody who was not the dream that had faded forever.'[14]

But there are no heroes, there is only an unfulfilled quest, and as Argentine, the black *nénène* or wet nurse of 'Des bouteilles dans les yeux', says, 'the day you can no longer respect your father you're alone', the day you can no longer respect your father you die. André catches pneumonia and dies of having waited for his hero in vain.

It is a small step from the anti-hero father to the father whom his child detests and would like to see dead. Between the two poles of this continuum, we find other images of the father, such as those offered by *Le Feu d'Espagne*: the guilty father, the jailer father, the murderous father (although the murder is only symbolic). But we do not have enough space here to investigate all these figures. We shall now concentrate on the Oedipus complex and on parricide, 'the murder of the father [being] the mythical prototype of the work of art'.[15]

In *Les Noces de la Vanille*, we again find the triangle as in Freud's schema, but it is a different triangle, which I shall describe as 'open', using a term adopted by André Green in his book *La Déliaison* to refer to a triangle which is not fixed but can take various forms. This triangle consists of the father, the son and a third figure who is the child's teacher. The boy is in love with his teacher and convinces himself that she loves him in return. However he soon discovers that the object of her affections is not him but his father. The father then becomes a rival, an enemy, 'the author and witness of the disappointment'[16] of the child, who swears to hate his father: 'I swear to hate you from now on.'[17]

The text contains an attempt at murder, at parricide against not the biological father but the father substitute, Esparon. Thus we see a transference of the son's aggressive drives on to a third party. It could be said that in diverting the murderous drive away from the real father and on to the father substitute, the text is censoring itself, as though it were seeking to deny the unthinkable, to silence the unnameable. There is thus a gap, a hole in the fabric of the text. A second triangle is grafted on to the first, consisting this time of Esparon, the father, the son and Marie-Thérèse, the son's fiancée. Marie-Thérèse is the object of desire of both father and son. To obtain this object, the son must 'kill' the father. But this parricide does not take place within the text since, when Esparon sets his heart on Marie-Thérèse, the son is in another place, far from Réunion and thus 'impotent'. Here again we can see a repression, a silence in the text. In the story 'Des bouteilles dans les yeux', the parricide motif can be seen again, but in a displaced form. A little boy, Emmanuel, is in love with his cousin, Hilda. It is considered sinful since Emmanuel is destined for the priesthood, and thus for purity. The boy has to hide his attraction from his parents, and particularly from his father, the supreme judge. The father's departure for work marks the moment when the door to the world of fantasy opens: 'when [the father] has been gone from the house for some time and Emmanuel can convince himself that he won't retrace his steps, he thinks of Hilda, he remembers their games and their words'.[18]

The father's return marks separation, the departure of Hilda. The father then becomes the 'executioner', the 'policeman'. The parricide consists in the transformation of the father into the figure of the devil, of Satan. For to call the father Satan is the same thing as killing him, as we can see here: 'The devil does not take on the shape of someone without at the same time making that person into the target of heavenly wrath;... It could not be worse if you poured poison into my glass.'[19]

The metamorphosis of the father leads us here to make links with the Polish writer of fantastical tales, Bruno Schulz, who excels in the art of the father's metamorphosis into an animal.[20] But Emmanuel's father is in deadly danger for only a brief moment. The end of the story shows him triumphing over the son: Hilda is sent home and Emmanuel loses his mother substitute, Argentine, because of the father. Alone, Emmanuel thinks only of death: 'What is loneliness, mother? Is it thinking endlessly of the eyes of the dead?'[21]

It is thus clear that in these texts it is impossible to eliminate the father, to do away with the omnipotent, omnipresent figure of the father. It is this omnipotence and omnipresence of the father that is dealt with in *Le Feu d'Espagne*, where a son, Manuel, is condemned to be the mirror in which the father contemplates his reflection: a differentiation without which the Same cannot become Other. At the end of the Massonian family romance, the gordian knot formed by the father remains complete; the text offers no resolution of the oedipal conflict. The text is the terrain of a game which produces multiple combinations based on the figure of the father. Like the artist of whom Sarah Kofman writes in *L'Enfance de l'art*, rather than creating or inventing, the writer recomposes and reworks the raw material, which is the conflict with the father: 'he does not create, nor does he invent, rather, he recomposes... with the aid of a specific and original form of writing'.[22] Thus we can see that in each case analysis of the relations between the text and fatherhood reveals a new configuration, as set out in Figure 14.1; in each of the texts mentioned the narrative function is taken on by a different figure: father substitute in *Le Notaire des Noirs*, the nameless son[23] in *Les Noces de la Vanille*, the biological father in *Le Feu d'Espagne* and an omniscient narrator in 'Des bouteilles dans les yeux'. Through writing, the writer invents, or rather reinvents himself, he symbolically kills his father and replaces the father's name with a new one, his own. As Guy Rosolato says in *Essais sur le symbolisme*, 'although the name is held in a lineage (that of the father) it also constitutes an origin once it is associated with the first work, it is the mark and proof of the second birth of the Ego'.[24]

The writer becomes both father and son, 'father since he is in practice the author of his work; son to the extent that the creation of this work has allowed him to be reborn'.[25] To rid himself of the 'smell'[26] of the father, one must, to paraphrase the African writer V.Y. Mudimbe, sound 'the cry and proof of this singular place', the place of the son, 'speak and produce'.[27]

Figure 14.1 Relations between text and fatherhood

	SON	NARRATOR	BIOLOGICAL FATHER	SUBSTITUTE FATHER
Les Notaire des Noirs	André	Substitute father	Absent	Narrator
Les Noces de la Vanille	X(nameless)	X	Present	Esparon
Le Feu d'Espagne	Manuel	Biological father	Present/ Narrator	Ludwig Kramer
Des bouteilles dans les yeux	Emmanuel	Omniscient	Present	–

Notes

1. Loys Masson was born in Mauritius on 31 December 1915. At the age of 23 he emigrated to France, where he lived until his death in October 1969, without once returning to his native island. From 1937 to 1969 he wrote prolifically; his work includes poems, novels, short stories and plays. Although little known by the general public, Masson won three literary prizes: the Deux Magots prize for *Le Notaire des Noirs* (1961), the Prix Antonin Artaud for his collection of poems *La Dame de Pavoux* (1965) and the Katherine Mansfield prize (awarded posthumously) for his story 'La Chose' in the collection *Des bouteilles dans les yeux*. Masson also received an award from the Del Duca foundation for his work as a whole.
2. Franz Kafka, 'Letter to his father' in *Dearest Father: Stories and Other Writings*, Ernst Kaiser and Eithne Wilkins trans. (New York: Schocken, 1954) p. 75.
3. Marthe Robert, *Roman des origines et origines du roman* (Paris: Grasset, 1972) pp. 43 and 46.
4. Loys Masson, *Le Notaire des noirs* (Paris: Laffont, 1961) p. 81.
5. *Ibid.*, p. 22.
6. *Ibid.*, p. 58.
7. *Ibid.*, p. 6.
8. *Ibid.*, p. 65.
9. *Ibid.*, p. 59.

10. *Ibid.*, p. 81.
11. *Ibid.*, p. 14.
12. *Ibid.*, pp. 18–19.
13. *Ibid.*, p. 244.
14. *Ibid.*, pp. 240–1.
15. Jean Le Galliot, *Psychanalyse et langages littéraires* (Paris: Nathan, 1975) p. 48.
16. Masson, *Les Noces de la Vanille* (Mauritius: L'Océan Indien, 1981) p. 29.
17. *Ibid.*
18. Masson, *Des bouteilles dans les yeux* (Paris: Laffont, 1970) p. 124.
19. *Ibid.*, p. 128.
20. See 'La Dernière fuite de mon père' in Bruno Schulz, *Le Sanatorium au croque-mort*, Thérèse Douchy, Allan Kosko, Georges Sidre and Suzanne Arlet trans. (Paris: Denoel, 1974).
21. *Des bouteilles dans les yeux*, p. 150.
22. Sarah Kofman, *The Childhood of Art: An interpretation of Freud's Aesthetics* (New York: Columbia University Press, 1988) p. 155.
23. The son who narrates *Les Noces de la Vanille* has no name. It would be interesting to explore this anonymity, given the importance of the name to the whole question of paternity.
24. Le Galliot, *op. cit.*, p. 52.
25. V.Y. Mudimbe, *L'Odeur du père* (Paris: Présence Africaine, 1982) p. 35 cited by Michael Syrotinski, 'V.Y. Mudimbe and the Francophone African Subject: Theories and Practices', paper given at the ASCALF conference, London, November 1995.
26. *Ibid.*, p. 13.
27. *Ibid.*, p. 35.

(Translated by Trista Selous)

15

Il Papa, Sade's *Pater* Beyond Compare*

Béatrice Fink

How can one describe, inscribe the Sadian father? When dealing with a text that tells it all, what remains to be told? Moreover, and paradox *oblige* (paradoxes are one of the mainstays of Sade's rhetorical agenda), the notions of gender and therefore of father are arguably liminal in the Marquis' prose. Sexual identity disintegrates in the magma of Sadian orgies. It is transmogrified into couplings, joints, crossovers, gear systems and other species of mechanical interplay set into motion by high carbon fuel. Nor should one forget that on the level of metaphor the overwhelming power, that which envelops and bears down on all others in Sade's cosmogony, is feminine and maternal, better yet step-maternal. The reference is to Mother Nature, bearing Matter Triumphant in her wake.

Yet, when all is said and done and the above reservations are taken into account, Sade's star player is without doubt the *pater familias*, be it in the shape of a firmly entrenched, hierarchised patriarchal system or that of the ubiquitous, hypertrophied phallic metonym. Male genitals, it should be mentioned, are most often lexically rendered in Sade's text by *vit*, a French term semantically linked to 'vital', and having by extension seminal and generative connotations, hence evocative of paternity. None of this is startlingly new, being well entrenched in Sade criticism. Hierarchised systems or microsystems in which *archein* – to command, to impose order – may be traced to male-founded filiation dot the Sadian landscape. In line with the Marquis' rhetorical recourse to clichés or dead metaphors, the reader in quest of the Sadian father is engulfed in phallomorphic clichés, that is to say in a display of figurative transpositions parading *seriatim* from the Surrealists to academics by way of *Tel Quel*.

The Reign of the Father, first in a series of Sade family papers (mostly unpublished letters) recently edited by Maurice Lever, encapsulates in its title the above-mentioned features under the double aegis of sovereignty and lineage.[1] Do these newly available materials reveal a hitherto unknown father-in-the-flesh by the name of Jean-Baptiste François Joseph, Count de Sade, progenitor of Donatien Alphonse François? Reality rarely lives up to fiction. Among the 800-plus letters in this volume, a mere two dozen refer to the future author and depict a disappointingly conventional father given the times and social milieu: kindly if somewhat distant, concerned, fussing over his son's education and what was originally mapped out as a military career. There is no inkling whatsoever here of fictionalisations to come. Regarding the count's offspring, a letter written when the son was twenty documents the 'sincere and tender friendship' that unites father and child.

As Denis de Rougemont might say, a successful relationship is one without a story. In order to narrate the father, the fictional mode best suits our purposes. In Sicily, a land where the not-so-unseen presence of the Mafia conjures up visions of Sadian power structures, two incidents were instrumental in dictating the present essay's subject. The first was a tour of Palermo's Chiesa del Gesù, a seventeenth-century Jesuit church overabundantly baroque given its manifold marble incrustations and surfeit of *trompe l'oeil* motifs. A *décor* depicting martyrised souls, a number of them in curiously unexpected positions, ornaments the church's inner recesses. Churches, specifically the excessively iconised variety, are indeed evocative of Sadian scenarios. In the Marquis' sign language, the omniscient, omnipresent and omnivisceral divine melds into an orgy of forms, colours, and postures, a dynamic coupling of *Eros* and *Thanatos*. Needless to say, it is the father who officiates.

The second incident was an encounter at a place where heaven meets earth – Rome's airport – with an irresistible Italian cake named 'Il dolce del Papa' (the Pope's pastry). I shall thus deal with the *pater par excellence*, the Holy Father, the Sovereign Pontiff enthroned on the Holy See. This spiritual surrogate father is one of two main characters in a lengthy episode of Sade's *Juliette*,[2] where he takes the form of a fictionalised version of Pius the Sixth, otherwise known as Braschi.

Before dealing with this pious personage, a quick glance at the rules of the Sadian game is in order. The Marquis' reader is faced with what might be termed a splinter-script insofar as the text relies on stylistic schisms and (if another consonance be permitted) ruptured rhetoric. The latter manifests itself in the constant intrusion of performance in discourse, the theatricalising of theory or *passage a l'acte* being an essential ingredient of Sadian *rhetoric*.[3] Thus the long (often overlong), ponderous philosophical pronouncements in which rhetorical sleights of hand abound are systematically transposed into live performances, the constant oscillation between pure and applied theory forming a sort of *locutio interruptus*. Appended to this swing of the pendulum is narrational displacement, since the exogenous narrator/orator changes positions when he/she more often than not comes on stage to take part in the action, thereby becoming endogenous to his/her discourse as object, set, or mere moving part. In this fashion total control of the word – through oration, narration, utterance – becomes an unconstrained discharge of energy and turns, into the uninhibited transgressive force that substitutes the unbound for the bound when discourse turns into action.

As to stylistic schisms, these manifest themselves linguistically in the shape of lexical confrontations or rather clashes triggered by means of incompatible juxtapositions (such as obscene/scientific/manneristic language) resulting in a disharmony or disequilibrium calculated to shock the reader and subvert established stylistic conventions. This effect is usually, but by no means solely, produced by a perfidious blending of literal and metaphoric terms, the latter tending towards flowery clichés with mythological leanings. These splintering and rupturing techniques are part and parcel of Sade's montage. Their role in the make-up of *Il Papa*, the overdetermined father, is especially effective in the present case since the two protagonists, Juliette and the Pope, are at once theoreticians and practicians, both extra- and intradiegetic characters.

Juliette is *New Justine*'s sequel. Together these companion novels constitute a highly expanded version of *Justine*, which is in turn an enlarged version of *The Misfortunes of Virtue*. *Juliette*, however, is unique in that, among other things, a non-negligible part of the heroine's peregrinations take place in Italy. Sade's only personally familiar foreign county was Italy. The novel's Italian sequence thus has a ring of regional authenticity and a richness of documentary detail lacking in his other foreign scenarios, and otherwise to be found only in his Provençal tales. The setting of the Vatican episode and its representational dimension are thus based on the real, not merely the conventional, and as such they enter into what constitutes the papal father. Another detail worthy of note: *Juliette* (1797) was drafted during the post-Revolutionary years. Decapitation both as reality and symbol, that of the sovereign and the gentry, that of the father and his prospective lineage therefore come into play, whether as *imaginaire* or as trauma. Parricide is the flip side of the overdetermined father.

Juliette, both heroine and principal narrator of the novel bearing her name, in constant pursuit of ever more sensational adventures, decides to travel to Italy, her main stopovers being Florence, Rome and Naples. At this point of the narration she has attained philosophical enlightenment, specifically where religion is concerned. In other words, she has turned into a radical materialist. Not only, as the author intimates, is she naturally 'predisposed' in this regard, but she is likewise a hardened libertine, having trained under the watchful eye of Saint-Fond (who is, as one might expect, Minister of Finance) as well as Noirceuil, her husband-to-be. She arrives in Rome with her equally libertine companion Olympe Borghese, and sets up an appointment with Pope Pius in the Vatican upon arrival. Sade's men of the cloth, be it noted, are reverse-image projections, choice targets in a hyperbolised satire of the Church and its institutions and, by extension, the Establishment at large. Be they in charge of enclosed communities cut off from society at large, such as monasteries, or merely adventuresome wayside encounters, whether humble monks or princes of the Church, they are almost invariably depraved and debauched, fictional ammunition meant to pulverise a vast array of 'prejudices'. These subversive antifathers nonetheless retain their paternal attributes in that the patriarchal hierarchy – the fold of the victimised faithful headed by a *pater familias* – remains in place. The *New Justine* abounds with just such creatures. In *Juliette*, where Sade's *machine infernale* goes into high gear, the road leads all the way to the ecclesiastical summit, a unique occurence in the Marquis' prose.

In the elaborate Vatican episode, an unseen yet very present priestly apanage surrounds Pope Pius by way of historical retrospective, with two particularly vicious cardinals (one of them being France's ambassador to the Holy See) in the foreground.[4] Nearly all of the high ecclesiastics appearing in retrospect are real-life characters taken from history or the contemporary period, not mere inventions. When Juliette enters this context and comes face to face with the Pope, she is introduced as 'the desired young Frenchwoman'.[5] This amounts to a transposed encounter between France, 'The Church's eldest daughter' (a standard reference to the French Catholic Church), and her holy father. Is this lexical foreplay blending incense with incest? Priests, it should be remembered, tend to call the members of their flock 'my child'.

Daughters can be capricious and demanding. Juliette accordingly states her terms: 1) that she be handed the keys to all of the Vatican's rooms; 2) that Braschi deliver a soliloquy on murder; 3) that he set up an orgy on the altar of Saint Peter's. The main attraction of the couple's subsequent key-laden house tour is the Vatican's celebrated portrait gallery, authorially placed under the sign of the key. The one portrait that stands out and merits commentary in this privileged domain is that of Saint Peter with the Three Keys, emblematic, as Braschi puts it, of unlimited power. The conflating of Pius and Peter, the archetypal holy father, is an ongoing process that picks up speed during the simulated mass that later takes place on the altar of Roman Christendom's holy of holies. Framed by the columns of Bernini's baroque canopy, the Pope is repeatedly iconised in a series of variations on the royal portrait theme. In this case it is live and encased in baroque surroundings overflowing with ornamental supernumeraries. Twenty adolescents of both sexes are poised near huge background screens, while three priests, six choir boys and an equal number of androgynous cherubs[6] are also in attendance. The list is endless. Clothes, when called for, are given the same minute attention as the decorative objects such as the oriental rugs, ottoman and garlands of flowers scattered about. The text reveals that this piece of staging is quite conscious on the author's part, with everything in this hothouse of excessive representation carefully positioned for wide-angle lens exposure, for the ultimate take of the ultimate father–daughter coupling. The ritualised orgy that follows is arguably the most intensely transgressive episode of all of Sade. Unremittingly obscene language enhances a sequence of cumulatively sacrilegious montages, with the papal reproductive organ, his *vit*, invariably at the controls.

This unholy scene is performed on the main altar of the church of the founding holy father, Saint Peter, he of the keys, earthly representative of the divine father. His descendant Pius the Sixth, depraved father and 'mitred philosopher' consolidates his power by thrusting his vital parts into the filial Juliette, likewise inserting in her body the eucharistic host and eternal father, Christ the Pancreator. However, the multilayered-father scenario merely follows a suitable curtain-raiser orchestrated by Juliette: a recital of the names of scores of unholy fathers complete with indications of their unmentionable crimes, in order, as Juliette the narrator puts it, to affirm Braschi's infallibility. In a *mise en abîme* as deep as the Vatican's portrait gallery is long, twenty-five popes file past: two Bonifaces, three Clements, one Stephen, three Gregorys, one Innocent, three Johns, one Leo, one Pascal, one Paul, two Piuses, one Sergius, two Sixtuses, one Alexander, one Benedict (Benoît), one Julius and one Urban. This resort to a proof-by-numbers strategy is quite typical of Sadian rhetoric and fits in nicely with the author's obsessive need to systematise. Here, however, the text takes us one step further. Juliette's litany also turns into a multifaceted mirror in which the Sovereign Pontiff's image is reflected ad infinitum. In the context of his ecclesiastical lineage, the Pope is quite literally projected as the ubiquitous paternal prince.

The obverse of filiation is discontinuity, and Sade is known for perversely destroying that which he constructs. His fiction is rife with cases of parricide and infanticide. While Braschi in person remains uncontested and unmolested as *pater* beyond compare (even though the key-laden Juliette manages to loot the Vatican's bottomless treasures before fleeing to Naples), he nonetheless delivers his promised disquisition on murder that is in fact its eulogy. The philosophical justification of such a stance lies in the contemporary materialist rallying cry, namely that birth, life and death are merely differing aspects of the same phenomenon in nature's unending cycle. In a universe governed by the destructive principle, the Pope declares, history provides us with numerous examples of social institutions that grant fathers the power of life and death over their children. Nor does Braschi forget to make a systematic defence of parricide,[7] sons being nothing more than potential fathers desirous of positioning themselves in their own father's place. Earlier in the novel Juliette's mentor Saint-Fond entrusts her with a mission: to assassinate his father. When she hesitates, being not quite the hardened libertine she later becomes, her other mentor Noirceuil firms her resolve by delivering an apology of parricide: what links are there to bind child to father? One neither chooses him nor can he be identified beyond a doubt (these are pre-DNA days). The father's identity is thus a matter of probability or conjecture rather than incontrovertible proof. At best, children are involved in a matter of guesswork. In the case of Saint-Fond's father, there are additional damaging circumstances on record: he is already sixty-six years old and soon meant to disappear in any case. Noirceuil remains adamant: 'He who kills an old man is merely helping nature accomplish her designs' (VIII, p. 244).

Doing away with the father also has distinct fringe benefits for Saint-Fond, who proceeds to inherit the former's immense wealth. A similar situation arises when the libertine Brisa-Testa, aided by his combined sister, spouse, and accomplice Clairwil, kills his father in a well-planned prandial murder whose grand finale occurs at the meal's end since the hapless father 'falls stone dead over dessert' (IX, p. 229). In line with the coincidence of *Juliette*'s genesis and the Revolutionary years, those of the real and symbolic beheading of a collective father, one should add Sade's rhetorical intent of fragmenting established filiation in order to replace it with an alternate system. Quite apart from a political reading of parricide, decapitation has further dimensions: in a world of perpetual motion power-seekers must continually reposition themselves in order to find their way to the summit.

The lethal sword, however, is double edged since those at the patriarchal summit want nothing more than to stay in place permanently and rid themselves of successors by preventive maintenance. Hence the resort to infanticide. Generally speaking, all sons and in certain cases daughters are a menace for the father in the Sadian context. Infanticide thereby becomes a pre-emptive strike in the art of self-defence. Returning to the Pope's disquisition, he praises infanticide in that it 'breaks the links of lineage' and 'buries a goodly number of seeds' (IX, p. 180). The most striking example provided is that of a redistribution of longevity: 'A king of the North whose name escapes me immolated nine of his children for the sole purpose, as he put it, of prolonging his days at the expense of those who were being deprived of them by him' (IX, p. 190). Albeit a manifestation of prejudice, according to Braschi, this form of behaviour is forgivable insofar as it is conducive to pleasure.[8]

The question of author intentionality inevitably rises to the surface. Is Sade indeed thoroughly committed to convincing his reader that a hierarchical microcosm based on male/female, master/victim dominance is in order? One centred on institutionalised phallocracy, on a patriarchal hierarchy? *Juliette*'s interstices reveal a greater degree of complexity than at first appears. As Maurice Blanchot so pointedly notes, Sadian logic leads not so much to supreme power as to supreme annihilation.[9] Inspired by Nature's ways, Sade is apt capriciously to destroy that which he has created, the paternal paradigm being no exception. Overdetermined, unholy fathers on the one hand, exterminated or exterminating ones on the other, when all is said and done, the whole fatherly equation is up in the air. But what about Juliette, the heroine who basks in glory at the novel's end and is the ultimate key-holder and keeper of the word? Has she the makings of a father? The textual picture is unclear. She may, however, be viewed as a man: does the reader not discover early on in the novel that she has a clitoris of gigantic proportions?

Notes

*This essay is the English version of a text originally drafted in French and entitled '*Il Papa*, père sadien hors pair'.

1. M. Lever (ed.), *Le Règne du père (1721–60)* (Paris: Fayard, 1993).
2. D.A.F. de Sade, *Oeuvres complètes* VIII and IX, (Paris: Têtes de feuilles, 1973). Parenthetical page references are to the edition above unless otherwise indicated.
3. An excellent analysis of Sadian theatrics or staging may be found in Roland Barthes, *Sade, Fourier, Loyola,* (Paris: le Seuil, 1970) pp. 127–74.
4. There is even a London connection since the list of wicked monsignors includes a bishop of London who takes pleasure in plucking the body hairs of all those unwilling to convert to catholicism.
5. All translations into English are mine.
6. The term Sade uses is 'ganymède'.
7. Here is an example: 'In which way can your father's body... be considered more precious in nature's eyes than that of your slave? ...That body so treasured under your laws shall be reproduced and metamorphosed just like that of the helot you hold in such contempt' (IX, p. 179).
8. Cf. on the case for infanticide: 'This right is firmly entrenched in nature; and what is one more entitled to dispose of than that which one has provided? If murderous crimes were rated according to their degree of evil (while containing none) infanticide would surely rank at the bottom' (IX, p. 180). Also 'In the kingdoms of Zopit and Tropodane, fathers strangle their own children, whether male or female, if they don't like their appearance and in Madagascar all children born on Tuesdays, Thursdays and Fridays are thrown to the wild beasts by the authors of their days' (IX, p. 188). With Sade, history often veers towards the fantastic!
9. Maurice Blanchot, *Lautréamont et Sade* (Paris: Minuit, 1963).

16

Kafka's 'Papa'

Sander L. Gilman

The central problem of *fin de siècle* 'human science' is stated in the subtitle of Friedrich Nietzsche's *Ecce Homo*: 'how one becomes what one is'. Jews lived in terror, even greater than Nietzsche's, that they were fated to become what they were said to be.[1] Nietzsche proposed, 'I am merely my father once more'. Certainly no 'case' in the history of becoming one's father is more compelling than than that of the Prague Jewish writer/civil servant Franz Kafka. In his 'Letter to his Father' (1919), since its publication one of the touchstones of Kafka interpretation, this anxiety is paramount. This letter, often quoted in 'oedipal' readings of Kafka's relationship to his father, is an elaborate fiction about Kafka's anxiety about his own body's predestination to become his father's. This is not the strong, paternal body, but the ill body of a father who manipulates his illness for his own ends, at his son's expense.

In 1911 Kafka wrote a short autobiography in his diary (*D1*, pp. 197–8).[2] In it he traces his lineage through the Löwys, his maternal family, which begins with his namesake, his mother's maternal grandfather, Adam (Amschel) Porias (1794–1862), 'a very pious and learned man' who 'bathed in the river every day, even in winter'.[3] These begats, in the matrilineal Jewish tradition, return to his mother's mother who 'died before her time of typhus'. Her death at the age of twenty-nine so affected her mother (Franz Kafka's great-grandmother) 'that she became melancholy' and committed suicide in 1860. Then he writes about his mother's great-grandfather, a miracle rabbi, whose four sons 'all died young', except for his namesake Amschel, who was known as 'Crazy Uncle Nathan', and one daughter, his mother's mother. One of the brothers converted and became a physician. What Kafka does not mention is that his mother, who had 'weeping spells and melancholy', was orphaned at three, and was raised with her two brothers and three half-brothers, one of whom, Kafka's uncle Rudolph, was also a convert. Kafka's father, according to the letter Franz never sent him, agreed that his wife's family was tainted by madness, demonstrated by their apparent hereditary predisposition to a whole range of illnesses for which madness was the master category. For Jews of the time, madness was definitively proven by symptoms such as melancholy or conversion, for only a mad person would try to convert out of a race. Kafka sees himself half-ironically as in that maternal tradition. In a letter to Hedwig Weiler from April 1909 he writes: 'If there is anything you want to know about me, my mother is due for an operation next week; my father is more and more on the downgrade; my grandfather collapsed unconscious today; and I'm not so well myself' (*LF*, p. 53).

Kafka's notion of inheritance is perhaps best documented in his story 'Eleven Sons' (1917), in which the inheritance of illness is central. Not only do the sons inherit the positive qualities of the parent but also their physical anomalies. The smaller left eye of the second son is equated with a 'small irregularity of the spirit, a kind of stray poison in the blood' (*S*, p. 420). The sixth son is not ill;

> his health on the contrary is very good – he sometimes staggers, especially at twilight, but he needs no help, he never falls. Perhaps his physical growth is the cause of this phenomenon, he is much too tall for his age. That makes him look ugly in general, although he has remarkable beauty in detail, in hands and feet, for instance. His forehead, too, is ugly; both its skin and its bone formation are somehow arrested in their development'. (*S*, pp. 421–2)

The eleventh son is the frailest, a frailty that masks an inner strength. It is not incidental that there are eleven *sons*. It is the masculinity of the father, which is the equivalent of his Jewishness, which is present in the sons. And along with all of the positive qualities ascribed to this inheritance, Kafka also stresses the pathological – the very form of the body reflects the inheritance from the father.

But it is not the illnesses ascribed to his mother's family that form the centerpiece of his concern, but rather his anxiety that he must become his father. He writes on 16 October 1911, 'the whole staff gave Father notice. By soft words, cordiality, effective use of his illness, his size and strength, his experience, his cleverness, he wins almost all of them back' (*D1*, p. 97). His father's heart pains haunt his own sense of himself. In the famed passage about the writing of his first great story, 'The Judgement', Kafka wrote on 23 September 1912: 'As the maid walked through the anteroom for the first time I wrote the last sentence. Turning out the light and the light of day. The slight pains around my heart' (*D1*, p. 276). He feigns 'nervousness and cardiac excitability' to quit the job he disliked at the Assicurazioni in July, 1908.[4]

There is a detailed literature that claimed that Jews had a much higher incidence of heart illness, which was nonetheless a vague category in the nineteenth century. The forensic psychiatrist Cesare Lombroso, in his 1894 study of Jews and anti-Semitism, argued that Jews in Verona between 1855 and 1864 showed a 9 per cent morbidity rate due to heart disease, as against 4 per cent for the general population.[5] Lombroso's explanation was the environment in which they were forced to live, their 'passionate temperament, the anxiety of wagering and profit, the force that results from poor living conditions'. This mix of predisposition and context was typical of debates about Jews and heart disease, but ultimately the Jewish character, Jewish nervousness, is the deciding factor. According to Martin Engländer, it is the 'struggle of modern life, the haste and drive, the hunt for happiness', coupled with the weakness of the Jewish nervous system caused by centuries of oppression, which are at the core of their 'nervousness and neurasthenia'.[6] According to the German psychiatrist Otto Binswanger, 'among the European nations the Jews supply, relatively, the largest contingent of neurasthenics'.[7] Even James Jackson Putnam, the leading American specialist in nervous diseases, could claim that without exception 'the psychoneuroses in general are particularly common to the Latin and Hebrew races'.[8]

This nervousness is represented in Kafka's own struggle with the trope of the inherent instability of the Jew. In February 1911, Kafka writes, 'as I was getting out of bed this morning, I simply collapsed, and for a very simple reason, I am badly overworked. Not in the office but because of my other work. To me this means leading a horrible double life, from which madness probably offers the only way out' (*D1*, p. 44). In July 1912, Kafka spent three weeks at Jungborn sanitarium because of 'a pathological nervous condition manifesting itself in nearly continuous digestive disturbances and sleep problems'.[9] (Kafka, like many Central Europeans at the *fin de siècle*, often spent his 'holidays' at health spas.) At least this was his claim when asking for extended leave. He observes his mental state as a sign of his own decline: 'Am I in decline? Almost all signs speak for it (coldness, apathy, state of my nerves, distractedness, incompetence on the job, headaches, insomnia); almost nothing but hope speaks against it' (*D2*, p. 140). In 1913, he records in his *Diaries* a list of his symptoms: '1. Digestion 2. Neurasthenia 3. Rash 4. Inner insecurity' (*D1*, p. 287). The neurasthenia of the Jew, like the Jew's hysteria, is a product of the Jew's inbreeding and the confining spaces of the city in which the Jew has been housed. Indeed, Kafka believes that he has found the cure for his neurasthenia in gardening, until he learns in May of 1913 that the local gardener had committed suicide. On 6 October 1915, he again notes: 'Various types of nervousness' (*D2*, p. 138).

But in a letter to his fiancée Felice Bauer on 5 November 1912, he attempts to persuade her that his health is fine, that his 'nervousness and cardiac excitability' are but the signs of a sensitive soul destined to be a writer: 'My heart may be comparatively sound, but for any human heart to stand up to the sorrows of bad writing and the joys of good writing is not easy. I was in sanatoria only on account of my stomach and my general weakness, not forgetting my self-enamored hypochondria. One day I shall have to write at length about all this' (*LF*, p. 27). Later, on 4 August 1913, he provides further documentation of the state of his heart: 'Lately, however, I have had palpitations, followed by stabs and pains in the region of the heart, which are no doubt caused largely, if not altogether by the unbearable separation from you. But they are also partly due to the fact that I have recently been swimming too much' (*LFe*, p. 296). His biographers record how Kafka attempted to alter his body through sports of all types, including swimming.[10] But he could not avert his destiny, which was to become his father and all that his father represented – the ill Alfred Dreyfus, the diseased Jew.

The analogy is not at all forced. For his father had in fact been a soldier. Between 1870 and 1880 Hermann spent three years in the Austrian army, quitting the service with the rank of corporal in the 11th Bohemian Infantry Regiment (the k.k. Kronprinz Albert von Sachsen Regiment) stationed at Pisek.[11] He evidently enjoyed his service in the military for he even enlisted after his draft period ended. Indeed, the image of his father as a healthy soldier haunts even Kafka's dreams. In 1916, he dreams of a regiment of soldiers marching by, whereupon his father comments, 'One has to see this, as long as one is able.'[12] For Kafka this attribute of the father is literally inscribed on the father's body. In 'The Judgement' (1912), in Kafka's account his first 'real' piece of writing, the ill father mocks his son in a very specific way. The father may be ill but in the eyes of the son, he is still 'a giant of a man' (*S*, p. 81). This sickly figure suddenly metamorphoses into his former self when he mocks his son because of his engagement: '"Because she lifted up her skirts," his father began to flute, "because she lifted her skirts like this, the nasty creature," and mimicking her he lifted his skirt so high that one could see the scar on his thigh from his war wound' (*S*, p. 85). This 'war wound' marks the father's body as the soldier's body, and mocks the son as a male in thrall to a woman and unable to serve. Kafka has the ill father enact the seductive woman's role! The scarred warrior and the feminised male Jew with a high voice merge in the figure of the father. Thus the 'son' who later writes to his father in 1919, 'You encouraged me, for instance, when I saluted and marched smartly, but I was no future soldier' (L, p. 120), uses his father's desire to have a soldier as a son in order to draw his own masculinity into question.

The father's unnamed illness in 'The Judgement' seems to make him into an invalid. In *The Trial* (1914), the lawyer to whom Joseph K's uncle brings him in the dead of the night clearly suffers from a heart condition. K's uncle asks immediately upon being told that his friend is ill: 'Is it his heart?' (*T*, p. 100). When they finally see the lawyer, the uncle attempts to dismiss his illness: 'Are you really in a bad way? I can't believe it. It's one of your heart attacks and it'll pass over like all the others.' But the lawyer's diagnosis is more pessimistic: 'Maybe, but it's worse than it's ever been before, I find it difficult to breathe, can't sleep at all, and am losing strength daily.' This exchange encapsulates the myth-making that Kafka is able to spin about heart disease. On the one hand, from the external point of view, it is not truly serious; it happens over and over again, but there is always a recuperation. Indeed, it might really only be a form of hypochondria. Thus it is analogous to the miraculous recuperation of the father in 'The Judgement'. On the other hand, as seen from within, it is a sign of morbidity, of the decay that will eventually lead to death. The lawyer's description of his symptoms, moreover, ring true as an image of Kafka's own 'illness' as well as those symptoms ascribed to his father.

By April 1916, Kafka was diagnosed as having a 'cardiac neurosis', for which the prescribed treatment (which he did not do) was electrotherapy, used for traumatic neurosis at the time.[13] His own reading of his ill body, perhaps already in the first stages of pulmonary tuberculosis, was in terms of mental illness. He writes on 1 September 1916: 'Since yesterday, after three days remarkably free of headaches, I have been feverish – from the tips of my toes to those of my hair. (My fits of despair send me not through a window, but to a doctor's office.)' (*LF*, p. 495) Somatic illness (fever) clarifies the mind (a point that Kafka will make after the first appearance of his pulmonary tuberculosis in 1917). His 'neurosis' does not drive him to suicide (as it had a number of his ancestors), but rather manifests itself in somatic form, as hysterical symptoms, for which he seeks treatment (as a Jewish patient) from a physician. He knows, however, that such a course of action cannot change the inevitability of the outcome of his illness unto death.

In the 'Letter to the Father' it is inheritance, becoming like his ancestors, but especially like his father, that is at the centre of his litany of woes: 'In this, by the way, I have inherited a great deal from you and taken much too good care of my inheritance, without, admittedly, having the necessary counterweights in my own nature, as you have' (L, pp. 117–18). Kafka is like his ancestors, but less than they. There has been a decay in his generation. And the sign of this decay is the sickly relationship between mind and body, the sick mind in the sick body or the sick body caused by the sick mind – *mens non sana in corpore insano*. This is the dominant model of inheritance for Kafka. Inheritance is the curse that his father recognises. His father condemns his grandson, Felix (Kafka's nephew), when 'he does anything that is in your opinion unclean, you are not content to say to him, as you used to say to me: "You are a pig", but add: "a real Hermann" or "just like your father"' (L, p. 125). Kafka's fear is that he will become 'just like his father', the parvenu with 'unclean' table manners (L, p. 124). The image of the pig, tortured in Kafka's place in his nightmares, is the Jew. Here is a further intrusion of Devil's Island and the Penal Colony into the domestic sphere. Kafka is the 'pig' and his father, the 'pig butcher'. This is the powerful father, a proud soldier like Dreyfus, who haunts Kafka's nightmares.

Kafka sees himself as a poor combination of the worst qualities of both sides of his family:

> I... a Löwy with a certain Kafka component which, however, is not set in motion by the Kafka will to life, business, and conquest, but by a Löwyish spur that impels more secretly, more diffidently, and in another direction, and which often fails to work entirely. You, on the other hand, a true Kafka in strength, health, appetite, loudness of voice, eloquence, presence of mind, knowledge of human nature, a certain way of doing things on a grand scale. (L, p. 117)

His younger sister Ottla, who rebels against her parents with Franz's support, on the other hand is 'a kind of Löwy, equipped with the best Kafka weapons' (L, p. 141). Kafka projects an ideal onto his father in order to imagine himself to have this potential, but his own body seems to have decayed next to his father's imagined health.

When bathing, Kafka feels himself to be 'a little skeleton, unsteady, barefoot on the boards'. The image of a skeleton with bare feet encapsulates all the contradictions in the discourse about the male Jewish body, acutely aware that it is being read for signs of difference: 'I felt best when you sometimes undressed first and I was able to stay behind in the hut and put off the disgrace of showing myself in public... I was grateful to you for not seeming to notice my anguish, and besides, I was proud of my father's body' (L, p. 121). Kafka himself is a sickly survivor, whose 'brothers died when they were small' (L, p. 117).

But there is a counterweight to this image, and that is the image of Kafka's father as the sick Jew. Like Dreyfus, the father's strength is revealed to have crumbled. Kafka records his father's complaints to him: 'I have never come to you when you were in the synagogue, never visited you in Franzenbad', where his heart condition was being treated (L, p. 115). Even among the ill, he appears healthy: 'In fact, in the group photographs taken at Franzenbad, for instance, you always looked big and jolly, among those sulky little people, as a king on his travels' (L, p. 144). Kafka has him accounting for his 'imperious temperament': 'In recent years you have been explaining this as due to your nervous heart condition. I don't know that you were ever essentially different. Rather, the nervous heart condition is a means by which you exert your domination more strongly' (L, p. 126). Here there is no question of the 'reality' of the father's heart condition – he is truly ill in Kafka's representation – but he still appears more healthy than the 'really' ill. The ambivalent representation of his father's heart condition represents his desire for a powerful father (whom he fears) and a sickly father (whom he fears to become). In addition, the heart condition comes to be an explanation for the erratic mental state of the father.

Kafka presents his own 'heart condition', or at least the feigned 'nervousness and cardiac excitability' by means of which he quit his job at the Assicurazioni in July 1908, as the result of his identification of his former employer with his ill but still abusive father:

> you gradually began to terrify me on all sides, the way you treated the staff. I don't know, perhaps it was the same in most businesses (in the Assicurazioni Generali, for instance, in my time it was really similar, and the explanation I gave the director for my resignation was, though not strictly in accordance with the truth, still not entirely a lie: my not being able to bear the cursing and swearing, which incidentally had not actually been directed at me; it was

> something to which I had become too painfully sensitive from home). (L, p. 136)

But the father's abuse is not random – it falls on those hirelings whom he feels are not carrying their weight in the business: 'your constant complaint about a clerk with TB: "The sooner that sick dog croaks the better". You called the employees "paid enemies"' (L, p. 136). Here the weak heart from which Kafka did not suffer is replaced with tuberculosis. This tactic is unmistakable in the fall of 1917. On 29 August 1917, Kafka writes to his sister Ottla about his first bout with tuberculosis. In this letter, Kafka begins to structure his tuberculosis as part of an inherited predisposition to mental illness rather than to somatic disease. Madness is the illness he inherited from his mother's family. Yet on 2 September 1917, he writes to Ottla that he has closed his 'cold, stale, ill-smelling' apartment, an act that he compares to dying, and has moved back with his parents. His coughing has become the prime symptom of his tuberculosis, and he lies awake in his parent's apartment where 'the door to the bedroom [was] left open so that I could hear Father coughing. Poor Father, poor Mother, poor Franz' (*LO*, p. 20). The father's heart condition has suddenly become marked by his coughing: Kafka has reshaped his father's illness to match his own symptoms.

Kafka maintained that all his illness was the result of his nervousness, an inherited hypochondria culminating in real illness, as real as the heart disease of his father:

> the worry about my health; it began imperceptibly enough, with now and then a little anxiety about digestion, hair falling out, a spinal curvature, and so on; intensifying in innumerable gradations, it finally ended with a real illness. But since there was nothing at all I was certain of, since I needed to be provided at every instant with a new confirmation of my existence, since nothing was in my very own, undoubted sole possession, determined unequivocally only by me – in sober truth a disinherited son – naturally I became unsure even to the thing nearest to me, my own body. I shot up, tall and lanky, without knowing what to do with my lankiness, the burden was too heavy, the back became bent; I scarcely dared to move, certainly not to exercise, I remained weakly; I was amazed by everything I could still command as if by a miracle, for instance, my good digestion; that sufficed to lose it, and now the way was open to every sort of hypochondria; until finally under the strain of the

> superhuman effort of wanting to marry (of this I shall speak later), blood came from the lung, something in which the apartment in the Schönborn Palais – which, however, I needed only because I believed I needed it for my writing, so that even this belongs here under the same heading – may have had a fair share. So all this did not come from excessive work, as you always imagine. There were years in which, in perfectly good health, I lazed away more time on the sofa than you in all your life, including all your illnesses. (L, p. 152)

The son's response to his illnesses, including his tuberculosis, cannot match the father's in his forbearance. What should be a narrative of illness is actually a narrative of acting ill out of psychic necessity. It is a narrative of hypochondriasis, notwithstanding Kafka's very 'real' tuberculosis. This is the story of the Jewish patient, whose anxiety is located in the body, but whose real source is the social displacement felt by Jews in *fin de siècle* European society.

The 'illnesses' of Kafka's childhood, from the dyspepsia to spinal curvature, mark his body as a diseased Jewish body. Now the theme of Kafka's letter is his anxiety about becoming his father, that is, becoming Jewish: 'Jewish schoolboys in our country tend to be odd' (L, p. 151). Indeed, Kafka attributes his special perceptual gifts to this nervousness: as a child, he had been 'acutely observant from sheer nervousness' (L, p. 148). He describes even his religious observances in terms of the congenital weakness attributed to the nervous *fin de siècle* Jew. Religious feeling at home was 'confined to the first Seder, which more and more developed into a farce, with fits of hysterical laughter, admittedly under the influence of the growing children' (L, p. 147). Hysteria characterised the response of the children to the idea of ritual, especially a child, like Franz. This is the nervousness, inherited along with his faith from his mother, capable only of a 'few flimsy gestures, little souvenirs of earlier times' (L, p. 148). Furthermore: 'As a child I reproached myself, in accord with you for not going to the synagogue often enough, for not fasting and so on' (L, p. 146). The refusal to attend synagogue is a sign of the changing manners of the westernised Jew. His father's atrocious table manners distinguish him as a partially acculturated westernised Jew. All of this is again little more than the 'historical character' of contemporary Prague Jewry. But the idea of Judaism as a 'gastronomic cult', or Ludwig Feuerbach's claim that the Jews see the world through their stomachs, are part and parcel of the idea of the Jew in the cultural realm of Prague.

The role of the father as a young *author's* ancestor is also important. Conventional wisdom at the turn of the century held that Jewish families were ill. Theodor Gomperz, a leading philologist of the late nineteenth century, could write in 1886 to his sister, 'looking around our family circle, there are not too many bright points. Nearly everywhere, at the least, irritable and excited nerves – the inheritance of a very old civilized race and of the urban life.'[14] The literary antidote to this inheritance was to be high culture. So it is in books that Kafka seeks a 'healthy' father and a 'healthy' son. Hermann Kafka reads Benjamin Franklin's memoirs, which his son gave him, 'because of the relationship between the author and his father, as it is there described' (L, p. 149). In the German edition available at the time, Franklin's father is introduced wisely talking the younger Franklin out of a wasted life as a poet and writer, and persuading him to become a printer instead.[15] The healthy father persuades his young son to do precisely what Kafka has no desire for – to take part in mundane reality as a replacement for the world of words.

Notes

1. Friedrich Nietzsche, *Ecce Homo*, R.J. Hollindale trans. (Harmondsworth: Penguin, 1983). On Kafka and Nietzsche see Patrick Bridgwater, *Kafka and Nietzsche* (Bonn: Bouvier, 1974).
2. All references to Kafka's works are to the following:
   T: *The Trial*, Willa and Edwin Muir trans. (New York: Schocken, 1984);
   S: *The Complete Stories*, Nahum N. Glatzer (ed.) (New York: Schocken, 1971);
   C: *The Castle*, Willa and Edwin Muir trans. (New York: Alfred E.Knopf, 1992);
   P: *Parables and Paradoxes* (New York: Schocken, 1963);
   L: 'Letter to the Father', Ernst Kaiser and Eithne Wilkens trans., revised by Arthur S. Wensinger in Franz Kafka, *The Sons*, introduction by Mark Anderson (New York: Schocken, 1989);
   D1: *The Diaries, 1910–1913*, Max Brod (ed.), Joseph Kresh trans. (New York: Schocken, 1948);
   D2: *The Diaries, 1914–1923*, Max Brod (ed.), Martin Greenberg and Hannah Arendt trans. (New York: Schocken, 1949);
   LF: *Letters to Friends, Family, and Editors*, Max Brod (ed.), Richard and Clara Winston trans. (New York: Schocken, 1977);
   LFe: *Letters to Felice*, Erich Heller and Jürgen Born (eds), James Stern and Elisabeth Duckworth trans. (New York: Schocken, 1973);
   LM: *Letters to Milena*, Philip Boehm trans. (New York: Schocken, 1990);

LO: *Letters to Ottla and the Family*, N.N. Glatzer (ed.), Richard and Clara Winston trans., (New York: Schocken, 1982).

3. On the family see Anthony Northey, *Kafka's Relatives: Their Lives and his Writing* (New Haven: Yale University Press, 1991); Ernst Pawel, *The Nightmare of Reason: A Life of Franz Kafka* (London: Collins Harvill, 1988) pp. 9–12.
4. Ernst Pawel, *The Nightmare of Reason: A Life of Franz Kafka* (London: Collins Harvill, 1988) p. 182.
5. Cesare Lombroso, *L'antisemitismo e la scienze moderne* (Turin: L. Roux, 1894) pp. 102–3. On the history of the idea of the heart and its illness, see H.P. Kafka, 'Silent Defects', *Journal of the American College of Cardiology* 13 (1989) 1451–2, and on the historical context of heart illness see Saul Jarcho (ed.), *The Concept Of Heart Failure From Avicenna To Albertini* (Cambridge: Harvard UP, 1980).
6. Martin Engländer, *Die auffallend häufigen Krankheitserscheinungen der jüdischen Rasse* (Vienna: J.L. Pollak, 1902) pp. 12–13.
7. Otto Binswanger, *Die Pathologie und Therapie der Neurasthenie* (Jena: G. Fischer, 1896) p. 46.
8. Alfred Lee Loomis and William Gilman Thompson (eds), *A System of Practical Medicine* (New York/Philadelphia: Lea Brothers, 1897–98) IV, p. 553.
9. Pawel, *op. cit.*, p. 260.
10. *Ibid.*, pp. 104, 134, 195.
11. Max Brod, *Über Franz Kafka* (Frankfurt: Fischer, 1977) p. 14.
12. Franz Kafka, *Tagebücher*, Hans-Gerd Koch, Michael Müller, Malcolm Pasley (eds) (Frankfurt: S. Fischer, 1990) p. 778.
13. Pawel, *op. cit.*, p. 343.
14. Cited by Peter J. Swales, 'Freud, His Teacher, and the Birth of Psychoanalysis' in *Freud: Appraisals and Reappraisals*, Paul E. Stepansky (ed.) (Hillsdale, N.J.: Analytic Press, 1986) p. 28.
15. Benjamin Franklin, *Leben und Ausgewählte Schriften* (Leipzig: Georg Wigand, 1838).

17

Death with Father in *David Copperfield*

Jeff Nunokawa

Remember this fantasy: the boy returns from school earlier than he was expected to find the father away, and the mother, infant brother and babysitter home alone:

> I had never hoped for this. I had never thought it possible that we... could be together undisturbed... there was no one to come between us:[1]
> [S]eeing me, she called me her dear Davy, her own boy! and coming half across the room to meet me, kneeled down upon the ground and kissed me, and laid my head down on her bosom near the little creature that was nestling there, and put its hand to my lips...
> 'He is your brother', said my mother, fondling me. 'Davy, my pretty boy! My poor child!' Then she kissed me more and more, and clasped me round the neck. This she was doing when Pegotty came running in, and bounced down on the ground beside us, and went mad about us both for a quarter of an hour. (P. 162)

By means of a simple eviction, the bleak house where all the yearnings of affection are punished becomes a happy home where all are permitted; by the excision of one figure, the forces of prohibition disappear from the family album; by the stroke of a single deletion, the repressive sentence is translated into the family romance, a story with no end in sight, since, excepting the father, additional characters only augment and amplify the maternal devotion which is the heart of the tale.

Like the pornographic fantasy, another scene infused with touching intensities different, but not altogether so, from the one reviewed here and whose devices of disinhibition are as routine as the everyday expectations they labour to suspend, the dream that comes true when young Davy comes home, for all its vivid outlandishness, fades into the common contours of a standard narrative. No less than the angel of the hearth, who, as everyone knows by now, can never really remain aloof from its gyrations, the oedipal horseplay that gently rocks the house is as durable as, if spicier than, any other domestic staple established before, by and beyond a novel like *David Copperfield*.

What distinguishes David Copperfield's happy day from other versions of the same old story told, or left untold, elsewhere, is less the banal erotics that it rehearses, than the frequency with which they can be found in the novel that bears his name. If, after the revelations of psychoanalysis and personal advertisements, our systems have absorbed any shock to be sustained from the *en famille* intrigues adumbrated by the household words of a nineteenth century narrative, we may be struck instead by the regularity with which the Victorian novel in general, and this one especially, plots the absence that the generic incest story requires.

The father whose prohibitions make days without him a rare treat is rare himself in the Dickens novel generally, and in this one especially; the regime of paternal rule that momentarily clouds the hero's erotic horizon is practically unique in the story whose title is also the name of the father only coincidently and on second thought, a regime as ephemeral as David's briefly endured if abundantly documented episode of *declassement*, the stint of factory labour which is the only interruption in the otherwise unbroken record of upward mobility that renders the personal history of David Copperfield and Charles Dickens an impersonal paean to the ideology of bourgeois meritocracy. Just as he rises from his excursion in the proletariat underworld to embrace the prosperity for which he has been destined from the start, David Copperfield, after his short spell under the stepfather's heel, resumes his proper station as the star of a fatherless household. The stepfather's reign is a spot of darkness between sunlit expanses unshadowed by any father at all.

A longing for 'the days' when 'there was no one to come between us' has little occasion to arise in *David Copperfield*, because the novel takes what would seem the most decisive steps to insure that the 'no one' in question never will. As if reading the forlorn wish that the father never come home as its command, the novel arranges alternative accommodations for him which would appear to insure that he never can: 'the quiet churchyard ... with the dead all lying in their graves at rest' (p. 62). The boy's prayer for the patriarch's 'vanish[ing]' is effectively granted as the given of the plot: 'My father's eyes had closed upon the light of this world six months, when mine opened on it' (p. 50). 'I had never seen my own father...my mother and I had always lived by ourselves in the happiest state imaginable.'

And the happy state underwritten by the death of one father is restored by the death of another; the paternal graveyard that underlies the happy home where the mother can adore her only child without interference extends to provide the premise for the house of married love, overseen by a wife whose undivided devotion is the angelic correlative of the mother's attentions. In a take-no-prisoners version of the romance narrative that defines the labour of love as the work of overcoming the patriarch's opposition, the death of the father is an indispensable prenuptial arrangement. An absolutist amplification of the patriarch's usual sense of property in his children, a trademark enhancement in the Dickens novel of affective and economic claims that are the stock of domesticity in more than the Dickens novel, precludes any settlement with the father for the hand of the daughter short of the offer that can't be refused. Nothing short of the death of the father will suffice to release the daughter from his grip.

But if the father's corpse fuels the heterosexual triumphalism that pervades *David Copperfield*, if it enables the male subject who is its featured player to secure without struggle both the mother and the bride who is her sublimated surrogate, it hardly abolishes the other in-house desire grounded in the oedipal plot, namely that of the son for the father himself. For as little Davy knows with the arrival of a step-father 'connected with the grave in the churchyard, and the raising of the dead' (p. 92), the earthly extinction of the patriarch fails to secure his disappearance from the family picture or, as an older David has reasons to learn, from the erotic investments which arise in its aura. Killing off the figure who interrupts intercourse between mother and son only works to transform the familiar, familial homosexual desire which takes the father for its paradigmatic object a love for the body and soul of the dead.

Listen to David now as he confesses his morbid fascination with the hard body of the man his mother marries:

> I could not [help] looking up in his face. He had that kind of shallow black eye – I want a better word to express an eye that has no depth in it to be looked into...I observed that appearance with a sort of awe...A squareness about the lower part of his face...reminded me of the wax-work that had travelled into our neighbourhood some half-a-year before. This, his regular eyebrows, and the rich white, and black, and brown, of his complexion – confound his

complexion and his memory! – made me think him, in spite of my misgivings, a very handsome man. I have no doubt that my poor dear mother thought him so too. (p. 71)

In a coincidence as commonplace as any arranged by the Victorian novel, the father who is the enemy of little Davy's desire turns out to be its object, as well. Explications of the oedipal scenario which illuminate the entanglement there of heterosexual investments with homosexual ones renders the revelation that little Davy desires his rival as much as he hates him as predictable as the discovery that the haughty scion of High Society is also the mother of a friendless child.

Less conventional though than the boy's helpless attraction to the figure of the father is his attraction to the ghost and the corpse that haunt it. The rigour of Murdstone – you will remember that this is the name of the stepfather whom David hardly ever mentions without affixing the adjective 'grave' to him – is in this passage sufficient to count as a full blown case of rigor mortis. Here the rigid face is difficult to distinguish from the mask of the dead; here the evil eye is superimposed on the glare of a ghost – the 'better word' that David 'wants to express an eye that has no depth to be looked into', but which compels the gaze nonetheless, is the line that Dickens is fond of repeating from Macbeth's confrontation with the spectre of Banquo, and that he comes close to quoting here: 'Thou hast no speculation in those eyes / Which thou dost glare with' (III.iv.1. 94–5). And here the love that generally goes by the name of hate is excited enough to surface as such. The stiff stepfather is sufficiently handsome in Davy's eyes to compel his confession of it not despite, but rather because of, his resemblance to the dead body he replaces.

Not nearly as handsome though as the 'good looking' 'senior', for whom David falls head over heels when he gets to school. The stepfather's dubious attractions are thin fare when they are set next to the charismatic Steerforth, whose 'ease of manner', 'animal spirits... delightful voice' and 'handsome face and figure' inspire a passion in David Copperfield intense and prolix enough to qualify as the *locus classicus* of male homosexual desire in the canonical Victorian novel; the thoroughly cold stepfather who attracts David despite himself couldn't seem less like the totally hot schoolboy at whose feet he would gladly lay down all he has, and whom he continues to adore, although more quietly, even after his disgrace. Such differences though, however striking, are not enough to keep the stepfather and the schoolmate from meeting at the grave of the father.

Various aspects of the father are inherited by the senior that David loves, albeit aspects as different from the ones that Murdstone usurps as day from night; what seems to the younger one the older boy's 'inborn power' is actually an eroticised echo of the paternal claim: 'You belong to my bedroom, I find . . . I feel as if you were my property' (p. 137), the older boy remarks, thus arrogating and sexualising the proprietorial prerogative of the patriarch's estate. Less directly, but no less powerfully, the 'enchantment' that David 'still believe[s]' Steerforth 'to have carrie[d]', an enchantment that triumphs over any resistance reality might offer to it is the residual spell of the books his father had left behind. Like the hero from the story that David draws out of his father's library and later recites to Steerforth long into the night, 'Captain Somebody [who] never lost dignity, from having his ears boxed with the Latin Grammar . . . a Captain and a hero, in despite of all the grammars of all the languages of the world', Steerforth, 'on whom [the teacher] never ventured to lay a hand since he felt [the boy's] superiority', is 'monarch' of the school where David is beaten everyday.

Steerforth is larger than life in more ways than one. Like his father's books, 'connected . . . in [David's] mind, with the churchyard', the hero that arises from them is put to rest with the dead:

> I thought of him very much after I went to bed, and raised myself, I recollect, to look at him where he lay in the moonlight, with his handsome face turned up, and his head reclining easily on his arm. He was a person of great power in my eyes; that was, of course, the reason of my mind running on him. No veiled future dimly glanced upon him in the moonbeams. There was no shadowy picture of his footsteps, in the garden that I dreamed of walking in all night. (P. 140)

David's yearning for Steerforth is never more acute – not to say definitive – than when the older boy lies asleep in bed, 'with his handsome face turned up', never more acute, then, than when his body verges on the condition of a corpse. The final sight of Steerforth allowed by David, allowed to David, who, even before it, had trained himself to think of the senior 'whom he loved so well still' as dead, merely confirms what is abundantly predicted by the sleeping body that the mind, if not the hands, of his sleepless roommate spends more than one night running over: 'I saw him lying [lifeless] with his head upon his arm, as I had often seen him lie at school' (p. 866).

And again like his father's books, the corpse of Steerforth is placed by David in the grave where his father lies; David's vision of the form he adores is lit by the light that illuminates the churchyard where 'the dead all l[ie] in their graves at rest, below the solemn moon' (p. 62); the garden that arises in the dream that follows this vision is the afterimage of the garden that 'faithful care had made' by his father's tomb (p. 378). Even the puzzling negation lodged in David's dream – 'There was no shadowy picture of his footsteps, in the garden that I dreamed of walking in all night' – obscurely returns to this burial ground, recalling 'One Sunday night', when young Davy required ocular proof that dead men don't walk: 'my mother reads to me [of] Lazarus... raised up from the dead. And I am so frightened that [she is] obliged afterwards to take me out of bed, and shew me the quiet churchyard out of the bedroom window, with the dead all lying in their graves at rest' (p. 62). In his love of the dead, David Copperfield is loyal to his father after all.

A final turn of the screw: the ghost story that Dickens tells enfolds the subject of desire along with the figure who inspires it in the father's shroud, enfolds him there by means of a temptation less terrorising than the 'unwholesome wind' arising from the churchyard in the shape of a man named Murdstone – 'I trembled, and turned white. Something... connected with the grave in the churchyard, and the raising of the dead, seemed to strike me like an unwholesome wind' – but no less appalling for that.

A temptation that works by means of love to secure the goals set out by Murdstone's mortifying regime, whose every measure is true to the implication lodged in the first syllable of his name: 'He beat me... as if he would beat me to death' (p. 108). A temptation as simple as the yearning that David admits in all but words as he watches, without touching, for who knows how long, the beautiful body in the bed next to his. Even on the ritual occasions when David isn't compelled to keep them to himself, his hands remain weighted down by a pressure of restriction hardly restricted to the nineteenth century novel: 'I grasped him by both hands, and could not let them go. But for very shame, and the fear that it might displease him, I could have held him round the neck and cried' (p. 345).

Unlicensed caressing between men, apart from the usual penalties mentioned here – 'shame, and the fear that it might displease him' – carries with it an additional surcharge in *David Copperfield*. The customary mortifications that are the usual sanctions imposed when one man touches another in an unexpected manner, place or time are augmented in the Dickens novel by a more acute variety of death sentence. Watch what happens to David when he succumbs briefly to the desire that he usually keeps under cover:

> [Steerforth] was so intent upon his own reflections that he was quite unconscious of my approach... He gave such a start when I put my hand upon his shoulder, that he made me start too.
> 'You come upon me', he said, almost angrily, 'like a reproachful ghost!' (P. 463)

This is not the only time in the Dickens novel when the rules governing bodily contact in the culture that it inhabits and helps to write are sufficiently taut to make violations of them a kind of capital offence. And in *David Copperfield,* where the phrase dead father is virtually redundant, where death and the patriarch are almost two ways of saying the same thing, for the hero to submit to this penalty is to take the place, by a means of a flickering identification with the ghost of Hamlet's father, of the figure that he never ceases to desire.

'What his remembrances of me were, I have never known... but mine of him were as the remembrances of a cherished friend, who was dead' (p. 516). Long after Steerforth is assigned to the grave, one of the countless paternal corpses strewn on the path of the marriage plot that the Victorian novel helped to write, his ghost continues to haunt David's heterosexual settlement, refigured there in the ambiguous angel who supplants the schoolmate as the object of the hero's devotion, the spectre 'still... near me, pointing upward', (p. 951) and beyond David's house, haunts a story of homosexual desire whose persistent power to entrance we have reasons of our own to know, a story of homosexual desire hard to tell from a book of the dead.

Note

1. Charles Dickens, *The Personal History of David Copperfield* (New York: Penguin Books, 1985) p. 162. All subsequent citations refer to this edition.

IV
Paternity, Sex, Gender and Succession

18

Why do Ogres Eat Babies? Monstrous Paternity in Myth and Fairytales

Marina Warner

Ogres who eat babies are familiar figures in fairytales. Charles Perrault's *Contes du Temps Passé*, published in 1697, contains 'Puss in Boots', 'Cinderella, or, The Little Glass Slipper', 'The Sleeping Beauty in the Wood' and other favourites and classics of the nursery.[1] They have been told to children, and almost exclusively to children, for nearly two hundred years. In the frontispiece to the first edition of 1697 the traditional storyteller, the crone or old wife of the old wife's tale, is shown sitting in front of the fire with the children of the household – they may be portraits of Perrault's own family – gathered around her. Yet three of these cosy fireside tales feature cannibal ogres who prey on children – and even on their own. In 'Hop O'My Thumb' (*Le Petit Poucet*), the hero finds himself lost in the forest with his brothers and sisters and takes shelter in the house of a giant, 'an ogre who eats babies', warns his grieving wife. In the English variations on this story, the ogre howls, as you will recall:

> Fee, fau, fum
> I smell the blood of an English man,
> Be he alive or be he dead,
> I'll grind his bones to make my bread.[2]

But Hop O'My Thumb is undaunted; he notices that the baby ogres sleep with gold crowns on their heads, and so he switches them for the caps of his own six brothers. The ogre comes fumbling in their bed for a night-time snack: 'Why, what a nasty trick I almost played on myself!' he says, when he finds the crowns. He changes direction, looking for the caps. 'With that, he slits the throats of his seven daughters'.[3] Gustave Doré's pop-eyed ogre, from his illustrations to Perrault of

1862, dominates a gothically black-comic illustration, fit to give anyone nightmares. In the morning, when his wife goes to the children's room, she finds her 'seven daughters, with their throats cut, swimming in blood'.[4] 'She responded with a fainting fit,' writes Perrault. 'Most women faint in similar circumstances.'[5] (This, by the way, is typical Perrault: dry, mocking worldly, weary and manipulative with his sophisticated ironical clichés.)

The word 'ogre' was introduced into English from French, via Italian, and the current in which it swam from the late seventeenth century was fairytales, both *The Arabian Nights* and the ornate, ironical French variety. Translations of Marie-Catherine d'Aulnoy's effervescent stories, as well as of Perrault's more succinct tales, introduced the word; in 'The Bee and the Orange Tree', she eavesdrops on the conversation of Ravagio and Tourmentine, who are 'tall as giants and their skin was pistol-proof'.[6] They are discussing a foundling human baby, Aimée, and the author has great fun with word play.

> Look, Ravagio, here's some fresh meat, nice and plump, nice and fat and tender, but I swear you won't get the tiniest nibble; it's a lovely little girl; I want to feed her up, we'll marry her to our ogre cub, they'll make us some ogrelings with extraordinary faces; they'll be the joy of our old age.[7]

The word's Italian predecessor, *ogro*, meaning monster, derives from the Latin Orcus, another name for Hades, or the God of the Underworld, hence Hell. Fans of Tolkein will recognise the origin of his 'orcs' here too.

Ogres' basic characteristics have proved remarkably stable since Polyphemus was first duped by Odysseus: in early modern fairytales, they are large, male, rich, strong, rapacious and very stupid, though Tourmentine the ogress is cleverer than Ravagio, we are told, and this is par for the course. Both sexes are very greedy, but they are fated to be outwitted, by tricks verbal or other, played on them by someone much smaller than themselves. They prey on children, but the pint-sized youngest child, like Hop O'My Thumb, or the small and cunning cat, like Puss in Boots, challenges them and overcomes them.

So what does this motif of the monstrous, bungling, paternal ogre mean, why does it continue to endure, and what relation does it bear to children, the specific chosen audience of such material?

The unholy combination of infanticide and cannibalism is a divine patriarchal prerogative, it could be said, part of the founding myth of the Greek divine pantheon itself, as told by Hesiod in the *Theogony*. Kronos, chief of the Greek gods in the first generation, as supplied by the genealogies of Hesiod's *Theogony*, is told that one of his children will supplant him, so he devours them one by one. Zeus survives as a baby only because his mother Rhea foils his father's plan when it comes to his turn to be eaten, as all his elder brothers and sisters have been before him. Rhea wraps up a giant stone in swaddling bands and Kronos swallows it happily.[8]

Rubens painted his ferocious image around 1636,[9] and Goya created a dark, even more desperate late painting, of around 1821–3, from the period of his deafness and seclusion.[10] He painted this straight onto the wet plaster of his farmhouse in the Quinta del Sordo: if you look carefully at the headless figure in the murderous father's jaws, the body is not a child's at all, but a youth's. It has very rounded, almost voluptuously painted buttocks, so rounded that I think this may be one of the god's daughters, not one of his sons, as more often expected, and no longer an infant, but a nubile young woman. In the pendant painting of Judith in the same house, Judith cuts off the lustful pagan Holofernes's head; Kronos begins devouring Hestia or Hera or Demeter head first. The inverted reflection then offers much matter for comment on male sexuality: before the restoration of the 1870s when Goya's Black Paintings were transferred from wall to canvas for exhibition in Paris in 1878, photographs were taken and show Kronos with a partially engorged penis, which was later painted out.[11] The story of Judith is a story of foiled seduction; here, in Goya's painting of Kronos, his famished assault on the body of one of his children arouses him – or his sexual excitement stimulates his murderous appetite. The ogre's hunger is sexual, his drive to incorporate has erotic force for him.

His devouring of a daughter brings into view another meaning of the image: the prohibition against incest.[12] Devouring here slips towards sexual union, and this has a twofold thrust: towards coupling with the female as a form of incorporation of the female. The father eats his own daughter: as he was born of woman, he now ingests female flesh in a chain consumption.

Both Rubens and Goya also disclose, by the way, one repeated, accepted but puzzling interpretation of the story in its visual transmission: in these paintings, the father of the gods eats his children in full savage consciousness that they are his offspring. The iconography of Kronos in the Renaissance shows him grasping his live children by a limb – sometimes upside down by one leg – or with one huge hand around their middles, and eating them whole, sometimes gnawing at their chests, sometimes stuffing the head whole into his mouth, sometimes, having chewed off a leg and forearm, attacking another part with bared teeth.

A discrepancy thus exists between the visual rendering and the texts: the logic of the narrative implies that, if Kronos could be tricked by a stone wrapped in swaddling bands, which he swallows as if it were simply a large pill of some kind, then he is not likely to have torn his other children naked limb from limb, piece by piece, gnawing and biting and chewing their undraped and vulnerable flesh as the artists almost all depict with appalled fascination.

Each of the famous Olympians, male and female – Hera, Demeter, Hades, Hestia, Poseidon – is devoured in this way at birth in the Hesiod foundation myth. Later, when Zeus grows up, he tricks his father into taking a purgative which makes him vomit: and one by one the gods are reborn whole from their father's belly. Again, this later segment of the myth contradicts the graphic depiction in Goya of Kronos's crazed gorging; but practical intelligence does not govern the incidents in stories of this kind, only symbolic desire: the sleep of reason engenders monsters. Kronos devours his children alive. This magical, implausible reprieve casts Kronos as a surrogate mother, giving birth to the gods and goddesses as the issue of his body, of his mouth. In this way, they re-enter the world, twice born of their father, begotten and brought forth. The devouring here acts as a prelude to birth; being eaten equals incorporation and this in turn stands for a surrogate though unwitting pregnancy – of the male.

The myth, as it grapples with the question about children's origin, passes through two phases before it interestingly suggests an answer: at first Rhea recognises Kronos's paternity by allowing him to eat his children and make them part of his flesh; secondly, Kronos reaffirms his biological paternity when he vomits them out of his mouth. But this anomalous behaviour implies the difficulty of male identity in the ordinary course of nature when it comes to parturition – later Zeus his son will give birth to Athena from his head in order to claim her as his true daughter. But Kronos's story – and indeed Athena's outlandish birth – both admit that the riddle cannot be solved except by prodigious, anomalous procedures, and this leads to an unspoken admission of the limits of paternal authority. The ogre, in the midst of asserting his absolute rights to incorporate, to make the child one with him, taking it into his body as if it were his own, has to accept defeat. The motif of the transgressive cannibal parent, as excess, as outrage, may serve to define limits in the more recognisable sphere of family conduct.

Kronos's devouring of his children follows his own act of parricide against his abusive father Ouranos, or Heaven. Kronos's mother, Gaia or Earth, hid her offspring from Ouranos's jealousy and then conspired with Kronos to castrate his father.[13] Hesiod gives the celebrated episode in the *Theogony*, with its fantastic consequence: Aphrodite, goddess of love and beauty, is born from the foam on the sea where Kronos has scattered his father's seed.[14]

Interestingly, later readers had difficulty in keeping the generations of filicides and parricides separate: The *Ovide Moralisé* of 1493 compresses the story into one vividly dramatic woodcut: Kronos, bleeding from the wound between his legs, devours a child, while his daughter rises on her shell beside him. Kronos here appears with the scythe of the planet Saturn, with whom he was identified in the middle ages, and on the helve of the scythe a dragon devours its own tail – another image of cyclical time, another expression of the desire for eternal return. The smiles on the faces of the onlookers seem to approve this divine refusal of the laws of nature.[15]

The vigorous woodcut dramatises the themes as well as the story with entertaining clarity: the issue at stake among ogres and cannibals is the onward march of time and within that, more particularly, the most fundamental social relation with which myths struggle: what relation exists between identity and origin? To whom do babies belong? Mothers or fathers? How does the natural – biological – origin convert into social relation? Who has control of children? In the woodcut from *Ovide Moralisé*, we see Kronos as a kind of unnatural mother, a man operated as it were to acquire a woman's bodily functions, a kind of sex-change: a man who gives birth twice over, through his mouth after he has eaten his children and through the semen frothing on the sea from his severed phallus. The medieval text's collapse of diachrony into synchrony opens a door onto one meaning of the death that the ogre and his food supply might signify: the jealousy of women's bodies as birthgivers.

In the middle ages and Renaissance Kronos was identified with Saturn, one of the planets, and the name Kronos (Greek Kappa) became assimilated to the word for time Chronos (Chi). Hence in traditional Zodiacal imagery and numerous astronomy and astrology treatises the complex figure of Saturn, presiding genius of Melancholy, holds a scythe and hourglass as he rides in his chariot round the wheel of the heavens; sometimes he is shown devouring his children, who are allegorised as the Hours. He comes to represent the unrelenting passage of Father Time, who devours all.

But the problem with this is that the story of Kronos and Zeus tells of time's eternal victory from the point of view of the vanquishing children who take over, not the triumph of the hoary old patriarch. The medieval and Renaissance allegory reassigns the laurel to the old because, in terms of chronology, the metaphor of the hours being inexorably swallowed up as Time rolls on works in a familar way. But it misses the point: it is an inadequate metaphor to capture all that is happening in the original mytheme of Kronos devouring his children. Kronos is attempting to halt time: the children represent the future generation and announce his redundancy, immortal or no: time will roll on *for him*.

The Grimm Brothers' extraordinary tale 'The Juniper Tree' could almost be read as a macabre recasting of this foundation myth for the modern nursery, in which mortals take the place of immortals and the ogre's attempt to destroy a member of the future generation is frustrated.[16] The wicked stepmother kills the child she has inherited from her husband's first marriage by dropping the lid of a trunk on his head and cutting his head off; she then adjusts it back on the child's body and props him up at the table, leaving his fatal injury for her own daughter to discover when she offers her stepbrother an apple and knocks his head off. The wicked woman then cooks the body and serves it up to her husband; he sups with relish on his son, not knowing of course what or who he is eating. Meanwhile the sister weeps, unable to share the meal. Later, however, the bones buried under the Juniper Tree will work their revenge on the cruel woman and the little boy who has been devoured will spring back again to life: incorporation into the father is not an absolute death. Paternity, in this fairytale as well as in the myth of Kronos, can bring forth the whole child again. 'The Juniper Tree', one of the most perfectly constructed of the Grimms' stories, was collected and passed on to them by the artist Philipp Otto Runge, who in his own paintings insists on the almost preternatural vitality of children.

The *Ovide Moralisé*'s mistaken conflation of Ouranos with Kronos was repeated much later by no less a figure than Freud who, in a passage critical of extended paternal authority in his own time, writes, 'Kronos devoured his children, just as the wild boar devours the sow's litter; while Zeus emasculated his father and made himself ruler in his place.' Freud comments, 'The obscure information which is brought to us by mythology and legend from the primaeval ages of human society gives an unpleasing picture of the father's despotic power and of the ruthlessness with which he made use of it.'[17] Later, Freud interpreted his mistake to examine the truthtelling value of such errors in *The Psychopathology of Everyday Life* and revealingly linked his conflation of Kronos and Ouranos to a remark his much older half-brother had made to him, when he told him: 'One thing you must not forget is that as far as the conduct of your life is concerned, you really belong not to the second, but to the third generation in relation to your father.'[18] Freud implies that his repression of the myth's sequence represents his own refusal to be considered so junior as to be his half-brother's son rather than his father's. Again, the myth of the murderous father repeats a lesson about genealogical time.

Both the Greek myth and the German Romantic fairytale encode resignation to the passing of time, the overtaking of age by the young, and the necessarily stepped character of the genealogical ladder through time. In Runge's portrait of his parents and his children painted in 1806, the two children are fingering lilies of the field, divinely granted life and beauty and splendour. They glow with colour and energy, while the grandparents, shaded and withered, recede into the background.[19] Runge responded to 'The Juniper Tree' and to fairytales in general because they are child-centred, proclaiming the resilience and the eventual emergence of the small as supreme.

Children themselves have adapted and internalised these themes; in order to feel he – sometimes, but not often, she – might prevail, the small person sometimes mimics the very threat he or she faces.

From a very early date children responded to the adult's bogeyman by defensive imitation. In play represented on Greek pots and Roman sarcophagi, children take on the role of the bogeyman ogre: the game consists of frightening the wits out of your playmates – how? By pretending to be an ogre. By putting on a monster mask with a big enough mouth to push your fist through and make-believe to grab your friends. The trope recurs, as in a drawing of the school of Mantegna, after a Roman original.

This theatrical defiance exemplifies a defence mechanism: internalising the aggressor in order to stave off fear. It is interesting that the trope can be found so frequently in classical sculpture and was later taken up by Renaissance artists. The ogre and his imitators present what is possibly one of those rare universal metaphors, for children still make up or pass on stories which star ogres. These are not fairytales but claim to be true – they are even sometimes presented as autobiographical. One group rings variations on the theme of paternal cannibalism and castration in a contemporary setting:

> There's the one about Jack: he goes into a butcher's and there was an attic, so he goes into the attic and he sees a hole, he says shit, what's that? So he gets his willy and he sticks it into the hole. Then a woman comes in and she goes: so there's no more sausages? and [the butcher] goes, no. And she says, 'Yes there is, there's one'. So, 'maybe it's the last one', so he grabs it and he cuts it off, Snip! Then he gives it to the woman. The woman eats it and next day she comes back and says, 'It was really good your sausage, have you got another one?' and Jack says through the hole, 'When it grows back.'[20]

The variants included by Claude Gaignebet, the folklorist who collected the material, sometimes tell the same story, but it is the *father*'s penis that is cut off. This variant also concludes with the line, 'When it grows back', spoken by the father.

In his analysis of the stories, Gaignebet does not think their ending savagely ironical, about a poor protagonist who is such a fool he doesn't know that penises don't grow back. He heard children telling the story without such cynicism and he praises their spirit of comic optimism, the rude health of their humour. He does also point out that these are boys' stories – told by boys and starring them frequently as victims in the first place, then as heroes. It is the first variant, in which the child's penis is eaten instead of a sausage, that seizes on the message of the myth of Kronos: that the young suffer the aggression of their elders but can comfort themselves that they will inevitably gain ground on the old. The variant which echoes the Greek myth more closely, and describes the (comic) castration of the father, contains the threat of repetition: the struggle will go on.

Notes

1. Charles Perrault, *Contes*, Gilbert Rouger (ed.) (Paris: Garnier, 1967).
2. Anon., 'The History of Jack and the Giants' in I. and P. Opie (eds.) *The Classic Fairy Tales* (London: Oxford University Press, 1974) p. 63.
3. *The Fairy Tales of Charles Perrault*, Angela Carter trans. (New York: Avon, 1977) p. 124.
4. *Ibid.*, p. 125.

5. *Ibid.*
6. *The Fairy Tales of Madame d'Aulnoy*, Anne Thackeray Ritchie trans. (London: Lawrence and Bullen, 1989) p. 145; see Ritchie, *ibid.*, p. 142.
7. *Tiens, Ravagio, voici de la chair fraîche, bien grassette, bien douillette, mais par mon chef tu n'en croquera que d'une dent; c'est une belle petite fille; je veux la nourrir, nous la marierons avec notre ogrelet, ils feront des ogrichons d'une figure extraordinaire; cela nous réjouira dans notre vieillesse.* (Madame d'Aulnoy, *Les Contes de fées* I (Paris: Mercure de France, 1956) p. 145.)
8. Hesiod, *Theogony*, lines 453–93 in *Hesiod and Theognis*, Dorothea Wender trans. (Harmondsworth: Penguin, 1973) pp. 38–9.
9. In the Prado, Madrid.
10. Janis Tomlinson, *Goya* (London: Phaidon, 1994) pp. 251 ff.
11. Nigel Glendinning, 'The Strange Translation of Goya's Black Paintings' in *Burlington Magazine* 117 (1975) 465–79; Maria del Carmen Torrecillas Fernandez, 'Nueva documentación fotografica sobre las pinturas del Quinta des Sordo de Goya' in *Buletin del Museo del Prado* IV, 17 (1985) 87–96.
12. I have written about the structural relation of cannibalism and incest in Marina Warner, *Managing Monsters: Six Myths of Our Time* (London: Vintage, 1994) pp. 65–79.
13. Hesiod, *Theogony*, lines. 155–82, pp. 28–9.
14. *Ibid.*, lines 159–206, p. 29.
15. See handcoloured frontispiece, *La Bible des poètes. Métamorphoses* (Paris c. 1485); frontispiece, different edition with woodcuts (Paris: Antoine Vérard, c. 1507).
16. *The Complete Grimm's Fairy Tales*, anon. trans. (London: Routledge, 1975) pp. 220–9.
17. Sigmund Freud, 'The Interpretation of Dreams' in the *Standard Edition*, James Strachey (ed. and trans.), with Alan Tyson, IV, p. 357.
18. Sigmund Freud, 'The Psychopathology of Everyday Life', *Standard Edition* V, p. 279.
19. 'The Artist's parents' (1806) in the Museum in Hamburg; reproduced in Robert Rosenblum, *The Romantic Child from Runge to Sendak* (London: Thames & Hudson, 1988) p. 38.
20. *Un coup c'était Cafougnette, y ren'tre dans une boucherie, puis y avait un grenier, alors lui y ren'tre dans l'grenier puis y voit un trou, y dit merde, qu'est-ce que c'est. Alors y prend sa bitte puis il l'enfonce dans l'trou. Alors v'là une femme et puis elle dit: y'a plus de saucisse? alors y dit, non. Et puis elle dit: si, y'en a une. Alors 'peut-être c'est la dernière' alors y prend, il l'coupe Zwitt. Alors y donne à la femme. La femme la mange et l'lendemain, elle revient et elle dit: – elle était bien bonne vot'saucisse, vous n'avez pas une autre et Cafougnette après y dit par le trou, 'quand er r'poussra'.* (Claude Gaignebet, *Le Folklore obscéne des enfants* (Paris: G.P. Maisonneuve et Larose, 1974) pp. 186–7.

19

Fathers as Mothers: the Myth of Male Parthenogenesis

Lynn Thomas

> Zeus! Why did you let women settle in this world of light, a curse and a snare to men? If you wished to propagate the human race you should have arranged it without women. Men might have deposited in your temples gold or iron or a weight of copper to purchase offspring, each to the value of the price he paid, and so lived in free houses, relieved of womankind.[1]

> After receiving the oracle, Cecrops convened all the citizens of both sexes to take a vote [as to who should be the presiding deity of Athens]. The men voted for Poseidon and the women for Athene. And as one more woman was found than men, Athene won. Poseidon was enraged... To placate his wrath, Varro says, the women were punished in three ways: they no longer could cast a vote, no newborn child would take the mother's name, and no one should call the women Athenians.[2]

Parthenogenetic birth to males is a motif which appears in several myths in the classical Greek and Indian traditions and is also found elsewhere.[3] The theme occurs in two main forms: firstly, and most radically, a complete process of physical birth from a male body involving parturition and some period of gestation, such as is found in the Greek myths of Zeus giving birth to Athene and Dionysus and the Indian myth of Māndhātar's birth from Yuvanāśva; and secondly, birth generated by semen alone without recourse to a female womb, such as is found in the Greek myth of the birth of Erichthonius and which occurs with some frequency in Indian mythology where such cases are labelled *ayonija* – non womb-born.[4]

The image of male birth, especially when it involves gestation and parturition, is one pregnant in every sense and appears to tap directly into contemporary concerns about gender relations and the role of patriarchy in the transmission of culture. Most scholars analysing the motif have viewed it in this light and argued that the image serves primarily to denigrate women and attest to the social and historical supremacy of men.[5] I would like to question these assumptions and examine the significance of parthenogenetic birth to males in more detail, paying special attention to its operation in the myth of Athene's birth from Zeus, which is probably the best-known example. As well as looking at the role and significance of the motif in that particular myth, however, I should also like to ask some broader questions of the topic. Firstly, is it possible to talk about male birth as a discrete motif which holds a similar significance in all the myths where it occurs, as the theories of these scholars would suggest? Secondly, does a closer examination of the material, in fact, bear out the argument that the image of male birth is primarily concerned with gender issues and the denigration of women? Finally, and with special reference to the theme of this collection, can the image of father as mother tell us anything significant about the nature of fatherhood? I shall begin by looking at the use of the motif in the myth of Athene's birth from Zeus.

ATHENE'S BIRTH FROM ZEUS AND HER SUBSEQUENT CHARACTERISTICS AND ROLE

The myth of the birth of Athene first appears in Hesiod's *Theogony* and I shall recount it in some detail. Zeus takes Metis, the goddess of Wisdom, as his wife but is warned by his grandparents Gaia and Ouranos that she will bear him a daughter followed by a son who will overthrow him:

> For her fate would be
> To bear outstanding children, greatly wise,
> First, a girl, Tritogeneia, the grey-eyed,
> Equal in spirit and intelligence
> To Zeus her father; then she would bear a son
> With haughty heart, a king of gods and men. (894–8) [6]

To forestall this, Zeus swallows Metis when she is pregnant with their daughter:

> But when she was about to bear her child
> Grey-eyed Athene, he deceived her mind
> With clever words and guile, and thrust her down
> Into his belly, as he was advised
> By Earth and starry Heaven. (888–91)

Some time later Zeus suffers from a terrible pain in his head and after consultation has Hephaestos split open his skull with an axe and Athene springs out, fully armed and uttering her war cry.[7]

Athene goes on to be Zeus's favourite child and she is portrayed as a dutiful daughter who upholds and validates his rule as well as the patriarchal norms which it represents. This is clear from the speech which Athene makes in defence of Orestes, on trial for the murder of his mother:

> No mother gave me birth.
> I honour the male in all things but marriage.
> Yes, with all my heart I am my Father's child.[8]

Athene's relationship with the male and male values can also be seen in her friendship with Odysseus and other heroes, a friendship which is clearly modelled on that between men.[9] It is also apparent in her enmity towards demonised or non-conformist women such as Medusa, whom she helps Perseus to defeat and whose head she wears on her *aegis*, indicating their antithetical relationship; or Arachne, whom she turns into a spider for the crime of *hubris* and for mocking the libidinous habits of the gods.[10] In fact, in her characteristics and physical portrayal, Athene represents such a masculine figure that Keuls can call her 'a sexless man-woman', 'stripped of any vestige of femininity'.[11]

As well as being Zeus's best-loved child, Athene is also essentially his heir, albeit in a situation where no heir can be explicitly acknowledged as Zeus must reign for ever. This relationship is clearly seen in the fact that Athene is the only deity to carry Zeus's *aegis*, the symbol of his sovereign power; and the only one to use his weapons.[12]

Athene is a virgin goddess, a characteristic which is strongly emphasised, but she is closely involved in one of the other Greek male birth stories, namely the birth of Erichthonius. The birth occurs when Hephaestos tries to rape Athene but she repulses him and he ejaculates against her thigh. The goddess wipes off the semen in disgust and throws it to the ground where it germinates. Earth hands the child born from the semen to Athene who places him in a chest for what is essentially the remaining period of gestation and then raises him as her own. As has been pointed out, the story thus manages to give Athene a child while re-emphasising her virginity and asexual nature at the same time. The child, Erichthonius, goes on to found Athens and institute Athene's worship there and the story of his birth from the earth serves as a charter myth for the Athenians' much vaunted autochthonous origins.[13]

The story of Athene's birth from Zeus and her subsequent role as his *de facto* heir, as champion of patriarchal rule and as patron deity of Athens, raise a number of questions for an understanding of this particular myth: first, why does Zeus swallow Metis in the knowledge that she is pregnant with a *daughter*? Why not wait till she is pregnant with the son against whom the prophecy had warned? Second, why swallow *Metis*? Why not simply swallow her issue as his father had before him? Third, why, of his many offspring, should a *female* play the role of heir and champion of Zeus's order? Finally, why, in particular, should a female be chosen as the presiding deity of Athens, a society whose startlingly misogynistic attitudes have been well documented? To start to find some answers to these questions it is necessary to set the events surrounding Athene's birth within the wider context of the unfolding pattern of theogony which precedes them.

READING THE BIRTH OF ATHENE IN THE CONTEXT OF HESIOD'S *THEOGONY*

The birth of the gods as narrated by Hesiod is carefully structured in a complex pattern of gender relationships, unnatural gestation and filial rebellion and Zeus's production of Athene clearly serves as the third tier of this pattern which resolves the conflict set up in the earlier stages and thereby ensures stability.

Tier one (Hesiod, *Theogony* 133ff)

In the first act of the theogony Gaia and Ouranos unite to produce the twelve Titans and two other sets of offspring who are monsters (*Theogony* 133–53). Ouranos is revolted by his offspring and imprisons them in Gaia; clearly, by the imagery used and subsequent details, in her womb:

And these most awful sons of Earth and Heaven
Were hated by their father from the first.
As soon as each was born, Ouranos hid
The child in a secret hiding-place in Earth
And would not let it come to see the light,
And he enjoyed this wickedness. (154–9)

Gaia, whom the text describes as 'strained and stretched inside her' (160) from this unnaturally prolonged gestation, hatches a plan and persuades the youngest Titan, Kronos, to agree to it:

Mother, I undertake to do the deed;
I do not care for my unspeakable
Father, for he first thought of shameful acts. (170–2)

Gaia forms a sickle and has Kronos hide inside her. When Ouranos comes to her 'longing for love' (176–7) Kronos castrates him and throws the genitals into the sea, where they give rise to the goddess Aphrodite.[14] Kronos now assumes the rule and the second act of the theogony is set to begin.

Tier two (Hesiod, *Theogony* 453ff)

Kronos forces Rhea and begets six children but he is warned by Gaia and Ouranos that one of his sons will overcome him so, as each child is born, he swallows it:

As each child issued from the holy womb
And lay upon its mother's knees, each one
Was seized by mighty Kronos, and gulped down. (459–60)

At Rhea's pleading, Gaia saves the youngest child, Zeus, and spirits him to safety, substituting a stone in his place:

Then,
To the great lord, the son of Heaven, the past
King of the gods, she handed, solemnly,
All wrapped in swaddling-clothes, a giant stone.
He seized it in his hands and thrust it down
Into his belly, fool! He did not know
His son, no stone, was left behind, unhurt

And undefeated, who would conquer him
With violence and force, and drive him out
From all his honours, and would rule the gods. (485–92)

Zeus grows to maturity and, along with Gaia, forces or tricks Kronos into vomiting up his swallowed children and the stone (493–500). He frees his uncles, whom Kronos had imprisoned, and in return receives the thunder and lightning with which he enforces his rule in heaven and on earth (501–6). After banishing Kronos and quelling a rebellion by the Titans, Zeus is urged by the gods to become king, inaugurating a rule which is presented as just and good and which clearly stands as the crowning purpose of the preceding action:

But when the blessed gods had done their work
And forcibly put down the Titans' claim
To honour, they fulfilled Earth's plans and urged
Far-seeing Zeus, Olympian, to rule
And be the king of the immortals. Thus
He gave out rank and privilege to each. (881–5)

Tier three (Hesiod, *Theogony* 887ff)

Immediately following his inauguration as king, and opening what is clearly the third tier of the theogony (not all of the Olympians have yet been produced), Zeus takes Metis as his wife and the events leading up to the birth of Athene take place. When these are read in relation to the previous two stages, and to Athene's subsequent characteristics and actions, a distinctive pattern emerges, with stages one and two in the theogony setting up a number of oppositions and tensions which Zeus's actions in stage three resolve; a resolution which is necessary for the establishment of the ordered world under the rule of its proper king:

1. Ouranos ♂ and Gaia ♀	Ouranos imprisons offspring in Gaia's womb (♀). Forced to release them (castrated). Ouranos is overthrown by his son, leading to an unstable situation which must be resolved.

2. Kronos ♂ and Rhea ♀ ↓	Kronos swallows offspring – *heen eskattheto nedyn* (487) – and imprisons them in his stomach (♂). Forced to release them (emetic). Kronos is overthrown by his son, leading to an unstable situation (*vide* Zeus's warning) which must be resolved.
3. Zeus ♂ and Metis ♀ ↓	Zeus swallows pregnant consort – *heen eskattheto nedyn* (890 and repeated at 899). = womb (♀) in stomach (♂).[15] Consents to release child. Daughter validates his rule and champions order and stability.

Reading the myth of Athene's birth in conjunction with the two stages of the theogony which precede it enables us to begin to find some answers to the questions which the story raised. It helps to explain, for example, why Zeus should swallow Metis rather than just her offspring, as swallowing the foetus while still in its mother's womb completes the pattern of female and male gestation set up in the earlier tiers of creation. It also helps explain why he should give birth to Athene himself after first engendering her in the original coition with Metis: by taking both male and female roles in the process Zeus resolves the tensions between father and mother which also characterised the previous attempts at reproduction, where fathers oppressed their wives and the wives conspired to have them punished.[16]

Most importantly, perhaps, the unfolding pattern of the theogony explains why Zeus should swallow Metis while pregnant with a daughter rather than the son he was warned against, as the third strand of tension to emerge is that between the desire for a son as heir to carry forward all that the father has achieved and the fear of a son as deposer who will overthrow the father and undo all that he has worked for. That this tension is the driving force of the theogony within the context of the establishment of the ordered universe as the work at hand is very clear from the wording of the warning given to Zeus by Ouranos and Gaia:

> In that way
> They said, no other god but Zeus would get
> The royal power over all the gods. (892–3)

Both Ouranos and Kronos refuse to allow a successor to carry the process of creation forward: they keep their children from birth and other gods must work against them to force a successor out. Zeus, however, while acting to avoid the overthrow of his rule, nevertheless does consent to the release of a child at the proper time, with other gods working with him to help it out.[17] By consenting to continue the line of succession, Zeus allows the necessary dynamism of forward movement into the process (a movement which cannot be denied, as the previous two tiers of the theogony show) but, by giving birth to a daughter, he breaks the cycle of filial rebellion which was hindering the establishment of order. The birth of Athene, therefore, resolves the tension which the theogony sets up. She is not just not a son, a negation of the threat which Gaia and Ouranos warn against. Rather, she represents the neutralising of the negative aspects of son as successor and deposer, while affirming the positive aspects of son as heir and champion. It is therefore not surprising that the goddess should uphold Zeus's rule and carry the aegis and weapons which symbolise and reinforce it. Nor is it surprising that she should have such masculine characteristics or be so celebrated by the Athenians: Athene is not, as has often been suggested, a father's vision of a perfect daughter but rather represents the fulfilment of a father's needs from a perfect, but unrealisable, son.

If Athene represents the completion of the divine creation in her role as daughter and heir, in her complementary role as mother and patron she allows the process to be taken to its logical conclusion with the establishment of Zeus's order in the mortal realm. In most cosmogonic accounts the end point of creation is the starting point for its narrators: the human world. Hesiod's *Theogony*, as the title makes clear, is primarily concerned with the gods and does not go on to provide the necessary bridge between the timeless world of the immortals and the historical world of human society. That link, along with much else, is provided by the story of Erichthonius, the more than adopted but less than biological son of Athene who comes to be seen as the founder of Athens.

There are several reasons for reading the story of Erichthonius as the concluding segment in the pattern of creation. Firstly, the details of his birth show a clear continuation of the concerns surrounding gender relations and the process of procreation which inform the three stages of the theogony proper, but takes the resolution further to avoid an act of coition altogether.[18] Secondly, through the relationship between the divine Athene, the semi-divine Erichthonius,[19] and the human city of Athens a clear connection is forged between the world of the gods, where the establishment of order is eternal and universal, and the world of humans, where it is rooted in the ordinances of a specific human society. Thirdly, the founding of Athens was blatantly set in this context by Athenians themselves. While the primary purpose of the myth of Erichthonius may have been to validate the autochthonous origins of Athenians and give them an incontestable claim to the soil of Athens, as most writers concur, it was certainly not lost on the inhabitants of that city that the story gave them a unique relationship with the most powerful of gods.[20]

Returning to the table of the theogony compiled above, therefore, Athene's dual relationship as daughter and mother enables us to now add a 4th and 5th stage to the process and bring it to a close.

4. Athene ↓	Female (♀) with the characteristics of a male (♂). Produces an heir (Erichthonius) who is born directly from semen and the earth without any act of coition.
5. Athens	Erichthonius is raised by Athene, founds Athens and institutes her worship there.

CONCLUSIONS

Placing the birth of Athene from Zeus squarely within its wider narrative context has enabled much to emerge from the myth which an isolated treatment of the motif would have lost. This has been useful for a greater understanding of this particular myth. It has shown a clear continuity between Zeus's production of Athene and the myths of Ouranos and Kronos which precede it: a continuity which is visible in the structure of the stories, the vocabulary employed, and the concerns about succession, gender relations and the process of reproduction which inform them. It has enabled the ending of the theogony to be joined to the founding of Athens to form an unbroken line of succession from the first cosmic union to its logical culmination in a concrete human society. It has also thrown light on several problematic areas within the story and Athene's subsequent characteristics and deeds.

However, returning to the broader questions raised at the outset, has it told us anything about the meaning of male parthenogenesis as a whole? Does it suggest that the motif is a universal one with a broadly similar significance in all its various manifestations? Does it bear out suggestions that the image serves primarily to denigrate women? And, finally, does it have anything significant to say about the nature of fatherhood? I would like to conclude by offering some tentative answers to these questions.

Although the birth of Athene is only one example of the use of the motif of male parthenogenesis, one of the things which has emerged most strongly from this study is the importance which the wider narrative framework holds for an interpretation of the image. The context of the unfolding theogony was seen to be so crucial for understanding the significance of Athene's birth from Zeus that it is hard not to conclude that other instances of the motif must likewise gain their meaning largely in relation to their context. Brief comparisons with the other myths bear this out. The birth of Dionysus from Zeus has more to do with concerns about mortality and rebirth than problems of succession.[21] The birth of the Indian hero Māndhātar from his father's side serves primarily to link him with Indra, the king of the gods,[22] while the version of male parthenogenesis found in the stories of birth from semen should clearly be read as a mythological rendering of contemporary physiological ideas which held that semen alone carried the power of reproduction while the womb was simply a vessel to contain and nurture it.[23]

However, although the central purpose of the image may differ in its various manifestations, a number of common themes do recur across the spectrum of male birth myths, namely, avoidance of the womb, either as a place of impurity or as unfit for heroes;[24] an emphasis on the continuation of male values, seen very clearly in Athene's validation of patriarchal norms and found elsewhere;[25] and an oblique but persistent connection between male pregnancy and prodigious and unnatural feats of swallowing which occurs in nearly every version.[26] It would appear then that although no universal significance can be assigned to the motif, this must be qualified by the fact that a number of important similarities can be found throughout the corpus.

Turning now to the question of whether the image of male parthenogenesis serves primarily to denigrate women, the answer must again be a qualified negative. As was clear from the analysis of the birth of Athene, the *primary* purpose of the story was to resolve the problems surrounding succession and Zeus's production of an heir from his own body was a solution necessitated by the logic of the myth. However, although the denigration of women may not have been the first concern of the myth, it certainly became a central feature in the way that the story was used. Aeschylus makes this clear in the version of the story which Apollo gives at Orestes' trial. Not only does he, erroneously, introduce Athene as one who was 'never bred in the darkness of the womb',[27] but he also uses her birth more generally to undermine and limit the female role in procreation:

> The woman you call the mother of the child is not the parent, just a nurse to the seed, the new-sown seed that grows and swells within her.
> The *man* is source of life – the one who mounts.
> She, like a stranger for a stranger, keeps the shoot alive unless god hurts the roots.[28]

At a deeper level, the denigration of women can also be found running through every aspect of the myth. It is impossible not to read the story of Athene's birth against the background of Greek and especially Athenian attitudes to women. As the first quotation opening this discussion shows, for the Greeks women were a necessary evil: a poison in the home which must be endured as the only means by which men could reproduce themselves. This attitude is clearly seen in the myth: most obviously, as Demand points out, in the fact that Zeus manages to fulfil the ideal of reproduction without women;[29] but also, and more fundamentally, in the way in which the myth brings together concerns about succession with the problems involved in gender relationships and an exploration of the male and female role in procreation, showing that these were closely related in the Greeks' minds. Athene herself also stands essentially as a symbol of women's oppression in the story. The relationship between mythical goddess on Olympus and real women in Athenian society is very clearly shown in the second opening quotation, where the raising of the goddess on her pedestal high above the city is accompanied by the downfall of human women and their loss of power and rights as citizens.

The denigration of women can also be seen as a subsidiary theme in the other myths of male parthenogenesis. The recurring idea that the womb is impure, unfit, or simply a housing for sperm clearly reflects the low status of women in the societies which produced it. Similarly, the use of the image of birth in the transmission of male values also undermines the status of women, with its identification of women with the biological and natural production of the unformed child as opposed to the male's social and cultural production of the refined and valued adult.

Turning then to the final question, can these myths of male parthenogenesis tell us anything significant about the nature of fatherhood? The story of Athene's birth from Zeus, which reflected more upon the problematic relationship between fathers and sons than anything else, would suggest quite strongly that they can. This suggestion is further born out by the fact that all of the myths display an obvious and underlying concern about the role of the male in the process of reproduction and show some attempt to resolve the insecurities that this raises when confronted with the far more evident role of the female. These insecurities can be seen most clearly in the birth from semen stories with their emphatic insistence on the male's role in reproduction and their reduction of the female role to that of mere receptacle.

Insecurity about men's broader role as fathers can also be seen in the myths' emphasis on the male role in the transmission of culture. If it is an incontestable fact that women produce the children, the myths make it clear that it is men who form them.[30] By giving greater value to this second birth from males the stories offer a reassurance which works on the level of both family and society. In exploring the idea of fathers as mothers, therefore, it would appear that these myths of male parthenogenesis serve, in part, as a vehicle whereby men may begin to overcome some of the fears and insecurities they may have about their role as fathers.

Notes

1. Euripedes, *Hippolytus* lines 616–24, cited N. Demand, *Birth, Death, and Motherhood in Classical Greece* (Baltimore: Johns Hopkins University Press, 1994) p. 134.
2. Augustine, *City of God* Book 18, Chapter 9, cited W. Blake Tyrrell and F. Brown, *Athenian Myths and Institutions* (Oxford: Oxford University Press, 1991) pp. 180–1.
3. The majority of these myths are not however concerned with parthenogenesis in the stricter sense of the word, i.e., birth from a virgin without any prior sexual encounter. In nearly all of the myths concerned some form of heterosexual encounter precedes the male birth and this distinguishes them from other instances where a male creator

god alone engenders divine or human offspring (e.g., the Hebrew God in Genesis; Ymir in Norse mythology; Marduk in Babylonian mythology, etc.) which I am not considering here.

4. The birth of the great warrior Droṇa is a typical example of these stories. After seeing a divine nymph the chaste sage Bharadvāja ejaculates and places the seed in a trough (*droṇa*) from which the eponymous hero is born: see *Mahābhārata* Book 1, Chapter 121, verse 5. This and all other references to this text are to V.S. Sukthankar, *et al.* (eds.) *Mahābhārata: Critical Edition* (Poona: Bhandarkar Oriental Research Institute, 1933–70). For an English translation see: J.A.B. van Buitenan trans., *Mahābhārata* (Chicago: University of Chicago Press, 1973, 1975) vols. 1 & 2.
5. Robert Graves, for example, reads the stories of Zeus giving birth as a mythological rendering of an historical process whereby the male deity usurped the parthenogenetic abilities of older goddesses: see, R. Graves, *The Greek Myths*, vol. 1 (Harmondsworth: Penguin, 1962) pp. 20f and 46f. Feminist scholars, such as Nancy Demand and Eva Keuls, argue that the myths reflect the reality of gender power in ancient Greece: see, E. Keuls, *The Reign of the Phallus* (Berkeley: University of California Press, 1993) pp. 34ff; Demand, *op. cit*. pp. 134–40.
6. Hesiod *Theogony*. This and all other references to the text are to D. Wender trans. *Hesiod and Theognis* (Harmondsworth: Penguin, 1973).
7. Hesiod makes no mention of Hephaestos in this context and simply has Zeus produce Athene from his head (lines 924–6). Hephaestos and the axe appear in Apollodorus, *Library* Book 1, Chapter iii, line 6 and Pindar, *Olympian Odes* Ode vii, line 34.
8. Aeschylus, *Eumenides* lines 750ff. This and all other references to the text are to R. Fagles trans., *The Oresteia*, (Harmondsworth: Penguin, 1972).
9. See, for example, her dealings with Telemachus, Odysseus' son, in book one of the *Odyssey*.
10. For an account of the Medusa myth see Apollodorus, *Library* Book 2, Chapter iv and for the story of Arachne see Ovid, *Metamorphoses* Book vi, verses 1–145. Arachne claims she is a better weaver than Athene and the goddess challenges her to a competition. Arachne weaves a picture of the gods' amorous pursuits while Athene herself weaves a picture of the naming of Athens.
11. Keuls, *op. cit.*, p. 38.
12. See, for example, Aeschylus, *Eumenides* line 837. On the significance of Athene's use of Zeus's aegis and thunderbolt see N. Loraux, *The Children of Athena*, C. Levine trans. (Princeton: Princeton University Press, 1984) p. 133.
13. On this see, for example, Tyrrell and Brown, *op. cit.*, pp. 138ff, who argue that the story of Erichthonius' birth serves to mediate between the biological reality of reproduction (two parents) and the Athenians' belief in autochthony. Loraux also discusses the role of autochthony in Athenian identity at length: Loraux, *op. cit.*, Chapter 1.
14. A myth which can also be read as a variation of male parthenogenesis.

15. As Tyrrell and Brown point out, the Greek for womb and stomach are the same – *nedys*: see Tyrrell and Brown, *op. cit.*, p. 23. This does not affect the force of the male/female opposition in the structure, however.
16. Ouranos and Gaia: 'But she... thought of a clever and evil plan... "My sons, whose father is a reckless fool, if you will do as I ask, we shall repay your father's wicked crime"' (lines 164–6); Kronos and Rhea: 'she begged the Earth and starry Heaven, her parents, to devise a plan to hide the birth of her dear son and bring the Fury down on Kronos' (lines 469–72).
17. As Loraux points out, descriptions and depictions of Zeus giving birth to Athene are full of allusions to actual childbirth: Zeus is 'delivered'; he is shown attended by midwives in vase paintings: see Loraux, *op. cit.*, p. 132. The pain which accompanies Athene's birth, a pain inflicted from within by the child ready to emerge, also suggests a birth which follows a gestation that has naturally come to term. This is also upheld by Apollodorus' account which has Hephaestos split open Zeus's head 'when the time came for the birth to take place', Apollodorus *The Library* Book 1, Chapter iii, line 6, J.G. Frazer trans. (London: Heineman, 1921).
18. The gender relations involved in the birth of Erichthonius are very complicated. He is the parthenogenetic son of a father (Hephaestos) who is himself the parthenogenetic son of a mother (Hera, according to Hesiod), but the heir of a mother who is the parthenogenetic daughter of a father and who has him while remaining a virgin through a coitus which is distanced (attempted rape) and a gestation which is distanced (she puts him in a casket). On the casket as the displaced womb of Athene see Keuls, *op. cit.*, p. 123; and on the message which the lack of a mother for Erichthonius gives to Athenian women see Loraux, *op. cit.*, p. 128.
19. The status of Erichthonius is rather ambiguous. While he is the offspring of a god's semen, his subsequent birth from the earth makes him autochthonous and he is often conflated with other autochthonous humans (and Athenians), namely, Erechtheus and Kekrops.
20. Both Herington and Loraux emphasise this point: see, C.J. Herington, *Athene Parthenos and Athene Polias* (Manchester: Manchester University Press, 1955) pp. 57–8 and 62–4; Loraux, *op. cit.*, pp. 130–7.
21. Dionysus is reborn from his father's body to save him from death in his mother's womb when she is consumed by fire. For the birth of Dionysus see Apollodorus *Library* Book 3, Chapter iv, line 3. Hesiod mentions Dionysus' birth briefly, but merely says that he was born of Semele: *Theogony* lines 940–3.
22. See *Mahābhārata* Book 3, Chapter 126, verse 1ff.
23. On this see: N. Tuana, 'The Weaker Seed: The Sexist Bias of Reproductive Theory', in N. Tuana (ed.), *Women and Science* (Bloomington: Indiana University Press, 1989). Demand points out that these theories were more likely to appear in the writings of philosophers than of physicians, who tended to lean more to an equal role for men and women, which again suggests that they were informed more by cultural bias than scientific observation: see Demand, *op. cit.*, p. 135.

24. Seen, for example, in Apollo's reference to the 'darkness of the womb' (Aeschylus, *Eumenides* lines 674–6) cited below; in the equation of the womb with mortality in the Dionysus myth; in the echo of Indra's own distaste for the womb as a 'bad place' (*Rig Veda* Book 4, Hymn 18, verses 1 & 2) in the Mandhatar myth; and in the total avoidance of the female in the birth from semen stories.
25. See, for example, Mary Carroll Smith, 'Epic Parthenogenesis', in A. Sharma (ed.), *Essays on the Mahābhārata* (Leiden: E.J. Brill, 1991), who argues that this is a predominant theme in the Indian birth-from-semen stories; and A.G. Epstein, 'Miscarriages and Miraculous Births in Indo-European Tradition', *The Journal of Indo-European Studies*, vol. 22 (1994) pp. 151ff, who offers a similar interpretation of a number of Indo-European stories in which men rescue and bring to term aborted foetuses.
26. Seen most clearly in the actions of Zeus and Kronos in the Greek theogony but found also in some versions of the birth of Dionysus (see M.L. West, *The Orphic Poems* (Oxford: Clarendon Press, 1983) pp. 140ff and, especially, pp. 161ff) and in several of the Indian myths. The connection between swallowing and male birth can also be found outside of the Indo-European corpus and is clearly an element of male parthenogenesis which would repay further investigation.
27. Aeschylus, *Eumenides* lines 674–6
28. Aeschylus, *Eumenides*, lines 665–70. The emphasis is the translator's.
29. Demand, *op. cit.*, p. 134. Not only does Zeus usurp women's role: he does a better job. When Hera tries to match Zeus's act she can only manage to produce the malformed god Hephaestos and the efforts of human women, too, are similarly undermined: while the birth of Athene was an ever-popular subject in Greek art, no image exists of women giving birth (see Loraux, *op.cit.*, p. 130, note 89; and also F. Lissarrague 'Figures of Women', in P. Schmitt Pantel (ed.), *A History of Women in the West* (Harvard University Press, 1992) p. 182).
30. An idea illustrated even more graphically in the myths of aborted foetuses which Epstein discusses: see Epstein, *op. cit.*

20

Dispossessing the Father in the Fiction of Michel Tournier

Mark Ferrigan

The anxiety of fatherhood informs the writing of Michel Tournier in both its fictional content and its wider literary context. Tournier's fathers often appear as ineffectual figures who are quickly eliminated from the texts they appear in, whilst his main characters betray an unmistakable reluctance to become fathers in their own right. Furthermore, Tournier's texts make constant reference to literary forefathers, often establishing a web of intertextual allusions and references so as to operate an ideological subversion of previous texts. The Bloomian overtones of Tournier's relationship with his literary fathers is clear and has already been commented on by critics; Michael Worton, for example, writes that 'Tournier's response to his acute awareness of literary influence is ambivalent. He feels both an almost angry envy and genuine loving gratitude.'[1] I examine some of the many negative images of fatherhood which appear in Tournier's fiction, arguing that the only real alternative to accepting fatherhood is – in the context of Tournier's writing – escape into a mythology of self-creation which serves both to deny the father and to preclude the possibility of becoming a father in one's own right.

On a thematic level, Tournier's major novels all focus on characters whose biological fathers are absent and who are also unable – or unwilling – to become fathers in their own right; Robinson, the hero of Tournier's first novel, *Vendredi ou les Limbes du Pacifique*,[2] is cut off from his parents and children when he is shipwrecked; Abel Tiffauges, the protagonist of *Le Roi des Aulnes*, is effectively abandoned by his father, who puts him into boarding school from an early age, whilst as an adult Tiffauges is emotionally and physically too immature – he is described as being 'microgenitomorphic'[3] – to sustain any relationship that could possibly lead to fatherhood. Again, in

Tournier's third novel, *Les Météores*, the relationship between the identical twins Jean and Paul is so deeply inward-looking that any attempt on their behalf either to establish a relationship with their father, or to assume the role of father in their own right, is doomed to failure. As Jean says: 'What about Edouard? I loved him dearly, and I still haven't got over his pitiful death. But the hard truth is that he wasn't cut out to be a father... Unless I was the one who didn't know how to be a son, because of being a twin, which distorted everything.[4]

Tournier's next major work, *Le Vent Paraclet*, continues in a similar vein. Although Tournier claims that the text is 'an intellectual autobiography'[5] there is substantial critical disagreement over how literally it should be read – Colin Davis, for example, warns that certain passages should not be taken 'too seriously',[6] whilst Françoise Merllié claims that *Le Vent Paraclet* is 'extremely dangerous for critics' as the book is, in her opinion, 'the most fascinating of novels, in the sense that the author constructs his own character before our very eyes'.[7] Whether fact or fiction, *Le Vent Paraclet* also marginalises father-figures. The hero-narrator's father is rarely mentioned, and when he does make an appearance, he is described as 'too discrete, too self-effacing to have ever wanted to mould his sons in any way' (p. 151).

Not only is Tournier's father effectively absent from the text, all other adult role models are denied: 'when I ask myself who I might call my mentors, I find only emptiness and disappointment' (p. 151). Although Sartre briefly won the young Tournier's respect, he too is quickly eliminated. The narrator suggests once again that the conflict inherent in any father–son relationship (whether metaphoric or literal) was responsible for his rejection of Sartre: 'This rejection of Sartre should be taken for what it was: a sort of elimination of the father by overgrown adolescents who were uncomfortable with the knowledge that they owed him everything' (pp. 161–2).

When actually faced with biological fatherhood, Tournier's creations fail their offspring in one of two ways; either they are prevented from performing the role of father by other stronger-willed family members, or they attempt to deny fatherhood by disposing of their children; Tournier's most prolific father, the ill-fated Edouard of *Les Météores*, is regarded by his wife Maria-Barbara as little more than 'the provider of the insignificant gesture which unleashes the creative process' (p. 12), whilst his son Jean regards his father as having been 'dispossessed' of his paternal function by his overbearing brother Paul (p. 464); Again, Gilles de Rais, the anti-hero of *Gilles et Jeanne*, abandons his wife and daughter in order to pursue occult experiments which involve the systematic torture and murder of other men's sons.[8]

This splitting of the biological and social chain serves a dual purpose in Tournier's writing; it appears both as the necessary precondition of each character's self-realisation, and as the price to be paid for there being a story to tell. Unfathered and unfathering, Tournier's creations are free to undertake personal transformation, yet the absent father continues to haunt their text. Tournier's characters initially respond to this absence by attempting to reintegrate themselves into the social and biological chain by reinventing familial – and specifically fatherly – relationships; when this strategy fails – as it invariably does – they resort to the creation of mythologies of self-generation in which they play the leading part. Robinson, in *Vendredi ou les Limbes du Pacifique*, initially attempts to replace his lost family by playing son, then lover, to his desert island. After copulating with the sand dunes Robinson becomes a father, as the aptly named Speranza gives birth to his 'daughters', white mandrakes. The strategy fails, however; Robinson catches Vendredi making love to the sand dunes, and realises that his 'right' of exclusive access to the mother's body has been infringed and that consequently his paternity has been thrown into doubt. Abandoning this approach, Robinson seeks refuge in fantasies of eternal youth and time standing still: 'my days stand on end, they no longer run into each other, [they] are no longer differentiated by the successive stages of a project being carried out, they are so alike that they merge perfectly into one another in my mind, and it seems as if I am constantly reliving the same day' (p. 219).

Abel Tiffauges, the hero of *Le Roi des Aulnes*, also experiences the failure of reinvented fathers. On the one hand Tiffauges plays father to the hundreds of adolescent boys at the élite Nazi school where he works, whilst on the other hand he attempts to father his own 'inner child': 'I carry him deep within me, this innocent, defenceless creature...who is so easily tricked, so slow to come to terms with misfortune... As if twenty years later I could carry his pain on my adult's shoulders and make him laugh, laugh!' (pp. 41–2).

The failure of these surrogate relationships is highlighted in the closing pages of the novel. Tiffauges makes no attempt to negotiate with the Russian soldiers, who then proceed to butcher his adopted children, whilst on the other hand Tiffauges' inner child – who has materialised as the young Jewish refugee Ephraïm – leads him to his death in the Prussian marshes. Through this inglorious end Tiffauges coincides with the mythological figures of the Erlkönig, thereby fulfilling his earlier claims of immortality and parthenogenesis: 'As old and immortal as the world, I can only have a putative mother and father and adopted children' (p. 14).

Surrogate fatherhood also makes a brief appearance in *Les Météores*, only to end, once again, in failure. Jean describes his meeting with the ageing American Ralph in the following terms: 'We immediately adopted each other, and although I don't know what happened in his mind or in his heart, I discovered in myself something I had never been before: a son. Ralph's old dream of becoming a father had suddenly come true' (p. 463).

Jean follows his new-found father to his home in Tunisia, yet no sooner have they arrived than Ralph's wife dies, and Ralph's personality disintegrates under the weight of 'senility and alcoholism' (p. 478). Jean has little choice but to relinquish his fantasy of adoption, and abandon his would-be father to his fate. This novel of inglorious paternal failure is saturated with images of self-creation which explicitly deny the possibility of fathering in one's own turn. As Paul never tires of saying, the twins are (at least in his imagination) 'a sterile, eternal couple, united in a perpetual loving embrace' (p. 197). Again, having boldly stated in *Le Vent Paraclet* that his own childhood was marked by an absence of paternal influence and significant others on which to model himself, the hero/narrator claims to have created himself *ex nihilo*: 'I am a pagan priest who reads his past, present and future by cutting open his belly and examining his own entrails' (p. 227).

The contrast between the breakdown of the father–son relationship and myths of self-generation appears in its starkest form in *Gaspard, Melchior et Balthazar*,[9] Tournier's rewriting of the three kings legend. In this story the conflict between generations is unmediated by any attempt to reinvent family roles. The kings who pay homage to Jesus are all orphans, in that their fathers are either dead or simply absent, whilst Herod, whose story is told in the central chapter, has his own sons executed and orders the murder of the Innocents. Herod's tale of infanticide is significantly flanked by two stories of fatherless generations, 'Goldenbeard or the succession' and 'The donkey and the ox'. The first story recounts the tale of an ageing king concerned about his succession, who is miracuously transformed into a young boy, whilst the second story recounts the equally miraculous – and fatherless – birth of Jesus.

As already mentioned, Tournier's writing betrays a distinct unease with relation to his literary precursors. This unease is most evident in his subversive rewriting – even appropriation of – other writers' work. In *Le Vent Paraclet,* Tournier comments on the similarity between a passage in his *Le Roi des Aulnes* and a scene in Alain-Fournier's *Le Grand Meaulnes*. Rather than acknowledge a debt to the literary 'father', Tournier claims that the passage is actually his, even if written over half a century later: 'this scene belongs more to me than to Alain-Fournier, because in *Le Grand Meaulnes* it only has an episodic, anecdotal character, whereas in *Le Roi des Aulnes* it prefigures everything that follows, and is quite clearly dependent on the notion of 'phoria' which is the novel's only subject'.[10] This argument leads to the conclusion that 'if one of them, Fournier or Tournier, had to be charged with plagiarism, Fournier would clearly be the guilty one' (pp. 55–6). Not only does Tournier charge Alain-Fournier with plagiarism, he also symbolically appropriates Fournier's text, in so far as the title of Tournier's novel ('Le Roi des *Aulnes*') may be read as a reworking of Fournier's title ('Le Grand Me*aulnes*'). Again, according to *Le Vent Paraclet,* Tournier's mother's maiden name was also Fournier – making the hero-narrator both Tournier and Fournier.

The most often cited example of Tournier's rewriting of his literary precursors is undoubtedly *Vendredi ou les Limbes du Pacifique,* which, it is often claimed, is a 'an ideological subversion' of Defoe's *Robinson Crusoe.*[11] This subversive rewriting of other writers' work may also be observed in the early collection of short stories, *Le Coq de bruyère,* where Tournier's target appears to be the writers of childrens' stories, notably Perrault and Grimm.[12] Thus the title story may be read as a subversive rewriting of Perrault's 'Bluebeard'. Like the original Bluebeard, Tournier's Baron de Saint-Fursy lives in a castle and is dedicated to the pursuit of women; just as Bluebeard forbids his wife to go into a certain room of the castle, where the remains of his previous wives are kept, so the Baron prevents his wife and servants from entering his office. The parallel is made explicit – and the intertextual stakes raised – when Tournier's text makes reference to a cinematic descendant of its literary precursor: 'huge posters announced that *Bluebeard* was showing that week at the Rex, starring Pierre Brasseur and Cécile Aubry' (p. 220).

Tournier thus problematises the intertextual chain by intercalating a second, iconographic, text between his story and Perrault's 'Bluebeard', effectively making his story a rewriting of a rewriting. The text–image–text structure is maintained in the story's dénouement; when the Baronness and her maid Eugénie do eventually break the

Baron's sanction and go into his room, they find not women's bodies, but their *photographic* representation: 'At that very moment Eugénie knocked over a huge pile of erotic magazines and photographs which spread out over the carpet. More of that filth! exclaimed the Baroness. I knew he was hiding them somewhere!' (p. 223).

In the same collection, the short story 'The Red Dwarf' may also be read as a subversive rewriting both of Perrault's 'Little Red Riding Hood' and Grimm's 'Snow White'. This time childish innocence is done away with as Tournier's dwarf (Lucien) sleeps with Snow White (Edith), murders her, and then sodomises the handsome prince (Bob). Alternatively, both Lucien's nickname 'the red dwarf' and his surname 'Gagneron' link him to the young heroine of Perrault's 'Little Red Riding Hood' ('petit *Gagneron/chaperon* rouge'). In Tournier's text, however, it is Little Red Riding Hood who kills (and rapes) the grandmother (Edith) and then manages to put the blame on the wolf (Bob). When Tournier's wolf eventually finds Little Red Riding Hood and begs for help, he not only fails to uncover her identity as the killer, but is forced to submit to the child's sexual fantasies: 'he came to his former rival's bed each night, and possessed him like a woman' (p. 118).

As I hope these two examples have demonstrated, Tournier's dialogue with his literary fathers is far from one of filial reverence. It would follow, at least from the patterns established in the novels, that once the (literary) father has been displaced the only course open to the Tournierean text is to attempt to generate itself. This is precisely what happens in the second collection of short stories, *Le Médianoche amoureux*.[13] Once again, the text presents the reader with a series of negative images of fatherhood; in 'Blandine or the father's visit', for example. Blandine's father attempts to use his daughter's influence over the narrator for his own ends; again, in 'African adventures', Hatem's father pimps his son to a French homosexual, despite the boy's evident disgust at sodomy. Perhaps the strongest image of failure – even catastrophe – of fatherhood in *Le Médianoche amoureux* is provided by the story 'Angus'. The hero of the story, Jacques, is born to Colombelle after she has been raped by Tiphaine, and the identity of the criminal father is hidden from the child. To avenge his daughter's rape, Colombelle's father makes Jacques swear that he will kill Tiphaine 'in single combat' (p. 209). Only when the sixteen-year old has challenged Tiphaine, and, against all the odds, defeated him, does he learn who his father is. Tiphaine's letter to Jacques, written on his death bed, makes it clear that as far as the father is concerned, father–son relationships are essentially rooted in conflict: 'I understand that a son should kill his father – that's natural' (p. 222), adding, somewhat ironically: 'We only met long enough to exchange a few blows, the last of which killed me. I wish you better luck with your offspring' (p. 223).

By so thoroughly discrediting fatherhood, *Le Médianoche amoureux* implicitly raises the question of its own literary heritage. Although Tournier occasionally acknowledges previous writers, literary influence is often passed over in silence. Thus for example, the title of the seventh story, 'Lucie or the woman without a shadow', alludes to Hugo van Hofmannsthal's 'Die Frau ohne Schatten', but Tournier leaves the reader to make the connection for him/herself. Even when literary debt is acknowledged, Tournier seems reluctant to accept wholeheartedly another writer's influence. Thus, while admitting that 'Angus' (the fourteenth story) was inspired by Victor Hugo's 'L'Aigle du casque', the author cannot resist pointing out that 'the story takes a very different turn to that told by Victor Hugo', ironically pleading for forgiveness: 'May the soul of Victor Hugo forgive my liberty' (p. 226).

Whilst problematising its relationship to its literary forefathers, *Le Médianoche amoureux* also encourages an image of itself as a spontaneously self-generated text; no explanation is offered for why the guests at the dinner party tell their stories, instead we are simply asked to believe that they 'happened' of their own accord: 'Neither Nadège nor Oudalle knew who thought of telling the first story. It was lost in the night, just like the second and third' (p. 40).

This image of textual self-generation is further emphasised by the way in which the stories echo and repeat each other, encouraging a reading which constantly moves backwards and forwards between stories, without ever establishing a hierarchy of influence or a point of origin. *Le Médianoche amoureux* eventually turns full circle as the closing words of the text ('You will be the high priest of my kitchens and the guardian of the culinary and manducatory rites which spiritualise meals') exactly repeat the closing words of the first story (pp. 42 and 268). In the context of Tournier's evident unease with father–son relationships, it is tempting to read this dramatic gesture of closure as a symbolic sealing of the text against the perceived threat of future generations of writers. Purportedly without origin and without end, Tournier's text denies paternal influence and pre-empts the threat of filial appropriation; intertextuality gives way to autotextuality, as textual self-generation replaces dialogue with the literary father.

It thus appears that the strategy of self-generation adopted by Tournier's characters, in response to the failure of fatherhood, is paralleled on a textual level as Tournier attempts to come to terms with his literary heritage. Just as his protagonists seek refuge in fictions of self-creation, so Tournier's writing attempts to clear a space free of 'paternal' influence in which the text may then freely generate itself. Furthermore, Tournier's practice of hermetically sealing his texts suggest that he is perhaps anxious to protect his work from appropriation by other writers. A further indication that Tournier has little intention of handing over his power to the next generation of writers was given in a recent film interview. Commenting on winning the Prix Goncourt for *Le Roi des Aulnes* by a first-ever unanimous vote, Tournier half-jokingly stated that he would use his new-found position on the Goncourt Jury to make sure that no other writer repeated this achievement.[14]

Notes

1. See in particular Michael Worton's article 'Ecrire et ré-écrire: Le projet de Tournier' in *Sud*, 61 (1985) 52–69.
2. Michel Tournier, *Vendredi ou les Limbes du Pacifique* (Paris: Gallimard, 1967).
3. Michel Tournier, *Le Roi des Aulnes* (Paris: Gallimard, 1970) p. 206.
4. Michel Tournier, *Les Météores* (Paris: Gallimard, 1975) pp. 463–4. All translations Mark Ferrigan.
5. Michel Tournier, *Le Vent Paraclet* (Paris: Gallimard, 1977) p. 7.
6. Colin Davis, *Michel Tournier, Philosophy and Fiction* (Oxford: Clarendon Press, 1988) p. 128, note 26.
7. Françoise Merllié in *Michel Tournier* (Paris: Belfond, 1988) p. 190.
8. Michel Tournier, *Gilles et Jeanne* (Paris: Gallimard, 1988).
9. Michel Tournier, *Gaspard, Melchior et Balthazar* (Paris: Gallimard, 1980).
10. *Le Vent Paraclet*, p. 55.
11. See, for example, Gerard Genette, *Palimpsestes: La Littérature au second degré* (Paris: Seuil, 1982) pp. 418–25, and Lynn Salkin-Sbiroli, *Michel Tournier, La Séduction du Jeu* (Geneva-Paris: Slatkine, 1987).
12. Michel Tournier, *Le Coq de bruyère* (Paris: Gallimard, 1978).
13. Michel Tournier, *Le Médianoche amoureux* (Paris: Gallimard, 1989).
14. Gérard Blain, *Michel Tournier*, video, 'Témoins' series (1983).

21

Molière's Disturbing Fathers

Tivadar Gorilovics

Molière paints a portrait of the society of his time and, in particular, of the bourgeois family.[1] Critics seem to agree that he was the first to take as his object, 'no longer isolated figures and stock types, but the richer reality of a family or a social setting, with their conflicts and their dynamism, with oppositions of light and shade, emotion and laughter.'[2] This *comédie bourgeoise* which Molière invented and which, incidentally, is fully realised in only a handful of plays,[3] obeys its own rules of dramatic composition, which Richard Monod has characterised thus: 'it imprisons the head of the bourgeois family in his own home with relatives, children, servants, visitors. For the very first time we see the bourgeois family from the inside.'[4]

Quite clearly, the central role is rightly held by the figure of the father, or occasionally the tutor, as is the case in *L'École des maris* or *L'École des femmes*. It should be noted that there is scarcely a single example of a Molière comedy from which this central figure is absent. It is not only the keystone of certain major works, but a constant element in the whole of his theatrical output. There is a single exception worth mentioning, one we must recognise as not insubstantial, and that is *Le Misanthrope*. However this exception merely proves a rule which is as applicable to the portrayal of the bourgeois world as it is to that of the aristocratic world presented in *Dom Juan*.

This said, commentators (at least those I have read) do not appear to have critically examined the strange way in which Molière presents the reality of the family in his work. Since the family is, by common definition, a group composed of father, mother and their children, it cannot be complete when one of these constitutive elements is missing. However, it would seem abundantly clear that the family in Molière's work is only very infrequently complete and this for the simple reason that the figure of the mother is almost invariably absent. One can count on the fingers of one hand those plays in which she is present: on the one hand are Angélique's mother, the aptly-named Mme de Sottenville in *Georges Dandin*, the cantankerous Mme Pernelle in *Le Tartuffe* and the unbearable Philaminte in *Les Femmes savantes*; on the other, by way of contrast with these disagreeable mothers, we may add the likeable princess Aristione from *Les Amants magnifiques* and the kindly Mme Jourdain from *Le Bourgeois gentilhomme*. If it is the duty of the mother to warm the hearts of the members of her family and, through the warmth of her presence, to ward off or counter the effects of the conflicts that threaten to undermine the family from within, then three out of the five mothers I have identified above are totally incapable of fulfilling this role. Nor do the two others, albeit made of finer stuff than the first group, correspond to the definition much better. The one mother figure who has the ability to trigger off feelings of love and tenderness appears only in a speech by Cléante in *L'Avare* and is not therefore directly involved in the action. This is Mariane's mother 'who is,' says Cléante, 'almost always ill and for whom this loving daughter professes feelings of friendship which are scarcely to be imagined. She tends her, shares her suffering and consoles her with a tenderness that would move you to the very soul.'[5]

In the absence of tender loving mothers, Molière could theoretically have put in their place affectionate fathers who were kind to their offspring. If he chose not to do so, we must assume that it is because such a substitution would have appeared to him to have been totally unrealistic.[6] It is not so much that the affectionate and sensitive father figure is completely absent from his drama, but rather that on the rare occasions when such a figure does appear, he has difficulty having himself taken seriously. Hence Sganarelle, in *Le Mariage forcé*, dreaming of conjugal bliss combined with family happiness, explains:

> I consider that . . . by getting married I shall be able to see myself live again in other little selves, that I shall have the pleasure of seeing creatures that have come from my body, little faces that will be as like to me as two peas in a pod, who will be continually playing in the house, and who will call me papa when I come back from town and will tell me a thousand pleasant little nonsenses.[7]

But this is a fifty-two year old bachelor speaking, expressing belated regrets at his childlessness which, for all the sympathy they may deserve, nevertheless bring a smile to the audience's lips.

What is significant in a different way is when paternal affection is no more than a front behind which the selfishness of the bourgeois may shelter. Such is the case of the Sganarelle of *L'Amour médecin* who initially pretends to be upset by his daughter's 'melancholy', whispering tenderly in her ear: 'Come along, open up your little heart to me. There, there, my sweet one, tell, tell, tell your little thoughts to your dear little darling papa.'[8] But at the very moment when his daughter is about to pour out her heart and confess that marriage alone will provide the remedy for her ills, this loving father has a sudden change of mood and, refusing to listen, begins insulting her: she is now a thankless child and a hussy whom he wonders whether he should not disown. Is this a metamorphosis? Not at all. It is simply a revelation of his true character which is that of a thrifty bourgeois and domestic tyrant. Sganarelle has accumulated a certain amount of wealth and does not want to part with any of it, especially as a dowry. He ends up shamelessly confessing as much: 'I was wise to forestall the open declaration of a desire that I am not prepared to satisfy. Has one ever seen anything more tyrannical than this custom to which they would like to subject fathers?... No, no I scoff at this tradition and I intend to keep both my wealth and my daughter to myself.'[9]

If we put together an identikit picture of these bourgeois fathers it would in truth be possible to think only of negative characteristics: even their common sense is terribly vulgar, as is the case with Gorgibus in *Les Précieuses ridicules* who, faced with the silliness of his daughter and his niece, is in the wrong by being right. These bourgeois who, with the rare exception of M. Jourdain and maybe one or two others, think only of accumulating as much money as possible are for the most part 'old men', in other words they are at least forty. This age seems to represent an important stage in the development of their chosen vice, at least if we are to believe *Sganarelle ou le cocu imaginaire*, in which the father's avarice is characterised as 'the most common of passions affecting old men, just as love is the one which holds sway in a young heart, and especially in that of a young girl.'[10]

These fathers are by definition right-thinking people full of platitudes and self-righteousness, completely preoccupied with the task of marrying off their daughters – who themselves clearly exist simply to add to their worries – as advantageously as possible. The solidly bourgeois Gorgibus of *Les Précieuses ridicules* naturally thinks that 'marriage is a holy and sacred thing' (IV, p. 268) that is to say, something far too serious to be considered an affair of the heart: 'I know their family and what they own,' he says of two of the young suitors, 'and I am absolutely resolved that you should arrange to take them as your husbands. I am weary of having to provide for you.' And should the young ladies prove recalcitrant, he threatens to have them locked up in a convent.[11] These bourgeois characters are also – and there is nothing at all surprising about this – completely hostile and insensitive to 'products of the mind', and this is a failing they retain even when they seem to be in revolt against those vagaries of fashion which simple common sense would condemn. In the argument of *Sganarelle ou le cocu imaginaire*, to which we have already referred, Molière says that Sganarelle recommends to his daughter 'that she read, rather than *Clélie*, some of those old books which give you some idea of the antiquity of the fellow and in which there is nothing that would not seem barbaric if compared with the style of the works of the illustrious Sappho'.[12] Gorgibus, the stereotype of the bourgeois as Adam has called him, 'is an old-fashioned Gaulois, and his ideas are of the ilk of those which were in vogue at the time of the League. . . . he observes indignantly the changes in the moral order, the triumph of gallantry, youth's taste for pleasure, the increasing freedom of women.'[13]

Domestic bliss does not exist in this universe: as we have seen, mothers are usually absent and when present they can be just as authoritarian as the men, as in the case of Mme Pernelle, or else blatantly usurp paternal power, as is the case with Philaminte. The family is in fact a battlefield where the absolute (or supposedly absolute) power of the father is at loggerheads with the children's desire to win their freedom or break away from paternal control, their efforts being supported by some more liberal uncle and, to much greater effect, by cheeky servants such as Dorine in *Le Tartuffe*. Most of Molière's comedies follow this pattern. It is true that the struggle is played out according to the rules of the comic genre and by its very definition the latter precludes any possibility of a catastrophic outcome; nevertheless, the comedy is not entirely devoid of seriousness. To borrow the words of a contemporary Hungarian author,[14] Molière did not joke where humour was concerned.

Yet even if we accept that the fathers he shows us angrily posturing are no more than figures of fun or characters without real weight who are incapable of frightening anyone, their words, their actions and especially their threats are far from being purely imaginary. When they stop themselves at the last minute from raising their hands to their children or give instructions for their daughters to be locked away in a convent, when they banish their sons from their houses and talk about disinheriting them, they are referring to very real forms of retaliatory action and it is here that they take on a disturbing aspect. They are also disturbing as a group in so far as they bear terrible resemblances to each other. They wield a power which is both real and symbolic, whose scope and character is clearly described by Harpagon's son when he explains to his sister, to whom he is confessing the fact that he is in love:

> Yes, I am in love. But before we go any further, I know that I am dependent on my father, and that the very name of son makes me subject to his will; that we should never give our word without the agreement of those who brought us into this world; that Heaven has made them the masters of our destiny, and given that they are not beset by any wild desires [which is in fact not at all the case since Harpagon, even at his age, wishes to marry!], they are in a position to make fewer mistakes than we and to see much better than we what is our best interest; that we should rather believe in the lights of their wisdom than in the blindness of our passion; and that the rashness of youth more often than not has terrible consequences.[15]

This is the very model of the social speech on the family and paternal authority, expressing as it does all the arguments ordinarily drawn upon to defend the institution of the family. However, and it is here that Molière re-establishes a sort of equilibrium between the defenders of the moral order and the younger generation which seeks to champion the rights of the heart and consequently the rights of the individual. It is true that scarcely has the model speech been uttered by Cléante than he brings the whole edifice crumbling down by saying, 'I tell you all that, dear sister, so that you don't need to take the trouble to tell me it yourself; because in fact the strength of my love will allow me to hear nothing of all this and I beg you not to remonstrate with me.'[16]

The happiness of the younger characters is not threatened solely by paternal power as a social institution, but also by some paternal vice or character defect which transforms the father into a sort of natural disaster which has to be suffered and against which protection must be sought since he threatens to ruin the entire family, as in *Le Tartuffe*, or at the very least, as is most often the case, the happiness of the younger characters. And so a struggle begins between the tyrant and his character defect (avarice, credulousness, hypochondria etc.) with the latter proving itself to be intractable. When their stories are complete, neither Arnolphe, nor Harpagon, nor Argan have undergone a change of character, and nor indeed has Orgon, who will henceforth be as absolute in his new-found scepticism as he previously was in his credulousness.

These fathers being what they are, that is to say insurmountable obstacles to the happiness of the younger characters and a hostile presence which more often than not inspires neither affection nor confidence, we cannot be surprised when we hear things said about them whose seriousness is mitigated only by the conditions in which they are spoken, that is to say the context of comedy. To wish for the death of a father, or even quite simply to consider it as a possibility, runs so counter to the most basic moral principles that it is normally seen as transgressing a taboo. The clearest example of this type of transgression is without doubt that of Dom Juan, who does not hesitate to vent his anger (itself perhaps a surpressed desire for a killing) against the father who hampers him in the exercise of his freedom as a great lord: 'Oh! die as soon as you can, it's the best thing you could do. Each of us must have his turn and it maddens me to see fathers who live as long as their sons.'[17]

It might be claimed that Dom Juan is a very special case and that may indeed be true. Yet Mascarille, Lélie's valet in *L'Etourdi*, says much the same thing though his importance as a character bears no relation to that of the son of Dom Louis. Mascarille says to his young master: 'Pay no attention to the advice of that old codger of a father, just keep on going and let the world go by' and, 'Your father shows an extreme reluctance to make all your dreams come true by an early demise',[18] a speech which, we may recall, awakens not the slightest reaction in the son, who is clearly not at all shocked by the verbal license of his servant. This brings to mind La Bruyère's telling words: 'Children might perhaps be more cherished by their fathers and, likewise, fathers by their children, if there were no such things as inheritances'; or this second observation by the same author: 'There are some very strange fathers whose aim in life seems to be to provide their children with reasons for consoling themselves when they die.'[19]

One could offer many more such examples and also bring out other aspects of the father/child relationship in Molière's work. I shall conclude with a quotation from *Sganarelle ou le cocu imaginaire* which throws a harsh light on the way Molière explored the terrain of fatherhood. When his daughter seems to be willing to bend herself to his wishes, Sganarelle, overcome with joy, says:

> Come closer, come here so I may kiss you,
> There is nothing wrong with such an action.
> When a father so wishes, he may kiss his daughter,
> Without there being any reason for anyone to cause a fuss.[20]

Nothing serves better than this curious remark, to which I shall refrain from attributing the hidden meaning which might be seen within it, to illustrate the insuperable distance which can separate a father from his daughter in that desert of love that is the world of the family.[21]

Notes

1. References to texts by Molière are from the two volume Pléiade edition edited by Georges Couton: *Oeuvres Complètes* (*OC*) (Paris: Gallimard, 1971).
2. Antoine Adam, *Histoire de la littérature française au XVIIe siècle* (Paris: Del Duca, 1962) III, *L'Apogée du siècle. Boileau-Molière*, p. 405. All translations from French by Patrick Corcoran.
3. On this point Adam quotes *Le Tartuffe, Le Misanthrope, Les Femmes savantes* and *L'Avare* (*ibid.*). Richard Monod (see following note) places five plays in this category, 'from *Tartuffe* to the *Malade imaginaire*'.
4. Richard Monod, entry on Molière, *Dictionnaire des littératures de langue française*, J.-P. de Beaumarchais, Daniel Couty and Alain Rey (eds) (Paris: Bordas, 1984) p. 1525.
5. *... qui est presque toujours malade, et pour qui cette aimable fille a des sentiments d'amitié qui ne sont pas imaginables. Elle la sert, la plaint, et la console avec une tendresse qui vous toucherait l'âme.* (*OC* II, p. 519.) It should be pointed out that this type of mother–daughter relationship, even if it clearly existed, was nevertheless far from typical. This at least is the view of Philippe Ariès in *L'Enfant et la vie familiale sous l'Ancien Régime* (Paris: Seuil, 1973) p. 7. The historical family 'had no affective function. That is not to say that love was invariably absent: on the contrary it is often discernible and sometimes from the moment of betrothal onwards...But [and this is the important point] tender feelings between partners in marriage or between parents and children, were not considered essential to a well-balanced family: they were simply an added bonus whenever they happened to exist.' In this perspective it is easier to understand why, in Cléante's eyes, the feelings of friendship which Mariane professes for her mother 'are scarcely to be imagined'.
6. As we have had occasion to see in the preceding note, such a position is not necessarily dictated by the realities of family life at the time.

7. *...je considère...qu'en me mariant, je pourrai me voir revivre en d'autres moi-mêmes, que j'aurai le plaisir de voir des créatures qui seront sorties de moi, de petites figures qui me ressembleront comme deux gouttes d'eau, qui se joueront continuellement dans la maison, qui m'appelleront leur papa quand je reviendrai de la ville et me diront de petites folies les plus agréables du monde.* (OC I, p. 718.)
8. *Allons donc, découvre-moi ton petit coeur. Là, ma pauvre mie, dis, dis, dis tes petites pensées à ton petit papa mignon.*
9. *...j'ai fait sagement de parer la déclaration d'un désir que je ne suis pas résolu de contenter. A-t-on jamais rien vu de plus tyrannique que cette coutume où l'on veut assujettir les pères?...Non, non: je me moque de cet usage, et je veux garder mon bien et ma fille pour moi.* (OC II, pp. 99 and 103.) Who could forget the famous scene from *L'Avare* with its leitmotiv 'Without a dowry' ('*Sans dot*')?
10. *...la passion la plus ordinaire aux vieillards, de même que l'amour est celle qui règne le plus souvent dans un jeune coeur, et principalement dans celui d'une fille.* See the argument of the first scene, OC I, p. 1225. Philippe Ariès, quoting the example of Molière's old men and how they still appear to be quite young in our eyes, writes 'We know very well that the onset of old age came early in bygone days.' (*op. cit.*, p. 50.) He adds: 'In general, before the 18th century, old men were considered figures of fun', (*ibid.*) and: 'In former times France showed little respect for old age: it was a time for retirement, for books, for prayers and for rambling speech.' (*Ibid.*, p. 51)
11. *...le mariage est une chose sainte et sacrée* (OC I, p. 268); and '*je connais leur famille et leur bien, et je veux résolument que vous vous disposiez à les recevoir pour maris. Je me lasse de vous avoir sur les bras.*' (OC I, p. 270.) Will they really be locked up? Gorgibus' final rejoinder could strictly speaking be interpreted in this sense. (*Ibid.* p. 287)
12. *...au lieu de la lecture de* Clélie *celle de quelques vieux livres qui marque l'antiquité du bonhomme, et qui n'ont rien qui ne parût barbare, si l'on en comparait le style à celui des ouvrages de l'illustre Sapho.* (OC I, p. 1225.)
13. Adam *op. cit.*, p. 275.
14. Frigyes Karinthy.
15. *Oui, j'aime. Mais avant que d'aller plus loin, je sais que je dépends d'un père, et que le nom de fils me soumet à ses volontés; que nous ne devons point engager notre foi sans le consentement de ceux dont nous tenons le jour; que le Ciel les a faits les maîtres de nos voeux, et...que n'étant prévenus d'aucune folle ardeur, ils sont en état de se tromper bien moins que nous et de voir beaucoup mieux ce qui nous est propre; qu'il en faut plutôt croire les lumières de leur prudence que l'aveuglement de notre passion; et que l'emportement de la jeunesse nous entraîne le plus souvent dans des précipices fâcheux.*
16. *Je vous dis tout cela, ma soeur, afin que vous ne vous donniez pas la peine de me le dire; car enfin mon amour ne veut rien écouter, et je vous prie de ne me point faire de remontrances.* Resistance then, resistance against the absolutist claims of paternal authority. But it should also be borne in mind that Cléante is not completely weaponless in this struggle with his

father since he possesses an inheritance from his mother which no-one can touch.

17. *Eh! mourez le plus tôt possible que vous pourrez, c'est le mieux que vous puissiez faire. Il faut que chacun ait son tour, et j'enrage de voir des pères qui vivent autant que leur fils.* (OC II, p. 73.)
18. *Moquez-vous des sermons d'un vieux barbon de père,*
Poussez votre bidet, vous dis-je, et laissez faire. (OC I, p. 56) and:
Votre père fait voir une paresse extrême
A rendre par sa mort tous vos désirs contents. (OC, I, p. 76.)
19. *Les enfants peut-être seraient plus chers à leurs pères et, réciproquement, les pères à leurs enfants, sans le titre d'héritiers.* In Chapter VI, '*Des biens de fortune*' of La Bruyère's *Les Caractères*. And, *Il y a d'étranges pères, et dont toute la vie ne semble occupée qu'à préparer à leurs enfants des raisons de se consoler de leur mort.* (Chapter XI, '*De l'Homme*'.)
20. *Approche-toi de moi, viens ça que je t'embrasse:*
Une telle action n'a pas mauvaise grâce;
Un père, quand il veut, peut sa fille baiser,
Sans que l'on ait sujet de s'en scandaliser. (OC I, p. 324.)
21. Xavier Martin, in his contribution to discussion at the Paternity/Fatherhood Colloquium at the French Institute, London, May 1995, noted the correlation between the increase in the power of the monarchy and in the family in seventeenth century France: legal experts in public law make reference to paternal authority in order to illustrate and justify royal authority; legal experts in private law make reference to royal authority in order to illustrate and justify paternal authority. At the time when Molière was writing, the juridical mechanism by which parents (fathers) maintained control over the matrimonial choices of their offspring (a mechanism which goes beyond any of the canonical laws which should theoretically have applied) is quite 'recent'. It dates from 1639 (Declaration of Louis XIII, sought by Richelieu.)

    We should also remember that, in a study published in *La France et les Français* (*Encyclopédie de la Pléiade*, Paris: Gallimard, 1972), Roland Mousnier has summarised this point as follows: 'While not approving marriages contracted without the agreement of the parents, the Council of Trent nevertheless declared them valid and indissoluble. French lawyers, bowing to social pressure, argued for the absolute authority of the father. Bodin even went so far as to claim the right of life and death over his children. An ordonnance of February 1557 allowed parents to disinherit those of their children who had married against their will. The ordonnance of Blois confirmed this in 1579. In 1639 an ordonnance was issued declaring rebellious children unworthy to succeed their parents'. (p. 1027.)

(Translated by Patrick Corcoran)

22

Shakespeare and the Misrecognition of Fathers and Sons

Lawrence Danson

I am going to look at some deferred, denied and disappointed reunions between Shakespeare's fathers and their estranged sons. But I begin, for the sake of a prefatory contrast, with Shakespeare's daughters, and specifically with those plays late in Shakespeare's career where the father's strong longing for reunion with his lost daughter is also, almost, a longing for union with a woman who must be simultaneously daughter, mother and wife. Pericles, who has fled down the years the dreamlike knowledge of an act of father–daughter incest which illogically but powerfully portends his own unenacted guilt, comes the closest of these Shakespearean patriarchs to fulfilling that fantasy of union; and his language of recognition, mixing pain with joy in ecstatic attainment, almost literalises the fact:

> Give me a gash, put me to present pain,
> Lest this great sea of joys rushing upon me
> O'erbear the shores of my mortality,
> And drown me with their sweetness – Oh come hither,
> Thou that begett'st him that did thee beget... (*Pericles* V.i. 196–200)[1]

In this great scene of anagnorisis, Pericles is granted not only recognition of the daughter who bears him (back) to life but, uniquely in Shakespeare, a concomitant recognition which further mystifies the moment with impossibilities: while still enclosed in mortality's 'muddy vesture of decay' (*Merchant of Venice* V.i. 64), he hears the immortal music of the spheres, which signifies the harmonising of all desire. It is a fantasy of begetting and begotten which converts the horror of incest to the promise of a virtually divine union.

What is accomplished in the action of *Pericles* with such literalness and flat-out emotional license appears in the tragedy of *King Lear*, not as fantasy but as mistake. Awakening from restorative sleep, but thinking that he is dead and in hell, Lear at first misrecognises what he takes to be the literally angelic Cordelia:

> You do me wrong to take me out o' the grave.
> Thou art a soul in bliss; but I am bound
> Upon a wheel of fire, that mine own tears
> Do scald like molten lead. (IV.vii. 46–9)

His wicked daughters had said that 'Old men are babes again'; Cordelia, ministering at Lear's re-awakening, in effect confirms that reversion of roles, but in a different modality. And in its eternity of blessings and forgivings, Lear's fantasy of life with Cordelia joyfully embraces the father's regression:

> Come, let's away to prison.
> We two alone will sing like birds i' the cage.
> When thou dost ask me blessing, I'll kneel down
> And ask of thee forgiveness (V.iii. 8–11)

But in *King Lear* this poignant first reconciliation of father and daughter is aborted; it becomes only another turn of the screw, leading to the reappearance of Lear carrying his daughter's dead body. Since at least the eighteenth century, this tragic ending, the death of Cordelia, has been a kind of audience limit-test of the emotionally and morally endurable. Dr Samuel Johnson confessed that he was, as he puts it, 'many years ago so shocked by the death of Cordelia that I know not whether I ever endured to read again the last scenes of the play till I undertook to revise them as an editor'.[2] I myself am not convinced that Cordelia's death is the only or even the most unendurable thing on Lear's great stage of fools. Freud in 'The Theme of the Three Caskets' identified Cordelia in Lear's arms as Death, the longed-for bride who brings as dowry the comfort denied by the niggardly reality principle: she is daughter as bride as ultimate bringer of impossible ease. The picture of the grieving father – the pathos of *his* loss, the embarrassment of *his* grief, this total indulgence in a male self-pitying fantasy – that I think is a picture which many men might find almost unendurable because it is so embarrassingly frank in its recognition of regressive neediness.

I shall recall one more father–daughter reunion before observing the very differently-troubled recognition scenes between fathers and sons. *The Winter's Tale* has a surplus of recognitions. The reunion of the lost daughter Perdita with her father Leontes is upstaged by her mother Hermione's de-monumentalizing; but that action, the restoration of the wife to Leontes, is dependent on the restoration of the daughter Perdita; and the likeness of mother and daughter, the doubling of their female image, plays out in another way the *Lear* fantasy of female forgiveness and nurture. Leontes' possessive jealousy resulted, sixteen years before, in the death not only of Hermione but also of their son, Mamillius. The play's romance ending pays its dues to reality in several ways. The living statue of the restored Hermione has withered and wrinkled and, more importantly for my purposes, the dead son Mamillius remains quite dead and his place in the romance of paternal reconciliation is taken by the daughter, Perdita.

My point is not to impeach the motives of Shakespeare's fathers but simply to notice the over-determined intensity of the father–daughter recognition scene and, now, to contrast those gloriously sentimentalised reunions with the reunions of Shakespeare's fathers and sons. In the late plays about fathers and daughters, Shakespeare writes, it seems to me, from the father's point of view: as playwright he occupies a father's subject position, almost to the extent of turning the female characters into objects of masculine wish-fulfilment. But in the father–son relations I am about to sketch, Shakespeare tends to write from the point of view of the son. In these encounters of a man with his male progenitor, the oedipal values are quite different: the reunion of Shakespeare's fathers and daughters is a male self-gratifying fantasy, but the reunions of father and son are accomplished, or not accomplished, or only partly accomplished, under the sign of the son's anxious aggressivity. These reunions come about not as the fantasised fulfilment of desire but under the sway of a reality principle, and what they recognise in their attenuated scenes of anagnorisis is a difficult compromise with the son's self-contradictory desires.

Despite the opposition of the eminent Shakespearean Stephen Dedalus, I begin, briefly, with *Hamlet*. In James Joyce's *Ulysses*, Stephen speculates that Shakespeare, who was (he thinks) cuckolded by his wife Anne, identifies not with Hamlet the son but with the cuckolded father, the ghost, Old Hamlet. Indeed, over-determination makes anything possible: every father is also a son, which is part of every father's and every son's problem. But much of the emotion the play generates for the murdered Old Hamlet is generated for him by his son, while the ghostly patriarch, with his dreadfully redundant 'Remember me', is the perfect disembodiment, as it were, of a son's double-bind: young Hamlet's piety, maybe any son's piety, demands that he outdo his father, succeeding, if not where his father has failed then still, unavoidably, succeeding by biological sequence. The one action is both reparation and repetition, both amends and aggression. Young Hamlet succeeds old Hamlet: the doubling of names implies the displacement which threatens or negates the father–son reunion. The father in this ghostly case, beckoning from some place always further off on the battlements, literally can never be embraced; he is psychic prohibition transformed to a condition of protoplasmic impossibility. Shakespeare's most culturally powerful drama of father–son recognition and reunion is a drama of something that can never be accomplished.

In this light it is interesting to speculate, as Stephen Dedalus does, on Shakespeare's own domestic drama. We know certain facts, empty of affective detail. We know, for instance, that William's father, John Shakespeare, was an up-and-comer in Stratford-upon-Avon civic life during his son's childhood. We know that when William was twelve or thirteen years old, John's economic situation sharply declined. Burdened with debt, he gave up his positions in town government. He may have become, literally, afraid to show his face out of doors: we know that he was charged with recusancy, probably not because of his religious scruples but because he feared that going to church would expose him to the debt-collector's warrant. So much is fact and reasonable interpretation; only a small speculative leap is needed to imagine the pubescent son's chaos of shame and anger as he watched his father's disgrace. There is one detail, somewhere between fact and gossip, especially poignant in this regard: according to the early Shakespearean scholar Nicholas Rowe (1709), John Shakespeare sent his oldest son to school 'for some time' and there he 'acquir'd that little *Latin* he was Master of: But the narrowness of his Circumstances, and the want of his assistance at Home, forc'd his Father to withdraw him from thence'.[3] Forced to leave school in order to help at home (a situation which may have made him more eager, at the age of 18, to marry the pregnant Anne Hathaway), the father's social catastrophe became the son's, an embarrassment, at least, and a potentially fatal thwarting of his talents.

The Shakespeare of this drama carries into manhood the anger that would make a son want both to rescue his father and to punish him, to make it up to the old man and to show up the old man; and he also carries the guilt his anger incurs. This Shakespeare makes a very successful professional life for himself in London, but he never abandons his Stratford home. In 1596 he achieves the family coat of arms his father had unsuccessfully sought: he succeeds where his father failed, paying homage while also rebuking the paternal source of shame and guilt, expiating the aggression he simultaneously commits. In 1597 young Shakespeare buys New Place, the second biggest house in town, again outdoing the father whose family fortunes he is repairing. In 1601 John Shakespeare dies, known to fame as the father of his son, and at approximately the same time that son writes *Hamlet*, about a son who finds peace for himself when he gives up trying to avenge the wrongs done his father and accepts with readiness the providence of his own fall.

William and Anne had their own family: a daughter, Susanna, born 1583, and twins, a boy, Hamnet, and a girl, Judith, born 1585. Hamnet died in 1596. So Shakespeare was the father of two daughters, whom he left in Stratford with his wife while he worked in London to become our 'Shakespeare'. For the moment, however, I am less interested in the paternal William's need for reunion with wife and daughters than in the filial William's contemplation of the impossible reunion of father and son.

We see the psychic economy of aggressive repetition, the son doing the father's work only better, in Shakespeare's second historical tetralogy. In the history plays, a Henry succeeds a Henry, as in the tragedy a Hamlet does a Hamlet. Prince Hal, like Prince Hamlet, is 'too much i' the sun'. He has two fathers, a good one and a bad one, a denying one and a permitting one, Henry and Falstaff. What is remarkable is how often, as well as how unsuccessfully, Hal gets to play out the reunion of father and son – a reunion which is achieved by displacing his fathers and which can never therefore be achieved at all.

In *Henry the Fourth Part I* Hal, whose whole life so far seems to have been dedicated to avoiding his father, is finally summoned to appear before Henry at court. This long-awaited meeting of father and prodigal son is rehearsed, before the fact, as a kind of play within the play between Falstaff and Hal. First Falstaff plays the part of father-king and Hal plays himself: 'Do thou', he directs Falstaff, 'stand for my father, and examine me upon the particulars of my life' (II.iv. 372–3). As Falstaff plays the role of fatherly inquisitor, this first reunion of father and son is a travesty: 'This chair shall be my state, this dagger my sceptre, and this cushion my crown' (II.iv. 377–8) says King Falstaff. Falstaff's concluding lines – the mock-father's lines in this staged reunion – are a weak defence of himself as mock-father, 'a goodly portly man, i'faith, and a corpulent; of a cheerful look, a pleasing eye, and a most noble carriage; and, as I think, his age some fifty, or, by'r Lady, inclining to three score' (II.iv. 417–19). Which Hal takes as his cue: 'Dost thou speak like a king? Do thou stand for me, and I'll play my father' (II.iv. 428–9). Falstaff makes the appropriate exegetical comment: 'Depose me?' And now it's Hal's turn to play the father, and Falstaff's to play the son. Hal's denunciation of Falstaff is vigorous, inventive, excessive. Under theatrical cover, when the father plays at being son and the son at being father, Hal can express a filial aggressiveness which only his real father (as we shall see) suspects is Hal's in propria persona. And Father Falstaff, assuming the voice of his fantasy son, defends himself with a poignancy that belongs to the already-defeated: 'But for... old Jack Falstaff, banish not him thy Harry's company, banish not him thy Harry's company – banish plump Jack, and banish all the world' (IV.ii. 472–5). Hal's answer comes, first as a voice in a play within a play, 'I do,' then in his own voice, 'I will'.

The answer is future-tensed beyond recall. Succeeding the father, which in this case will also mean succeeding where his father failed, is a temporal inevitability despite all Hal can do to avoid it. In the tavern, Hal deposes the false father (the father of permission) in the voice of the real father (the father of prohibition). From either position – deposing a father or speaking as a father – it is a rehearsal for the ambiguous act of succession toward which the two parts of *Henry the Fourth* inexorably move him.

The real event of which the scene with Falstaff is the mockery occurs – or, more to the point, fails quite to occur – in Act III. It does not begin well, as Henry figures the delinquent Hal as God's revenge and scourge, the hot vengeance and the rod of heaven to punish his own father's mistreadings (paraphrasing III.ii. 4–11). In this scene, which replays in earnest the tavern's travesty, Hal can only promise future reformation; and the incomplete reunion breaks off, as that earlier play-within-the-play did, on a future tense: Hal promises that he '*will* redeem all this... And in the closing of some glorious day, / Be bold to tell you that I am your son' (III.ii. 132–4).

Part II of *Henry the Fourth* deserves to be treated as more than merely more of the same; but here I pause only at the extraordinary scene when at long last Harry meets Harry. There is a nightmarish – or, if it's not played carefully, a comic – quality to the whole business. Hal sits by his father's sick-bed and moralises on the burdens of kingship, the burdens metonymised as the crown which lies on his father's pillow. The crown is the cause of royal insomnia, a troublesome bedfellow, 'polished perturbation, golden care, / That keeps the ports of slumber open wide / To many a watchful night' (IV.v. 23–5). But this king is not awake, therefore (since all living kings have insomnia) he must be dead. Hal's response to his father's death is, once again, future-tensed with purposiveness:

Thy due from me
Is tears and heavy sorrows of the blood,
Which nature, love, and filial tenderness
Shall, O dear Father, pay thee plenteously.

(IV.v. 37–40)

More present to Hal is the other side of the father–son reciprocity: 'My due from thee is this imperial crown'. Hal puts the crown on his head, and exits; at which point, of course, the King awakes.

Hal's reaction to Henry's untimely recovery, 'I never thought to hear you speak again', elicits Henry's most famous line, 'Thy wish was father, Harry, to that thought' (IV.v. 92), where the wish to remove the father becomes a kind of motherless fathering to the thought of its accomplishment. Hal's excuse for his self-coronation draws on the rhetoric of the heavy crown, the killing burden of king which, counter to logic, makes kingship (like fatherhood) a cause for the audience's pity. It is not hypocrisy, or not just hypocrisy. This grimly absurd scene of premature inheriting reveals a Hal who is guilty for doing what he should do, what he must do. Inheriting a father's heavy crown, Hal also inherits a son's heavy guilt.

Guilt is the subject of the father's last speech to his son: it is Henry's weary admission of how, by 'bypaths and indirect crook'd ways / [he] met this crown' (IV.v. 183–4). Although Henry assures his son that the soil of the achievement goes with him into the ground, he also warns that the results are still to come, in the form of civil insurrection and, by implication, in the hereditary insomnia which comes with the crown and which, as we find in *Henry the Fifth*, does in fact afflict the son. To be this father's successor is to succeed to guilt and its self-inflicted punishment.

Prince Hal's story is a version of the Prodigal Son's story, and it is a story John Shakespeare's son returned to several times in his career before he retired to Stratford to occupy his own dead father's place and title. Perhaps his oddest rescension of it is in *The Merchant of Venice*, a play much troubled with fathers. There is Portia's absent one, Jessica's present one (Shylock), and the ones to whom Shylock is loyal, 'Father Abram', Isaac, and Jacob. The father I am interested in for the moment is a parodic Isaac, a blind patriarch who possesses the blessing; and the son is a parodic Jacob, a trickster who takes his father's blessing. The father, Old Gobbo, enters the play at the moment when young Lancelot Gobbo decides to follow the fiend's friendly counsel to run away from his master the Jew (a father-figure who is 'the very devil incarnation' [II.ii. 25]). At that moment of filial defection, on comes 'my true-begotten father, who, being more than sand-blind, high-gravel-blind, knows me not' (II.ii. 32–4), for as Lancelot says, 'It is a wise father that knows his own child' (II.ii. 73–4). Lancelot decides that he will 'try confusions with him' (II.ii. 34–5): he will stage a recognition scene in the key of absurdist comedy. The humour of class-conflict, as Old Gobbo insists that his son is plain 'Lancelot' while Lancelot insists on being called 'Master Lancelot', is Lancelot's fantasy of outdoing his father; and quickly that aggressive fantasy becomes the more acceptably aggressive fantasy of being grieved over by his father – that is, of being forgiven for his aggression even as he continues it in a different mode by extorting his father's sorrow: 'Talk not of Master Lancelot, Father, for the young gentleman... is indeed deceased, or, as you would say in plain terms, gone to heaven' (II.ii. 57–62).

But having confused him so thoroughly, Lancelot now has to convince the blind father that he is, after all, his son. So he kneels, and Old Gobbo, touching his son's head instead of his chin, feels (as Isaac did when Jacob took the blessing) an unusual hairiness. It is not much as a token of recognition, but it accomplishes as much anagnorisis as the Gobbos will achieve.

This inset comedy of Lancelot and his blind father is not, when you think about it, a whole lot sillier than the bloodily tragic 'sub-plot' it presages in *King Lear*: again a blind father meets an alienated son who, to borrow Lancelot's phrase, tries confusions on the old man and eventually receives his blessing in a recognition scene so delayed and attenuated that, dramatically, it almost doesn't happen. I spoke at the start of this essay about the odd protraction, or repetition, of the Lear–Cordelia recognition and reunion. I conclude with the apparently motherless men in the play's other unhappy family, the Gloucesters.

Edgar the legitimate and Edmund the bastard seem to divide the son's role into good and bad as schematically as Lear's daughters divide their roles. But in the Gloucester family, the dramatic filiations are more complicated than the biological. Edmund the 'natural' son follows a mother-goddess named Nature, whose law is individualist aggression against the 'plague of custom' and the 'curiosity of nations' which bind 'honest madams' issue' (I.ii. 1–9). But it is in Edgar's name that he writes a forged letter urging parricide as a solution to 'the oppression of aged tyranny' (I.ii. 51), which keeps a son's inheritance from him until he is too old to enjoy it. Like the wicked daughters Goneril and Regan, but also like the prodigal son Prince Hal, the issue for Gloucester's issue is the timing of succession. In the aftermath of the forged letter – that is, in the whole extravagant business of Edgar's disguise as Poor Tom, leading his blind father to Dover Cliff and beyond – the clear division of labour between Edmund's filial aggression and Edgar's filial piety erodes. Edmund forges a fictitious letter about Edgar's supposed wish to supplant his father and Edgar now expiates that attributed wish by creating a fiction of himself as dispossessed person. Edgar's fiction abases him in humblest piety but it also fulfils the worst-case scenario which motivates the letter's theory that sons should dispossess fathers: Edgar's role as Bedlam beggar might justify an Edmund (doubly debarred from legal succession, as bastard and as younger son, and therefore dependent on Gloucester's charity) in taking arms against 'the oppression' of an older generation's economic tyranny. And in leading Gloucester to 'Dover Cliff', Edgar simultaneously enacts the wish expressed in the forged letter (he facilitates his father's death, or seeming death, in the seeming leap over Dover Cliff) and in the same set of overdetermined gestures he expiates that parricidal wish in a fury of self-abasement, taking for himself 'the basest and most poorest shape / That every penury, in contempt of man, / Brought near to beast' (II.iii. 7–9).

On the Elizabethan stage, a little disguise went a long way and it would indeed be a wise stage-father who knew his own son if the son merely shifted his shirt. But Edgar as Tom takes disguise to a kind of vanishing point, where he challenges the constructed line between man and beast and where he can proclaim, in his oddly modular formulation, 'Edgar I nothing am' (II.iii. 21). And as nothing-Edgar, as the inherited lack named Poor Tom, he can (in what is surely one of the most disturbing actions the son of John Shakespeare ever created) oversee his unseeing father, leading him to a feigned death, protracting the moment of anagnorisis beyond any canon of realistic motivation. And when that long-delayed recognition comes, it comes anticlimactically, narrated as an off-stage event:

> [I] Led him, begged for him, saved him from despair;
> Never – O fault! – revealed myself unto him
> Until some half hour past, when I was armed.
> Not sure, though hoping, of this good success,
> I asked him his blessing, and from first to last
> Told him our pilgrimage. But his flawed heart –
> Alack, too weak the conflict to support –
> Twixt two extremes of passion, joy and grief,
> Burst smilingly. (V.iii. 195–203)

The recognition of blind father and beggar son is one of the 'trifles', as they are called on stage (V.iii. 301), which pale into insignificance before the image of Lear with Cordelia in his arms. And in dramaturgical terms the anticlimax is unavoidable: how could any play bear more than one heart-rending reunion-in-death? But the evidence throughout Shakespeare's career suggests that the complement of the playwright's strong urge to father–daughter reunion is his equally strong avoidance of the father–son reunion – a reunion he is nonetheless drawn repeatedly to attempting. Edgar's ostensible reason for his delay in revealing himself to Gloucester has the feel of a rationalisation: 'Why I do trifle thus with his despair / Is done to cure it' (IV.vi. 33–4); and possibly it feels like a rationalisation because what Shakespeare really delays or defers could be the intolerable recognition that *Edmund's* wish, the bad son's wish to supplant the father, is also always the good son Edgar's unavoidable destiny.

Notes

1. Quotations from Shakespeare are taken from *The Complete Works*, David Bevington (ed.), 4th edn., (NY: HarperCollins, 1992).
2. W.K. Wimsatt Jr (ed.), *Samuel Johnson on Shakespeare* (NY: Hill and Wang, 1960) p. 98.
3. Reprinted in E.K. Chambers, *William Shakespeare: A Study of Fact and Problems* (Oxford: Clarendon Press, 1930), II, p. 264. Rowe's statement probably derives from the second-hand information of the actor Thomas Betterton. Chambers sees 'no reason to reject' the story (I, 17); but many scholars tend to ignore it, possibly because the idea of Shakespeare's 'little *Latin*' sounds too conveniently mythical.

23

'Father and Mother is One Flesh': Hamlet and the Problems of Paternity

Ann Thompson and Neil Taylor

Shakespeare's *Hamlet* must be one of the world's best-known stories. It has for example been filmed more often than any other narrative with the single and rather surprising exception of *Cinderella*.[1] Yet people get it wrong. The printer of the 1623 First Folio text apparently made a slip in Hamlet's apology to Laertes just before the duel in the final scene. In both the 1603 and the 1604 Quarto texts, Hamlet claims that any wrong he has done Laertes (by killing his father, for example, and driving his sister to madness and death) was committed accidentally: 'I have shot my arrow o'er the house / And hurt my brother, (V.ii. 243–4).[2] In the Folio text he says 'I have shot my arrow o'er the house / And hurt my mother'. Horace Howard Furness in his 1877 Variorum edition of the play quotes Joseph Hunter's 1845 speculation in support of 'mother': 'The change in the Folio might have been made by Shakespeare after he retired to Stratford, the passage as it originally stood coming too near to an incident which had recently occurred in the family of Greville in that neighbourhood, where one of them had by misadventure killed his brother with an arrow.'[3] Furness nevertheless prints 'brother' as do all other editors of the play, including those who privilege the Folio as Shakespeare's own revision of his earlier text; they assume 'mother' is simply a misreading and correct it without feeling any need to comment.

More recent errors are perhaps equally understandable. We are in the process of collecting examples, but here are two we have come across recently. The first is from an account of a presentation by Elaine Showalter at Duke University in 1984 headlined 'Showalter states importance of Hamlet's Ophelia': 'Before a large crowd in Zener Auditorium, Elaine Showalter, a Rutgers University professor of English, lectured on "Representing Ophelia: Women, Madness and the Responsibilities of Feminist Criticism". She focused on the critical interpretations of Ophelia, sister to Hamlet in Shakespeare's play.'[4] We need hardly say that the error was made by the reporter, not by the speaker. The second is from the publicity brochure for the autumn 1994 season of Shakespeare films at the Barbican: 'Following his renowned versions of *The Taming of the Shrew* and *Romeo and Juliet*, Franco Zeffirelli returned to Shakespeare with an inspiring and exhilarating interpretation of *Hamlet*. Mel Gibson impresses as the Prince commanded to murder his brother in the immortal story of intrigue, madness and despair.'[5] This season of films was sponsored by British Airways and our colleague Janet Beer suggested that the brochure might have been compiled by an air hostess who missed some important scenes as she was handing out the drinks.

We want to argue that these errors are not only understandable but in a sense revealing of something about the play and our reading of it. To put it simply, since we can only gesture towards a much larger argument in the space available, we are proposing to claim firstly that *Hamlet* is significantly concerned with sibling relationships, and especially relationships between brothers, and secondly that the Freudian and post-Freudian mode of reading the play as a paradigmatic representation of the Oedipus complex has resulted in a general neglect or distortion of this element. It would not be wise, particularly in the context of this collection, to deny that *Hamlet* is concerned with fathers, but it is also concerned with brothers.

The story begins with fratricide. As the Ghost puts it, 'Thus was I, sleeping, by a brother's hand / Of life, of crown, of queen at once dispatch'd' (I.v. 74–5). Even the murderer stresses the particularly shocking nature of this crime: 'O, my offense is rank, it smells to heaven, / It hath the primal eldest curse upon't, / A brother's murther' (III.iii. 36–8).

Editors duly note that Claudius is thinking here of Cain's murder of his brother Abel in Genesis 4.11–12, a reference which has been anticipated in Claudius' own bland mention of 'the first corse' at I.ii.105 (seen as a revealing irony or what we call a Freudian slip by some commentators) and which recurs in the graveyard scene when Hamlet watches the Gravedigger throwing up a skull: 'That skull had a tongue in it, and could sing once. How the knave jowls it to the ground, as if 'twere Cain's jaw-bone that did the first murder!' (V.i. 75–7).

Shakespeare seems to have been intensely aware that 'the first murder' in Judaeo-Christian tradition was not a parricide (more common in stories of the Greek and Roman gods) but a fratricide. His History plays are scattered with references to Cain and Abel. In *Henry VI Part I*, for example, Humphrey, Duke of Gloucester, accuses the Bishop of Winchester of having contrived to murder 'our dead lord' (meaning Henry V), but is defied by him: 'Nay, stand thou back, I will not budge a foot: / This be Damascus, be thou cursed Cain, / To slay thy brother Abel, if thou wilt' (I.iii. 38–40). Winchester was in fact half-brother to Gloucester's father, Henry IV.

A confusingly similar situation arises at the beginning of *Richard II* when Bullingbrook accuses Mowbray of plotting the death of a later Duke of Gloucester whose '...blood, like sacrificing Abel's, cries, / Even from the tongueless caverns of the earth, / To me for justice and rough chastisement' (I.i. 104–6). The implication here is that it is Richard rather than Mowbray who was ultimately responsible for shedding the blood of his kinsman (in fact his uncle). By the end of the play Bullingbrook, now Henry IV, has also shed the blood of a kinsman, his cousin Richard, and acknowledges that he must 'With Cain go wander through the shades of night' (V.vi. 43).

Two plays later in the sequence, Northumberland welcomes the total subversion of order:

Let heaven kiss earth! now let not Nature's hand
Keep the wild flood confin'd! let order die!
And let this world no longer be a stage
To feed contention in a ling'ring act;
But let one spirit of the first-born Cain
Reign in all bosoms, that each heart being set
On bloody courses, the rude scene may end,
And darkness be the burier of the dead! (*Henry IV Part II*, I.i. 153–60)

The same association with universal fratricide is evoked by Constance in *King John* when she compares her son Arthur to Cain 'the first male child' and implies that he is likely to die at the hands of his relatives, in particular his uncle John (III.iv. 79).

None of these murders is literally a fratricide, but the story of Cain and Abel is clearly an important touchstone for the hostility between male relatives and the competition between male heirs which was for Shakespeare one of the most horrific components of the civil broils of medieval history. It has often been noted (particularly by frustrated student readers) that the History plays contain a large number of consanguineously related English nobles who are difficult to distinguish from each other; writing about the discrepancies between the two texts of *Henry V* as regards the presence or absence of such characters as Warwick, Westmoreland, Gloucester, Clarence and Bedford, Gary Taylor for example sensibly remarks that most of them never achieve individuality anyway, but what is important is that 'Shakespeare surrounds Henry – particularly in difficult moments – with people he can quietly turn to and call "uncle" or "brother"'.[6] Similarly on the negative side, we get used to the accumulation of references to men killing their uncles, nephews and cousins, and occasionally (as in the symbolic tableau in *Henry VI Part III*, II,v) their fathers and sons. (Perhaps the only actual fratricide in the whole sequence is Richard III, who arranges the death of his brother Clarence.)

Curiously, *Hamlet* is the last of Shakespeare's plays to contain an explicit reference to the story of Cain and Abel. And the plot also ends with a kind of fratricide as Hamlet twice refers to Laertes as his brother before they kill each other. T.J.B. Spencer, editor of the Penguin *Hamlet*, has a note on the first instance of this (V.ii. 243–4 quoted above) which says 'As Ophelia's brother, Laertes might have been Hamlet's brother-in-law. But the allusion would be awkward'.[7] 'Brother' could indeed be used to mean 'brother-in-law' in Shakespeare's time. Claudius has not only murdered his brother but married his brother's wife, a fact which Hamlet harps on when scolding Gertrude in the closet scene: 'You are the Queen, your husband's brother's wife, / And would it were not so, you are my mother' (III.iv. 15–16). He makes a bitter point of the rhyme: 'A bloody deed! almost as bad, good mother, / As kill a king, and marry with his brother' (III.iv. 28–9).

Such a marriage was forbidden by the Church, as it is stated in the *Book of Common Prayer*: 'A woman may not marry with her husband's brother', and Henry VIII had rather famously, if belatedly, confirmed this doctrine. In the play, Claudius has formally introduced Gertrude to the court as 'our sometime sister, now our queen' (I.ii. 8). Hamlet in the closet scene accuses her of mistaking one brother for the other – 'What devil was't / That thus hath cozen'd you at hoodman-blind?' (III.iv. 76–7) – but he does not pursue the accusation that she was involved in his father's murder, focusing instead on what he sees as her incestuous second marriage. This, according to Joel Fineman, threatens the dialectic of Difference and No Difference which is at the heart of Shakespeare's exploration of symmetrical patterns of doubles and brothers:

> Gertrude, the 'imperial jointress' on account of whom 'the time is out of joint', represents far more than the simple point of difference between the two brothers. For it is her sensuality that has abolished Difference in Denmark. By sleeping first with one brother and then with the second – by sleeping, that is, both with Hamlet's father and with Hamlet's brother – Gertrude makes it finally apparent that there is in Denmark No Difference at all, at least no difference around which a secure, a sacrally corroborated masculine identity can be organized. (pp. 89–90)[8]

We are singling out Fineman's essay, first published in *The Psychoanalytic Review*, from the large number of psychoanalytic readings of *Hamlet* because it does pay attention to the importance of brothers – but it turns out that it can do so only by reading the fraternal relationship as a displacement of the paternal one. 'Hamlet', says Fineman, 'becomes Claudius' brother when Claudius becomes Hamlet's father' (p. 76), and the link between father and brother constitutes 'the projection of duality onto Oedipal triangularity' (p. 77). 'To Shakespeare, at least at this point in his career, parricide gains meaning, and thereby loses its horror, when it is re-understood as fratricide' (pp. 78–9); 'One dares to kill the father only when he is recognised as an equal, a rival, a brother' (p. 91).

Fineman's is a subtle and nuanced reading of the play, explicitly influenced by the arguments of René Girard in *Violence and the Sacred*[9] that all myths are at bottom fratricidal myths 'for they all address themselves to a fundamental need to distinguish hero from villain, good from bad, in such a way that social value is itself corroborated' (Fineman, p. 86). But it does not answer our desire for an interpretation which will prioritise fraternal relationships *in their own right* rather than as a version of something else. Is this simply because the whole Freudian and post-Freudian tradition of analysis, of real-life relationships as well as of fictional ones, has a lot to say about parents and children, but relatively little to say about siblings?

We want to turn now to real-life relationships. It is distinctly unfashionable to raise biographical issues in Shakespeare criticism these days, but Eric Sams has done so in his recent book, modestly entitled *The Real Shakespeare*,[10] in which he claims that Shakespeare wrote the early, lost version of the Hamlet story known to scholars as the *Ur-Hamlet* and usually attributed to Thomas Kyd. This play was clearly in existence by 1589, whereas the earliest version of *Hamlet* as we know it dates from around 1600 or 1601. Most scholars will not be convinced by Sams on this point, but one of his arguments for Shakespeare's authorship of the early version is that whoever wrote it changed the name of the hero from Amleth to Hamlet, and that Hamlet was the name of Shakespeare's only son who was born in 1585 and died in 1596. This is itself controversial, as all biographers insist that Shakespeare's son was called Hamnet rather than Hamlet, and named after Hamnet Sadler, Shakespeare's Stratford friend, but Sams rightly points out that this man is called Hamlett Sadler in Shakespeare's will and that the spellings seem to have been interchangeable. (There is also the tantalising parallel of Katherine Hamlett who drowned in the Avon in 1579; the Stratford inquest determined that her death was accidental and that she should therefore, like Ophelia, be allowed Christian burial.) It is not appropriate here to enter into extended speculation about Shakespeare's own relationships with his father (who died in 1601), his three brothers, or his son, but we do want to emphasise that for Shakespeare Hamlet or Hamnet must have been defined not only as a son, but, being one of a pair of twins, as a brother, poignantly recalled after his early death, by the surviving twin, Judith, the real-life 'sister to Hamlet'.

* * *

We are engaged in a joint project, a new edition of *Hamlet* (to be published in 2000 AD as one of the third generation of the Arden Shakespeare series). Producing a satisfactory edition of Shakespeare's *Hamlet* takes a long time – perhaps 400 years? The first attempt was made in 1603, when the First Quarto (Q1) was printed. The following year a very different and much longer text came out – the Second Quarto (Q2). In 1623, seven years after Shakespeare's death, another, fairly different and somewhat shorter, text was included in the First Folio (F1) of Shakespeare's *Complete Works*. Since then, countless editors have taken up the challenge. It took Harold Jenkins twenty or more years to produce his 1982 second generation Arden version.[11] Since then other major, scholarly editions have appeared, none of them in agreement with Jenkins, or one another, or anyone else, ever. Do we have any chance of producing an off-spring which satisfies the whole scholarly family?

The first half of this essay has argued for the substitution of one familial focus for another, shifting attention, at least momentarily, away from fathers and towards siblings. The fact is that each of us plays more than one familial role – by the very act of being born, a man or woman can become immediately not just a son or daughter, but a grandson or granddaughter, a nephew or niece, a brother or sister, an uncle or aunt, or a second cousin three times removed.

By marrying into another family, or by having a child, additional roles and relationships are acquired. By marrying twice and having further children with a new partner, the relationships complicate and enrich. Oedipus was much richer than most of us. He not only had two fathers and two mothers from an early age but, by marrying Jocasta, he made his father his brother-in-law, his son his brother, his daughters his sisters. It meant he became his own mother's husband, and therefore his own (third) father. When he realised this, he blinded himself, not only as punishment for such greed but, in Freud's eyes at least, as a symbolic act of self-castration,[12] lest he father further fathers.

It has long been noticed that *Hamlet* is constructed so as to encourage a kind of typological parallelism between elements in its story. Indeed Hamlet himself was the first to engage in this kind of analysis of the text: he compares his father to Hyperion (III.iv. 55–6), his mother to Niobe (I.ii. 49); he asks his mother to compare and contrast the portraits of the man he wants to call father and the man he doesn't want to call father (III.iv. 53–4); he criticises himself for being unable to perform the role of revenge-hero as well as the Player can act (II.ii. 550–69) or Fortinbras can kill (IV.iv. 32–53); and finally, he reflects on Laertes, the man committed to an act of double revenge (a son for a father and a brother for a sister), discerning in Laertes' plight the 'portraiture' of his own double obligation to avenge the loss of his father's life and his mother's honour (V.ii. 75–8). Hamlet's habit of mind involves repeated acts of substitution, Hyperion for father, Niobe for mother, and, as the lines we quote in our title make clear, mother for father.

Analysts outside the play have found in it a still more complex network of parallels. When we hear Polonius telling Hamlet that he once played Julius Caesar and was killed by Brutus in the Capitol (III.ii. 103–4), we not only recognise the irony that Polonius is soon to die in earnest at Hamlet's hand but think back to Hamlet's father, who was killed by Claudius, and forward to Claudius, who is killed by Hamlet at the end of the play. When we hear Hamlet ask the Player to tell Dido's tale to Aeneas (II.ii. 446), we remember how Pyrrhus lost his father and wreaked his revenge on the father of all fathers, Priam, but we also think of Ophelia as Dido and Hamlet as Aeneas. Fortinbras lost his father but his uncle rules; Lucianus kills a king and woos his queen, but since he is the king's nephew, this encourages parallels with Claudius killing Old Hamlet, Hamlet killing Claudius, and even Hamlet's Oedipal designs on his mother – seeking to be a little more than kin.

Hamlet's predilection for mental substitutions is reflected in his punning, the way he plays off kin and kind, son and sun. Puns test out different signifieds on the same signifier. They too are acts of substitution. The very plot of *Hamlet* is founded on certain acts of substitition and exchange – a brother for a brother, a husband for a husband, a father for a father. It begins and ends with a wager, an agreement that what's mine, my property or my life, is potentially yours and what's yours is potentially mine. The outcome may be tragic but many of the events would be at home in French farce – in Act II scene ii Claudius is often played as being unable to distinguish between Rosencrantz and Guildenstern, a pair of interchangeable twins (33–4); in Act III scene iv, Gertrude hides one man behind a curtain just before another comes to visit her in her room, then her husband interrupts them by wandering in in his night-gown; the best-laid plans go astray in Act V scene ii, when Laertes picks up the wrong sword and Gertrude picks up the wrong drink. Claudius may have popped in between the election and his hopes, but once the farce is over Hamlet has the last laugh by substituting Fortinbras for Claudius (V.ii. 355–6) and reversing the outcome of the initial wager between Fortinbras' father and his own.

This act by which Hamlet disinherits himself reminds us that the plot is constructed on an act of disinheritance – the wager between the kings of Norway and Denmark ensured that one or other would end by disinheriting his son (I.i.80–95). But any discussion of Hamlet's inheritance presupposes knowledge of the source of that inheritance. In a paper delivered in Tokyo in 1991, Ruth Nevo referred casually to Hamlet's 'unacknowledged doubt about his own paternity'[13] and Michael Neill, having heard that phrase, published an essay in 1993 in which he wrote of 'the shocking possibility that lies, only half-articulated, beneath Hamlet's reaction to Claudius' magnanimous assumption of paternity: "a little more than kin, and less than kind". For if his aunt-mother is the whore that her precipitate marriage seems to make her, what guarantee remains of Hamlet's "true" paternity?'[14]

Neill remarks in a footnote that this shocking possibility, that Hamlet's father was not called 'Hamlet' but 'Claudius', has been 'strangely ignored by earlier commentators'. But was it there to be ignored? Who created this shocking possibility – Shakespeare, Nevo or Neill? Who is Father, the reader or the author? Or both? Shakespeare begat Hamnet/Hamlet, but was he the only begetter of Hamlet? Is he alone Father and Mother of that mother and father of a play?

The answer has to be no. Not because there are Baconians or Oxfordians to question his paternity but because, although a little book called *Hamlet* was delivered and doing well as early as 1603, there is a sense in which 400 years later, mother is still in labour. Or, in the post-post-structuralist spirit of celebrating the rebirth of the author, should we say 'father is still in labour'? Like the theses/faeces of Father Luther, as fathered by John Osborne, Shakespeare's prince is still going a very slow progress through the guts of an author.

In this case, then, the writer's block is caused by the shape and size of the foetus: it is a monstrous birth, not so much of an artistic failure[15] as of an impossible object. Hamlet's father told him to revenge his foul and most unnatural murder (I.v. 25) but then added, nicely providing him with a clashing ethical imperative, 'Taint not thy mind, nor let thy soul contrive / Against thy mother aught' (I.v. 85–6). The text we have inherited from Shakespeare needs editing, but it arrived with a clash of imperatives: 'This is Shakespeare's *Hamlet*, improve him, but don't do anything his father wouldn't approve of.'

Why does *Hamlet* need editing? Because it is not one text but three (Q1, Q2 and F1), not even non-identical triplets but three distinctly different-looking siblings (although with a family resemblance) yet each bearing approximately the same name. In fact there are four texts called *Hamlet*. Every time an editor gets to work on the play, a mysterious changeling child materialises out of thin air, a fourth text smuggled in by the fairies, the product of an incestuous union of scholars (a kind of writers' guild). Each editor has spawned his (they are almost always men, they are almost always fathers) own new text of *Hamlet*, so that now there are no longer four texts, there are probably at least 4,000. That fourth text is either something which those previous editors genuinely believed Shakespeare once wrote, but which has got lost, or else it is something which they believe he should have written but which he never got round to writing. The object is an impossible one because there are now so many *Hamlet*s. More are born every year and there can never be any telling which, if any, are legitimate, and which, if any, are bastards. We have only got a five year gestation period to go about our 'father's business', otherwise the General Editor will be on to us, admonishing us as naughty children. (To complicate matters still further one of us, Ann Thompson, *is* one of the General Editors!)

We began by saying that *Hamlet* is one of the world's best-known stories, 'Yet people get it wrong'. We then provided examples of people innocently misquoting either the plot or the text of *Hamlet*, substituting for Shakespeare's ideas their own. We would like to close with two observations. The first is that it is interesting, not to say embarrassing, to discover that we are as capable of misquoting the play as anyone else – and in particular that we should go astray in such company on the sensitive issue of Hamlet's father. For the title of the essay we originally submitted for publication (a title which was accepted, and which we are now fond of and wish to retain!) contains a fiction of our own making. We were trying to quote the lines (virtually identical in Q2 and F1): 'Father and mother is man and wife,/ Man and wife is one flesh'.[16] But we came up with something different, something which collapses Hamlet's statement so that there is a statement about a biological relationship alone, rather than a biological relationship *and* a legal relationship.

But there is something else to notice here, and it leads to the second observation. Q1 is rather different from the lines in Q2 and F1: it reads 'My mother is your wife, man and wife is one flesh'.[17] The Hamlet of Q1 does not call Claudius his father, the Hamlet of Q2 and F1 does. So Q1 tells a different story from that told in either Q2 or F1. Q1's Hamlet can never bring himself to call his uncle his father. Q2 and F1 portray a man who, having resisted that idea, suddenly finds it acceptable here.

How can you get the story wrong if there is no such thing as the right story? Paul Werstine and others have pointed out how different are the stories told by Q1, Q2 and F1.[18] Only Q1 has the ghost of his father entering 'in his night gowne'.[19] Only Q2 has the ambiguity of Hamlet saying he has 'a father kill'd, a mother stain'd' (IV.iv. 57). Only F1 and Q1 have Hamlet calling his mother as he climbs the stairs. Barbara Mowat has pointed out how every editor between 1709 and 1980 produced a conflated text, drawing in different proportions on Q1, Q2 and F1 and therefore creating a new text.[20] Our own reading suggests that this is also true of most editors since 1980. If we put together their arguments we have to acknowledge that there is not just a fourth story claiming to be *Hamlet*, but that as edition succeeds edition the story continues and new stories about Hamlet are therefore created. If we look back we have also to acknowledge that the story of Hamlet is at least 1,000 years old,[21] that Shakespeare's version or versions arose in the second half of its history and that the history of the play on the stage is a story of even more stories of Hamlet. Garrick was a great Hamlet but the text he presented in 1772 was a travesty of what we would regard as Shakespeare's play.[22]

Shakespearean editors inevitably engage in a Bloomian Oedipal conflict with earlier editors. How pleasant it is to demolish the labours of one's forefathers! To open G.R. Hibbard's Oxford edition,[23] for example, and find that, having presumably spent many years tracking down every compositor's error in every copy of Q2 and F1, and having gone to the lengths of printing all the Q2 only passages in a separate Appendix, Hamlet's speech beginning

> How stand I, then,
> That have a father killed, a mother stained

does not end

> O, from this time forth,
> My thoughts be bloody, or be nothing worth

but

> O, from this time forth,
> My thoughts be bloody, or be northing worth (*sic*!).[24]

Claudius believes the supposedly mad Hamlet, now embarked on a ship of fools,[25] has gone west. Hamlet is mad enough, and prescient enough, to think that the moment of leaving Denmark is the moment to harbour bloody thoughts about the man he is leaving behind in the east. But Hibbard confounds them both and sends him north (or is it north-by-north-west?) – an unconscious election that he should alight on Norway.

Ah, life is sweet! Until, of course, our own edition comes out. In the light of our own capacity for error it's probably not wise to crow. Let us will labour on, but from now in silence – the unspeaking in pursuit of the uneditable.

Notes

1. This claim was made by Luke McKernan of the National Film and Television Archive in a programme note for the June 1994 season of *Hamlet* films at the National Film Theatre, London. McKernan is co-author with Olwen Terris of *Walking Shadows: Shakespeare in the National Film and Television Archive* (London: British Film Institute, 1994).
2. Quotations and references are to *The Riverside Shakespeare* (Boston: Houghton Mifflin, 1974).
3. Joseph Hunter, *New Illustrations of the Life, Studies, and Writings of Shakespeare* (London: J.B. Nichols and Son, 1845) II, p. 265.
4. Bob Hoge, *Duke University Chronicle*, 3 February 1984.
5. Anonymous compiler of publicity brochure for *Shakespeare on Film*, part of the *Everybody's Shakespeare International Festival*, Barbican Centre, London, October–November 1994.
6. Gary Taylor (ed.), *Henry V* (Oxford: Clarendon Press, 1982) p. 61.
7. T.J.B. Spencer (ed.) *Hamlet* (Harmondsworth: Penguin, 1980) p. 352.
8. 'Fratricide and Cuckoldry: Shakespeare's Doubles', reprinted in Murray M. Schwartz and Coppélia Kahn (eds), *Representing Shakespeare* (Baltimore: Johns Hopkins University Press, 1980) pp. 70–109.
9. *Violence and the Sacred*, Patrick Gregory trans. (Baltimore: Johns Hopkins University Press, 1977).
10. Eric Sams, *The Real Shakespeare* (New Haven: Yale University Press, 1995). See also Sams' note 'Hamnet or Hamlet, That is the Question', *Hamlet Studies* (1995) pp. 94–8.
11. Harold Jenkins (ed.), *Hamlet*, The Arden Shakespeare (London: Methuen, 1982).
12. 'The self-blinding of the mythical criminal, Oedipus, was simply a mitigated form of the punishment of castration – the only punishment that was adequate for him by the *lex talionis*' (Sigmund Freud, 'The Uncanny' (1919) in *The Standard Edition of the Complete Psychological Works of Sigmund Freud* XVII, J. Strachey trans. (London: The Hogarth Press, 1955), p. 231).
13. 'Mousetrap and Rat Man: An Uncanny Resemblance', in Tetsuo Kishi, Roger Pringle and Stanley Wells (eds), *Shakespeare and Cultural Traditions* (Newark: University of Delaware, 1994) p.357.
14. '"In Everything Illegitimate": Imagining the Bastard in Renaissance Drama', *Yearbook of English Studies* 23 (1993) 271–2.
15. T.S. Eliot famously called *Hamlet* an artistic failure in his *Atheanaeum* essay on '*Hamlet* and his Problems' (1919), reproduced in H. Bloom (ed.), *Hamlet* (New York: Chelsea House, 1990) pp. 43–6.
16. Q2: 'Father and Mother is man and wife, / Man and wife is one flesh'; F1: 'Father and Mother is man and wife: man and wife is one flesh'.
17. Page 84, line 1, in Graham Holderness and Bryan Loughrey (eds), *The Tragicall Historie of Hamlet Prince of Denmarke* (Hemel Hempstead: Harvester Wheatsheaf, 1992).
18. Paul Werstine, 'The Textual Mystery of *Hamlet*', *Shakespeare Quarterly* 39 (1988), 1–26.

19. Page 81, line 1, in Holderness and Loughrey's edition.
20. Barbara Mowat, 'The Form of *Hamlet's* Fortunes', *Renaissance Drama* 19 (1988) 97–126.
21. Hamlet's ancestors include not just Amlodi in Nordic legends, but a wider network of relations including Havelok the Dane, King Horn, and Bevis of Hampton.
22. For example, in Garrick's treatment Hamlet did not arrange the deaths of Rosencrantz and Guildenstern, Claudius did not poison the drink, Gertrude died off-stage of guilt, and Laertes, having neither poisoned his sword nor died, ended the play ruling Denmark jointly with Horatio.
23. G.R. Hibbard (ed.), *Hamlet*, The Oxford Shakespeare (Oxford: Clarendon, 1987).
24. Appendix A (xiii), p. 365, 57–8.
25. See Michel Foucault's chapter on the 'Stultifera Navis', in his *Madness and Civilisation: a History of Insanity in the Age of Reason*, R. Howard trans. (London: Tavistock, 1967) pp. 3–37.

24

Mystical Estates and Legal Fictions: Modernism's Apostolic Successions

Stan Smith

A NECESSARY EVIL

> A father, Stephen said...is a necessary evil....Fatherhood, in the sense of conscious begetting, is unknown to man. It is a mystical estate, an apostolic succession from only begetter to only begotten.... Paternity may be a legal fiction. Who is the father of any son that any son should love him or he any son?...What links them in nature? An instant of blind rut.

Stephen Dedalus, attempting with ponderous playfulness in *Ulysses* (1922) to prove that Shakespeare was his own grandpa, identifies some of the key concerns of an emergent Modernism, linking authorship and authority, sexuality and textuality, paternity, patronage and patriotism.[1] For W.B. Yeats, Irish nationalism has not broken with the imperial power until, like Moses, it has killed the Egyptian, the adoptive patriarch.[2] The father is symbolically deposed in Pound's 'Hugh Selwyn Mauberley' as the collective old men with their 'old lies' responsible for the Great War, as he is in Eliot's 'Gerontion' and *The Waste Land*.[3] The procedure is theorised in the critical writings of all three poets as a seizure of power on the site of Tradition, a 'making it new' in which a younger generation appropriates and reconfigures the whole cultural apparatus and canon, in the process killing the father.[4] I want here to sketch out the lines of a larger argument by focusing on a key moment in the emergence of a Modernist aesthetics, in the writing of T.S. Eliot.

KILLING THE FATHER

It is now generally agreed that *The Waste Land* is a poem about the aftermath of the Great War, and the disintegration of the patriarchal Empires in revolution and anarchy which it occasioned. One of the key notes Eliot added to the poem when it was published in book form is a quotation from Hermann Hesse's *Blick ins Chaos* attached to lines 366–76, the section about 'hooded hordes' swarming over endless – in the original draft 'Polish' – plains and about the cracking, reforming and bursting of cities like Vienna, the collapse of which haunted Eliot's imagination in his letters home and which clearly had some deeper, personal significance.

The passage from Hesse depicts a chaos which originates from a distinctly Slavic degeneration consummated by the October Revolution, a spirit of destruction at once loathsome and fascinating, in which 'Already half of Europe, already at least half of Eastern Europe, on the way to Chaos, drives drunkenly in spiritual frenzy along the edge of the abyss, sings drunkenly ... as Dmitri Karamazov sang', while 'The offended bourgeois laughs at the songs; the saint and seer hear them with tears'.[5]

The crime of which Dmitri Karamazov is accused in *The Brothers Karamazov*, and in which all the other brothers, particularly Ivan, are in different ways implicated, is of course parricide – the murder of a drunken, destructive and abusive father. Of Ivan, the writer and revolutionary, Dostoevsky wrote that he represents 'the synthesis of our modern Russian anarchism': 'To our foolish but terrible Russian socialism (for our youth is mixed up in it) [Ivan's 'negationist' philosophy] is a *directive* and, it seems, a very powerful one: the loaves of bread, the Tower of Babel (that is, the future reign of socialism) and the complete enslavement of the freedom of conscience – that is what the desperate negationist is trying to achieve.'[6]

Eliot had read the whole of Dostoevsky with avidity on his first visit to Europe in 1911. In any post-1917 reading of *Karamazov*, the theme of a collectively willed parricide cannot be dissociated from the chaos of a Russia and a Europe now in revolutionary turmoil, in the imperial heartlands of Munich, Berlin, Budapest and Vienna. Hermann Hesse, the source of Eliot's note, himself provides the link. *The Waste Land* was first published in October 1922 in the first number of the journal Eliot edited, *The Criterion*. The same issue contained the plan of a novel by Dostoevsky, the importance of which for Eliot is clear from his letters, and an article by Hesse on 'Recent German Poetry'. Of the latter Eliot wrote to F.S. Flint in July 1922 that it was one of 'two things which I want to be in the first number'.[7] If one looks at the piece one can see why. In many ways it can be seen as an extended footnote to the first publication of the poem. It is certainly one of its continuing intertexts.

Addressing the 'immense postwar significance' of 'the new psychology, whose harbingers were Dostoievski and Nietzsche, and whose first architect is Freud', Hesse observed that

> Two principal themes are everywhere predominant: rebellion against authority and against the culture of that authority in process of downfall; and eroticism. The father thrust against the wall and condemned by his son, and the youngster, hungry for love, who endeavours to sing his sexual passion in new, free, lovelier and true forms: these are the two figures that are everywhere to be found.... The experience and impetus behind all these revolutions and innovations are clearly discernible in two powerful forces: the world-war, and the psychology of the unconscious founded by Sigmund Freud. The experience of the Great War, with the collapse of all the old forms and the breakdown of moral codes and cultures hitherto valid, appears to be incapable of interpretation except by psycho-analysis. Europe is seen by the youth of today as a very sick neurotic, who can be helped only by shattering the self-created complexes in which he is suffocating. And the otherwise tottering authority of the father, the teacher, the priest, the party, and of science finds a new and terrible antagonist in psycho-analysis.[8]

These young men have renounced the name of the Father. Instead, their hearts belong to Dada. According to Hesse, 'The knowledge of the collapse of pre-war culture and the eager acceptance of the new psychology as – at last – a science in the making, these are the foundations on which the young men of today are beginning to build'. But 'The large majority of these young men give one exactly the same impression as the half-analysed psychopath, who knows indeed the first main results of his psycho-analysis, but is unaware of its consequences.... Beyond this, there is nothing but obscurity and aimlessness'.

This throws new light on the disjunctive dialogue of the 'neurotic' upper-class couple in the 'Game of Chess' section of *The Waste Land*. In that section, the War has clearly affected the working-class Lil, whose husband's demob has consequences tangential to paternity in her abortion. But the idea that these other exchanges primarily reflect the personal life of Tom and Vivienne Eliot has obscured another possibility: that the man here is a war veteran, the victim of catastrophic neurasthenia. Certainly his reactions are very similar to those explored in Rebecca West's contemporaneous novel *The Return of the Soldier* (1918), where the breakdown of the officer back from the Front also problematises the whole issue of fatherhood and patrilineal inheritance.

Paternity, and its problematic nature, is in fact a key theme of *The Waste Land*, and it is figured in curiously Freudian hints throughout the text. Eliot had certainly encountered Freud's work. Indeed, he picks him out as archetypically Viennese in a context which also alludes to many of the preoccupations of *The Waste Land*, particularly its anthropological ones, in a dismissive remark in 'Euripides and Professor Murray' (1920) about 'the present day', in which:

> we have acquired sociology and social psychology, we have watched the clinics of Ribot and Janet, we have read books from Vienna and heard a discourse of Bergson; a philosophy arose at Cambridge; social emancipation crawled abroad; our historical knowledge has of course increased; and we have a curiously Freudian-social-mystical-rationalistic-higher-critical interpretation of the Classic and what used to be called the Scriptures.[9]

There is a significant omission in *The Waste Land*'s note about Tiresias, 'the most important personage in the poem, uniting all the rest'. The note cites a passage from Ovid about Tiresias' sex-change operation, but contains no reference to his part as a surrogate father in *Oedipus Rex*, where he warns Oedipus against too much knowledge (against knowledge, specifically, of the primal crimes of parricide and incest). Tiresias' appearance in the play (of which Murray had produced a popular translation in 1911) is, however, clearly recalled when *The Waste Land* speaks of his walking by the walls of Thebes, and is obviously relevant to a poem which speaks of dangerous knowledge and dangerous ignorance, dead fathers and murmurs of maternal lamentation.

One of the 'books from Vienna' which I think Eliot had read develops Freud's idea of the Oedipus Complex in a way which is centrally relevant to the poem. That book is *Totem and Taboo* (1913), published in an English translation by A.A. Brill in 1918.[10] In one of *The Waste Land*'s many intertextual citations, there is a peculiar alteration of

Eliot's source on which I have never seen any critic remark, but on which Freud's book can throw some light. There seems no particular explanation for it, and yet its sheer gratuitousness suggests it must be meaningful. It is, in one sense, a Freudian slip. The citation, of the ostensibly orphaned Ferdinand in *The Tempest*, occurs in lines 191–2 of *The Waste Land*:

> Musing upon the king my brother's wreck
> And on the king my father's death before him.

The allusion is picked up in line 257, 'This music crept by me upon the waters', echoing Ferdinand's response (I.ii.390 *et seq*.) when he believes himself the sole survivor of the shipwreck in which his father has drowned:

> Sitting on a bank,
> Weeping again the king my father's wrack,
> This music crept by me upon the waters...

The music is Ariel's, whose song, 'Full fathom five thy father lies', enchanting though it is, carries a grievous burden. The song has already been echoed parenthetically by the clairvoyante Madame Sosostris in line 48 of the opening section: '(Those are pearls that were his eyes. Look!)'; and it is reiterated in the fraught exchanges of the neurotic couple in 'A Game of Chess': 'I remember / Those were pearls that were his eyes'.

Eliot's substitution of the 'king my brother's wreck' for 'the king my father's wrack', and the half-citation of 'the king my father's death before him' are both unnecessary, and therefore significant: an overloaded seme. They have a precedent in another substitution of young for old buried in the poem's formative unconscious. Anthony Hands records that Eliot claimed 'the young man carbuncular' of line 231 was based on the 'Old man eloquent' of Milton's sonnet 'To the Lady Margaret Ley', another orphaned child, 'Daughter to that good earl, once President / of *England's* Counsel'.[11] According to Milton, the 'sad breaking of that Parliament / Broke him' (one recalls the 'broken Coriolanus' of *The Waste Land*), 'as that dishonest victory / At *Chaeronea*, fatal to liberty / Kil'd with report that Old man eloquent'. Milton's allusion is to the death of Isocrates, allegedly on hearing of the victory of Philip of Macedon (the subsequently murdered father of a more famous son) over the Theban and Athenian armies in 338 BC –

which goes some way to explaining the presence of Athens in Eliot's list of collapsing cities, along with Vienna and London. Ley's daughter, Milton concludes, 'Though later born, then to have known the dayes / Wherin your Father flourisht', nevertheless resurrects him in her own person: 'by you / Madam, me thinks I see him living yet'. Milton's phrasing, unconsciously perhaps both for him and Eliot, in turn calls up Hamlet's fraternal exchanges with Horatio about his own father's relations with the brother who has killed him: 'My father, methinks I see my father.... In my mind's eye.... The king my father!'[12] The last phrase, of course, leads us back via *The Tempest* to Eliot's poem.

It is difficult to see what precisely is going on in these multiple and recessive substitutions, but something is. Eliot's own father, Henry Ware Eliot, had died in January 1919, while the poem was gestating, and Eliot was currently in correspondence about the death with his own older brother who, sharing the father's forenames, was clearly the heir to the patronym. The most intriguing clue to what is happening here is supplied by *Totem and Taboo* where, at the end of a lengthy discussion of the originary crime in which the primal horde overthrows and kills the father and institutes the rule of a brother-clan, Freud concludes that 'An event such as the elimination of the primal father by the company of his sons must inevitably have left ineradicable traces in the history of humanity; and the less it itself was recollected, the more numerous must have been the substitutes to which it gave rise.'[13] And then, in a footnote, to illustrate this process of substitution, he cites Ariel's song:

> Full fathom five thy father lies;
>   Of his bones are coral made;
> Those are pearls that were his eyes:
>   Nothing of him that doth fade,
> But doth suffer a sea-change
> Into something rich and strange.

RICH AND STRANGE

Eliot's reference to 'hooded hordes' may add a Freudian frisson to the image of anarchic forces swarming once again on the frontiers of Europe. I don't intend to pursue here the extent to which the emergence of the brother-clan out of the primal horde by way of an originary parricide is a theme of *The Waste Land* – though it is clearly related to the poem's use of the motif of the dying god from *The Golden Bough*, a work which Freud cites at length in his own study. I want to explore instead, taking the clue from Hesse's essay, the peculiar significance of this conjunction for a Modernist aesthetics. For the most striking thing here is that Ariel's song is used more than once by Eliot as the very model of the way in which art works on and transforms (in Freud's words 'substitutes for') the real. The most obvious example of this is in the essay 'Shakespeare and the Stoicism of Seneca' in 1927, linking two of Eliot's literary father-figures, Shakespeare and Dante, whose 'brave attempts to fabricate something permanent and holy out of his personal animal feelings... can all be matched out of Shakespeare. Shakespeare, too, was occupied with the struggle – which alone constitutes life for a poet – to transmute his personal and private agonies into something rich and strange, something universal and impersonal.'[14]

There is, from this passage, a complex of filiations (I use the word advisedly) running throughout Eliot's work. What I want to focus on is the idea that the relation of art to reality, via Freud and Hesse, is seen as an act of ritual parricide in which the body of the material world (including one's own life seen as other, as belonging to the father) has to be killed in order to be resurrected as 'something rich and strange', the work of art. In this perspective, artistic creation, in the words of 'Tradition and the Individual Talent' (1919)[15], requires of its author 'continual self-sacrifice... continual extinction of personality'. This conjunction lies behind the peculiar antiseptic, clinical quality of this essay's 'Impersonal theory of poetry', adumbrated in the year of his father's death. It accounts for the way the essay first kills off the father: 'We dwell with satisfaction upon the poet's difference from his predecessors, especially his immediate predecessors' – and then immediately reinstates him as a tribal totem investing with his authority every aspect of the new creation: 'we shall often find that not only the best, but the most individual parts of [the new writer's] work may be those in which the dead poets, his ancestors, assert their immortality most vigorously'. In this way, the parricide is reunited with the primal father he has overthrown, so that 'His significance, his appreciation is the appreciation of his relation to the dead poets and artists.... you must set him, for contrast and comparison, among the dead.' Significantly, one of the literary instances Eliot adduces to illustrate 'the difference between art and the event' is 'the murder of Agamemnon' (the consequences of which for his children, Orestes and Electra, prefigure the dilemma of Hamlet).

What we see here, in fact, is Freud's thesis that, out of guilt at the primal murder, the brother-clan of sons reinstates the image of the dead father as a totemic ancestor, whose post-mortem authority invests and ratifies all their deeds. The libidinal charge is such that, in describing the process of artistic creation, Eliot feels compelled to evacuate all human agency and presence from the process by means of his famous analogy with a laboratory experiment in which two gases achieve chemical fusion through the intervention of an inert catalyst in a glass retort. His insistence, in this essay, that a man is *compelled* (a significant word) 'to write not merely with his own generation in his bones, but with a feeling that the whole of literature of Europe from Homer... has a simultaneous existence and composes a simultaneous order', reinstates the murdered father at the heart of that new Tradition created by the 'supervention of novelty'. The phrase 'in his bones' (one recalls those bones the dead men lost in rats' alley – an allusion to the trenches? – in *The Waste Land*) reminds the triumphant son of his own mortality, prefigured in the father's, for which it is punishment. Such deep anxieties can be repressed only by insisting, in the most generalised of terms, that although everything has changed, nothing has, really. 'The existing order is complete before the new work arrives', Eliot says, and the 'supervention of novelty' totally restructures the whole, if only ever so slightly; but at the same time this revolution 'abandons nothing *en route*... does not superannuate either Shakespeare, or Homer, or the rock drawing of the Magdalenian draughtsmen.'

The presence of Freud's theory is, I think, rather confirmed by this last, unexpected reference to 'the Magdalenian draughtsmen': a lengthy footnote in *Totem and Taboo* refers to 'the carvings and paintings of animals in the French caves' to expound modern ideas about 'the magic of art'.[16] With more time, I would want to follow the implications of this through to Eliot's wider criticism, but I can here refer only to the essay on 'Hamlet and His Problems', written again in the year his father died, 1919, and republished simply as 'Hamlet' (no problems) in the *Selected Essays*.[17]

The essay first of all separates off the work of art, '*Hamlet* the play' from 'Hamlet the character' as 'the primary problem'. (Note, however, that the original title speaks of 'his', not 'its' problems.) It then proceeds, in terms themselves heavy with affect, to identify a classic Freudian cathexis in a play which is, according to Eliot, 'full of some stuff that the writer could not drag to light, contemplate, or manipulate into art', and to speak of Hamlet the character as 'dominated by an emotion which is inexpressible, because it is in *excess* of the facts as they appear'. This arises, according to Eliot, because it is 'a play dealing with the effect of a mother's guilt upon her son', in which 'Shakespeare was unable to impose this motive successfully upon the "intractable" material of the old play' by Thomas Kyd on which it is based.

The 'intractable' textual material of the older play, like the intractable material in Hamlet's unconscious, is something which Eliot also represses in his discussion: it is the corpus/corpse of the murdered father. For Freud the cause of Hamlet's delays is obvious: his unconscious identification of father and uncle, so that the desire to avenge his father's death is constrained by the taboo upon killing the (in this case surrogate) father – the deepest, libidinally charged desire of the sons, as expounded in *Totem and Taboo*. Hamlet senior, and his murder, the 'motive and the cue for passion' with which Hamlet reproaches himself, are not even mentioned in Eliot's essay, though their repression everywhere issues in precisely that kind of 'bafflement at the absence of objective equivalent to his feelings' which Eliot attributes to Hamlet, and the absence is made the more conspicuous by the acknowledgment that the source play centres on 'the difficulty of assassinating a monarch'. Significantly, the play Eliot adduces in contrast to *Hamlet* as 'Shakespeare's most assured artistic success' is *Coriolanus*, from which the hero's father has been totally erased, to be replaced by a phallic mother who also usurps the function of his wife, a play whose protagonist speaks of wanting to 'stand / As if a man were author of himself / And knew no other kin' (V.iii. 35–7).[18] The parricidal subtext invades the essay's most famous critical coinage, in the unexpected citation of Lady Macbeth's guilty sleep-walking to illustrate the nature of the 'objective correlative'. For, we may recall, Lady Macbeth had shrunk from murdering Duncan because he reminded her of her father as he slept, and Macbeth in killing him has murdered sleep itself.

Freud's essay, 'Some Character Types Met with in Psycho-analytic Work', first published in German in the journal *Imago* in 1916, in a section whose very title, 'Those Wrecked by Success', recalls Ferdinand's 'wreck/wrack', discusses *Macbeth* at some length in terms which prefigure Eliot here, concluding that:

> [T]he whole play ... is sown with references to the father-children relation. The murder of the kindly Duncan is little more than parricide; in Banquo's case, Macbeth kills the father while the son escapes

> him; and in Macduff's, he kills the children because the father has fled from him. A bloody child, and then a crowned one, are shown him by the witches in the apparition scene; the armed head which is seen earlier is no doubt Macbeth himself. But in the background rises the sinister form of the avenger, Macduff, who is himself an exception to the laws of generation, since he was not born of his mother but ripp'd from her womb'.[19]

Though the essay was not translated into English until 1925, Eliot's German was sufficiently good for him to be studying Husserl and other German philosophers in the original at Marburg University in 1914. There are good grounds for suspecting that Eliot may have read this newly published essay while undergoing treatment for his nervous breakdown in Lausanne by disciples of Freud.

'Hamlet' joins 'Tradition and the Individual Talent' in being the source of one of Eliot's most widely influential aesthetic ideas: in this case that 'objective correlative' illustrated in the Lady Macbeth example. Central to this much-disputed concept is, as we might expect, the conversion of the raw material of life into the 'something rich and strange' of art. At its repressed core sits the slain father. Indeed, when Eliot speaks of Hamlet's verbal playing, he does so in phrases which could refer to his own assumption of an antic disposition in his poetry, in either the 'continual self-sacrifice . . . continual extinction of personality' of 'Tradition', or the self-effacement of a Prufrock who protests 'I am not Prince Hamlet, nor was meant to be'. The words could also describe the paralysis of *The Waste Land,* and recall Eliot's own comments elsewhere on the automatic writing in which that poem finally finds cathartic release: 'The levity of Hamlet, his repetition of phrase, his puns, are not part of a deliberate plan of dissimulation, but a form of emotional relief. In the character Hamlet it is the buffoonery of an emotion which can find no outlet in action; in the dramatist it is a buffoonery of an emotion which he cannot express in art'.

'The intense feeling, ecstatic or terrible, without an object or exceeding its object', which Eliot attributes here to both Shakespeare and Hamlet (authorial father and textual son) is, he says, 'something which every person of sensibility has felt', though it is also 'doubtless a subject of study for pathologists'. Its intensity can be explained if we see it as a guise for a symbolic cultural parricide like that of the Russian revolutionaries and the Karamazov boys, effecting a sea-change which converts the murdered father into something rich and strange. *The Waste*

Land is, like *Hamlet* in Eliot's description, the site of an 'insoluble puzzle', and Eliot's verdict on the play holds for his own poem also: 'under compulsion of what experience he attempted to express the inexpressibly horrible, we cannot ever know.' Except that, with the help of Freud and his intercessor Hesse, we can suspect that the corpse so conspicuously planted in the garden at the end of 'The Burial of the Dead' by Stetson (Stepson?) is that of the primal father himself, and the guilt and anxiety which everywhere pervades the poem, and Eliot's criticism, is that of the parricidal son who seeks to resurrect the murdered Father in the body of his text and at the heart of his new-made Tradition, with bones of coral and with pearls for eyes.

I want to conclude by returning to *Ulysses*, whose serial publication Eliot had arranged and whose 'mythical method' Eliot offers as the model of how art transforms the 'immense panorama of futility and anarchy which is contemporary history' in a famous review in 1923.[20]

HIMSELF HIS OWN SON

Stephen Dedalus knew all this stuff, as he makes clear in his disquisition on Shakespeare, or, if I may be pardoned the bilingual pun, Shakes-père. Dedalus plays upon the coincidence of the dramatist's own dead son having the name of Hamnet, but then goes on to overthrow the paternal imago by dissolving the unitary Shakespeare into a portmanteau brother-clan of imputed authors, 'Rutlandbaconsouthamptonshakespeare or another poet of the same name in the comedy of errors'. And the words in which he does this recall his departure at the end of *A Portrait of the Artist as a Young Man*, to become his own and his father's father by forging, in the smithy of his soul, the uncreated conscience of his race:

> Sabellius, the African, subtlest heresiarch of all the beasts of the field, held that the Father was Himself His Own Son . . . When Rutlandbaconsouthamptonshakespeare or another poet of the same name in the comedy of errors wrote Hamlet he was not the father of his own son merely but, being no more a son, he was and he felt himself the father of all his race, the father of his own grandfather, the father of his unborn grandson, who, by the same token, never was born. . . . Himself his own father, Sonmulligan told himself.[21]

The syntactical ambiguity of the penultimate 'his' (i.e. either his *grandfather*'s or *his own* grandson) avenges the primal parricide by slaying in advance the perpetrator, leaving him unborn. The same double movement lies behind something I cannot explore here, the convergence of the buried father and aborted child in 'A Game of Chess'. (The memory of a dead child is also at the heart of *Return of the Soldier*.) Killing the father, literally or symbolically, is the foundational modern act. It is in this spirit that Dedalus rejects Leopold Bloom's overtures to become a surrogate father. In the same spirit, Joyce himself kills off the much-loved father Paddy Dignam, as well as Bloom's own father, in what increasingly seems like a very suspicious suicide. (In the *Odyssey*, Odysseus' father Laertes, the name Shakespeare gives to Polonius' son, is still alive. Eliot, incidentally, remarks on how unnecessary and extraneous is the Polonius–Laertes material in *Hamlet*.) Most significant of all, perhaps, is Joyce's major departure from his source in not having Bloom/Ulysses kill the brother-clan of suitors besieging Penelope/Molly. (They are all, in the *Odyssey*, of Telemachus' age.)

The revolting sons of Modernism everywhere substitute for the patriarchal lineage (the name of the Father) the self-constituting brother-clan of generation, coterie, social group, or political movement, elevating nurture over nature, replacing biological diachrony with the synchronic cultural formation, a perpetual contemporaneity which was the Modern. But they also carry with them the guilt of that crime. In its strategies of self-authorisation, replacing loyalty to the fatherland with the solidarity of the generational brother-clan, Modernism thus parallels the mass-movements of right and left that emerged from the *fin de siècle* and shaped European history for half a century, in which parricidal revolutions ended by devouring their children. The rupture with genealogy that Modernism initiated is still with us, inscribed in the very word with which we signal our own current cutting-adrift: 'Postmodernism'.

The manifesto of that new inscription is, perhaps, Salman Rushdie's *Midnight's Children*.[22] Rushdie's wholly postmodern children are not the scions of their biological or cultural parents but the creatures of an unprecedented moment of rupture and scission, the chimes of midnight on which their nation was born. The book's restless protean narrative repeatedly rewrites its various pasts in the process of finding new lineages, shifting patrimonies, for itself and its hero, the changeling Salim Sinai. For if Salim is 'fathered, you understand, by history' (p. 118), that history is itself an endlessly altered inheritance, with no *real* past, only a complex of hypperreal narratives. As Salim says, expressing the true postmodern condition, 'my inheritance includes this gift, the gift of inventing new parents for myself whenever necessary. The power of giving birth to fathers and mothers which Ahmed wanted and never had' (p. 108). Ahmed, supposed progenitor of his line, had always longed for various fictional ancestors and had invented a lineage for himself (p. 110). Salim's conclusion, however, is the truly postmodern one: 'in the end, everyone can do without fathers' (p. 66). Thus this child of the century's midnight confirms the destiny Stephen Dedalus had mapped out at its beginning, a projection founded on the 'incertitude' and 'unlikelihood' of the mystical estate of fatherhood: in Stephen's words, 'On that mystery and not on the madonna founded and founded irremovably because founded, like the world, macro- and microcosm, upon the void'. Merely, that is, a legal fiction.

Notes

1. James Joyce, *Ulysses* (London: The Bodley Head, 1937) pp. 195–6.
2. See W.B. Yeats, 'Samhain: 1901', in *Explorations* (London: Macmillan, 1962) p. 83: 'Moses was little good to his people until he had killed an Egyptian; and for the most part a writer or public man of the upper classes is useless to this country till he has done something that separates him from his class.'
3. Ezra Pound, *Hugh Selwyn Mauberley* (London: Ovid Press, 1920); T.S. Eliot, *Poems* (New York: Alfred Knopf, 1920); 'The Waste Land' in *The Criterion* I, 1 (1922). I have discussed these issues from a different angle in Stan Smith, *The Origins of Modernism: Eliot, Pound, Yeats and the Rhetorics of Renewal* (London: Harvester Wheatsheaf, 1994).
4. An older Eliot, discussing with an arched eyebrow the 'Youth of today' in 'Thoughts after Lambeth' (1931), manages in a parenthesis to dismiss both the concept of thinking in generations and the original impact of his poetic revolution: 'I dislike the word "generation", which has been a talisman for the last ten years; when I wrote a poem called *The Waste Land* some of the more approving critics said that I had expressed the "disillusionment of a generation", which is nonsense. I may have expressed for them their own illusion of being disillusioned, but that did not form part of my intention.' A page or so later, moving from his 'low opinion...of Youth' to 'that vacuous word "religion"', Eliot makes an apparently gratuitous leap: 'Dr Sigmund Freud, with characteristic delicacy of feeling, has reminded us that we should "leave Heaven to the angels and the sparrows"; following his hint, we may safely leave "religion" to Mr Julian Huxley and Dr Freud'.

T.S. Eliot '*Selected Essays* (London: Faber & Faber, 1951) pp. 368 and 370. The intent of the present essay is to suggest that this is not for Eliot a gratuitous constellation of associations. It is perhaps significant in this context that Freud's providential sparrows recall *Hamlet* V.ii. 118–19: 'Not a whit, we defy augury: there's a special providence in the fall of a sparrow' – Hamlet's words just before he meets for the first time since his return to Denmark the stepfather who he now knows had plotted to kill him, as he had killed his father, and whom he will shortly kill.

5. Translation in B.C. Southam, *A Student's Guide to the Selected Poems of T.S. Eliot* (London: Faber & Faber, 1981) p. 106.
6. Quoted in David Magarshack, Introduction, *The Brothers Karamazov* (Harmondsworth: Penguin, 1958).
7. Valerie Eliot (ed.) *The Letters of T.S. Eliot, vol. 1, 1898–1922* (London: Faber & Faber, 1988) pp. 542–3
8. Hermann Hesse, 'Recent German Poetry' in *The Criterion*, I, 1 (1922) 90–1.
9. T.S. Eliot, 'Euripides and Professor Murray' in *The Sacred Wood* (London: Methuen, 1920) p. 75.
10. Sigmund Freud, *Totem and Taboo: Some Points of Agreement between the Mental Lives of Savages and Neurotics*, A.A. Brill trans. (London: Routledge, 1919); all subsequent citations in my text refer to the *Standard Edition* in the Penguin Freud Library 13, *The Origins of Religion*, Albert Dickson (ed.), James Strachey trans. (Harmondsworth: Penguin, 1990). Freud's essay, 'Dostoevsky and Parricide' is extremely pertinent to this discussion of Eliot, developing at some length the claim that 'It can scarcely be owing to chance that three of the masterpieces of literature of all time – the *Oedipus Rex* of Sophocles, Shakespeare's *Hamlet* and Dostoevsky's *The Brothers Karamazov* – should deal with the same subject, parricide'. (Penguin Freud Library 14, *Art and Literature*, pp. 441–60) Unfortunately for this argument, it was not written until 1926–8, nor translated into English until 1929. Nevertheless, it demonstrates an area of common ground between poet and psychoanalyst.
11. Anthony Hands, *Sources for the Poetry of T.S. Eliot* (Oxford: Hadrian, 1993) p. 100. In the light of Eliot's subsequent use of this turbulent period, in 'Little Gidding', as a figure for the breaking and reconstitution of the English tradition, it may be that he found some particular affinity with this sonnet: Charles I's 'sad breaking of that Parliament' was famously resisted by Eliot's putative ancestor, Sir John Eliot, who was thereupon dispatched to the Tower.
12. *Hamlet* I.ii. 160–258.
13. *Totem and Taboo*, p. 217.
14. Eliot, *Selected Essays*, p. 137.
15. *Ibid.*, pp. 13–22, quotations *passim*.
16. *Totem and Taboo*, p. 149.
17. Eliot, *Selected Essays*, pp. 141–6. It appeared under the earlier title in *The Sacred Wood*.
18. The plot (or the witches' brew) gets even thicker if we pause to consider what Coriolanus signifies at the end of *The Waste Land* (410–17) in a paragraph, isolated by the capitalised command 'DA' at start and

finish, which ends with the image of a key turning in a prison lock, while 'aetherial rumours / Revive for a moment a broken Coriolanus'. Eliot's note refers perfunctorily to Dante's *Inferno* XXXII. 46, the episode in which Count Ugolini tells of his Pisan incarceration with his sons and grandsons, their death by starvation, and his subsequent cannibalism. Before they die his children urge him, in filial piety, to sate his hunger on their flesh, of which he is the author. Ugolino descries in their faces 'the image of my own', and Dante calls Pisa 'a modern Thebes'. In the unconscious of Eliot's text the original Oedipal site and the myth of the child-devouring Saturn converge, by way of a brother-clan who slay the father to avert a similar fate, in a figure whose condensation and intensity conceal an emotion too excessive to be dragged into the light or manipulated into art.

19. Sigmund Freud, *Einige Charakter Typen Aus der Psychoanalytischen Arbeit*, in *Imago* IV, 6 (1916) reprinted in German in 1918 and 1922, first English translation 1925. This translation: The Penguin Freud Library 14, *Art and Literature*, p. 305. A thoroughgoing Freudian deconstruction of Eliot's essay might seize upon the fact that it makes much of *Hamlet*'s source text, by *Kyd* (the child is father of the man?) and link this to his opening remark, speaking of those writer-critics such as Goethe and Coleridge who have attempted to father images of themselves on the text ('the substitution – of their own Hamlet for Shakespeare's'), that 'We should be thankful that Walter *Pater* [my emphasis] did not fix his attention on this play, (*Selected Essays*, p. 141). But I would not want to do this.
20. T.S. Eliot, 'Ulysses, Order and Myth' in *The Dial* 75 (1923) 480–3.
21. Joyce, *loc. cit.*
22. Salman Rushdie, *Midnight's Children* (London: Picador, 1981). Page numbers refer to this edition.

Epilogue

So, have the preceding pages brought us any closer to defining paternity, fatherhood and the relationship between the two? Undoubtedly not: twenty-four different writers have suggested at least twenty-four different ways of understanding who or what the 'father' is. Does this then suggest that the whole notion of fatherhood as we in the West understand it is in crisis, falling apart? Far from it, because, as this book has shown, 'fatherhood' as a concept has always been in process, tugged this way and that between the discourses of art, science and the law, its definition and redefinition being crucial elements both in the establishment of social stability and in movements for cultural change. As our authors have discussed, each historical moment, including our own, reworks the father's role and there is no reason to suppose that this process will not continue. However, changes in the respective socio-economic positions of adult women and men and their children – those not-quite-adult 'young people' – over the past fifty years or so have introduced a new element into our current redefinitions of fatherhood, of which this book itself is a manifestation. Over at least the last millennum and a half, the father's place and authority were established largely by fathers themselves, whether the biological variety or their symbolic counterparts, fathers of religion, clan or nation. We have seen in the preceding chapters how some mothers, daughters and sons have rebelled against paternal law, while others have conformed to its demands. Today however, advances in reproductive technology and genetic engineering and shifts in the social structures of authority have meant that determining the father's role has ceased to be a matter for fathers alone. While, as we have seen, some post-modernists may declare themselves ready to 'do without' them, in practice, and despite cloning, it seems unlikely that fathers will disappear. On the other hand fatherhood has become a topic for general debate in which everyone, fathers, mothers, children, employers, social workers and people in general, has an axe to grind and accommodations of one sort or another must be reached. For fathers this means uncertainty, for the rest of us that the days of a simple choice between rebellion or conformity to father's will are over; we are all implicated both in the question of what a father is and in its possible answers. We cannot foresee how fatherhood will evolve but, by asking questions about its past and present, this book written in a plurality of voices may help to shape its future, with all the cultural repercussions that implies.

Trista Selous

Index